Jaroslav Kušnír

**American Fiction:
Modernism-Postmodernism, Popular Culture,
and Metafiction**

This book is a result of research on American literature which was awarded a governmental grant by the Slovak Ministry of Education. The theme of research is Americká literatúra v kontexte premien [American Literature in the Context of Changes] VEGA 1-9339-02.

The book was also sponsored by a VEGA grant 1-9340-02 Z vývinovej problematiky moderných germánskych a anglosaských literatúr [Development of Modern Germanic and Anglo-Saxon Literatures].

This book was reviewed by:

                Doc. PhDr. Josef Grmela, CSc.
                Doc. PhDr. Michal Peprník, PhD.
                Doc. PhDr. Bohuslav Mánek, CSc.

Jaroslav Kušnír

AMERICAN FICTION: MODERNISM-POSTMODERNISM, POPULAR CULTURE, AND METAFICTION

ibidem-Verlag
Stuttgart

Bibliografische Information Der Deutschen Bibliothek

Die Deutsche Bibliothek verzeichnet diese Publikation in der Deutschen Nationalbibliografie; detaillierte bibliografische Daten sind im Internet über <http://dnb.ddb.de> abrufbar.

∞

Gedruckt auf alterungsbeständigem, säurefreien Papier
Printed on acid-free paper

ISBN: 3-89821-514-8

© *ibidem*-Verlag
Stuttgart 2005
Alle Rechte vorbehalten

Das Werk einschließlich aller seiner Teile ist urheberrechtlich geschützt. Jede Verwertung außerhalb der engen Grenzen des Urheberrechtsgesetzes ist ohne Zustimmung des Verlages unzulässig und strafbar. Dies gilt insbesondere für Vervielfältigungen, Übersetzungen, Mikroverfilmungen und elektronische Speicherformen sowie die Einspeicherung und Verarbeitung in elektronischen Systemen.

Printed in Germany

To my family

TABLE OF CONTENTS

ACKNOWLEDGEMENTS 9

CHAPTER I
BETWEEN MODERNISM AND POSTMODERNISM:
DONALD BARTHELME'S NOVELS *SNOW WHITE* (1965) AND
***PARADISE* (1986)** 13

CHAPTER II
POSTMODERNISM AND POPULAR CULTURE 37

   II.1 The Western 43

      II.1.1 Parody of the Western in American Literature (E. L. Doctorow's *Welcome to Hard Times*, 1960; and Robert Coover's *The Ghost Town*, 1998) 43
      II.1.2 Reconsideration of Nature, Myths and Narrative Conventions of Popular Literature in Richard Brautigan's Novel *The Hawkline Monster: A Gothic Western* (1976), or Gothic Novel and Western in One 55
      II.1.3 Parody of the Western (Film): Robert Coover's *Adventure! Shootout at Gentry's Junction* (1987) 64

   II.2 Pornography 79

      II.2.1 Pornography, Western Myths and Violence in R. Coover's *Spanking the Maid* (1982) 79
      II.2.2 Pornography, Artificiality and Technology: R. Coover: *Lucky Pierre in the Doctor's Office* (1994) 88

   II.3 Fairy Tales as Popular Culture 101

      II.3.1 Subversion of Myths: High and Low Cultures in Robert Coover's *Briar Rose* (1996) 101
      II.3.2 Parody in Robert Coover's *Pinocchio in Venice* (1991) 113
      II.3.3 From Experience to Postmodern Sensibility (Robert Coover: *The DOOR: A Prologue of Sorts*, 1969) 123
      II.3.4 Popular Culture, Media and Parodic Contexts of R. Coover's *For the Kiddies: Cartoon* (1987) 134

   II.4 Popular Autobiography and Travel Book in One (Richard Brautigan's *An Unfortunate Woman: A Journey*, 2000) 142

CHAPTER III
POSTMODERNISM AND METAFICTION 151

III.1 Metafiction in Robert Coover's Fiction (*The Marker* and *The Hat Act, 1969*) 151

III.2 Allegorical Metafiction— Paul Auster's *The Locked Room* (1985) 165

III.3 Crossing the Genres— Fact or Fiction? Kurt Vonnegut's *Timequake* (1997) 184

NOTES 203

WORKS CITED 207

ACKNOWLEDGEMENTS

This book is a continuation of my previous study on American postmodern fiction entitled *Poetika americkej postmodernej prózy: Richard Brautigan and Donald Barthelme* [Poetics of American Fiction: Richard Brautigan]. Prešov: Impreso, 2001. While in my first book I dealt with various aspects of American postmodernist fiction in connection with parody and its relation to history, popular culture and fantasy as manifested in the novels by Richard Brautigan and Donald Barthelme, this book explores various aspects of American postmodernist fiction as manifested in other works by Richard Brautigan (*An Unfortunate Woman: A Journey*. New York: St. Martin's Press, 2000), Donald Barthelme (*Paradise*, 1986), and especially in the works by other American postmodernist authors such as Robert Coover, E. L. Doctorow, Kurt Vonnegut and Paul Auster. The scope of this book ranges from a single work to a comparative study of different authors' works ranging from short story to novel. Using Brian McHale's theory of postmodernist fiction (*Postmodernist Fiction*. London and New York: Routledge, 1987) to show a difference between modernist and postmodernist Literature, Chapter I gives an analysis of two novels by Donald Barthelme (*Snow White*, 1965; and *Paradise*, 1986), the author who has traditionally been considered to be an iconic postmodernist author. Analyzing these two novels, I have tried to show not only differences between modernist (*Paradise*) and postmodernist literature (*Snow White*), but also Donald Barthelme's return to more traditional modernist poetics in the last phase of his literary career (his novel *Paradise*). Chapter II is a continuation of my previous book's Chapter II, and points out the way postmodern literature uses the narrative strategies of popular literary genres such as the western and pornography, but also fairy tales, popular autobiography and travel books to undermine not only traditional and mimetic representation of reality (through parody, irony, grotesque, and satire), but also the way the parodies of these genres give a critique of some aspects of American cultural identity and experience (the American Dream, individualism, consumerism). Analyzing two of Robert Coover's short stories (*The Marker* and *The Hat Act*), a novel(lla?) by Paul Auster (*The Locked Room*, which is a part of Paul Auster's *The New York Trilogy*, 1985), and the most recent novel by Kurt Vonnegut (*Timequake*, 1997), the last chapter shows different ways postmodern authors create metafictional effect that I consider to be one of the most significant manifestations (but not the only one) of postmodern literature. At the same time, the last chapter offers a typology of metafiction. Although metafictional elements occur in the literary works discussed in other two chapters as well, I have selected the works in which these metafictional elements dominate and point out a relation between fiction and reality. I will point out the way these works turn the reader's attention to language and its functioning at the construction of (linguistic) reality and meaning.

A slightly different version of this book was published in a limited edition as *American Fiction: Modernism-Postmodernism, Popular Culture, and Metafiction*. Prešov, Impreso, 2003. Some of the chapters and sub-chapters included in this book were presented as papers at various international conferences in the USA, Austria, Poland, Hungary, the Czech Republic and Slovakia, and were further revised and extended. Shorter versions of one chapter and some sub-chapters of this book were originally published in the conference proceedings (Kušnír, J. "What is and What is Not Postmodernism: [Mis]Understanding Donald Barthelme's Novel Paradise." Sweeney, M., Peprník, M.(eds.): *[Mis] Understanding Postmodernism & Fiction of Politics, Politics of Fiction*. Olomouc, Universita Palackeho Olomouc, Olomouc, 2003. 131-148; Kušnír, J. "Life and Death in the American Novel." *The 6th Conference of British, American, and Canadian Studies (Proceedings)*. Opava: Slezská univerzita v Opavě, 2001.100-106; Kušnír, J. "Metafiction in Robert Coover's Fiction ("The Marker" and "The Hat Act")". Bényei, T., Morse, D.E., Szaffkó, P., Virágos, Z. (eds.). *HUSSE Papers 2003 (Literature and Culture). Proceedings of the 6th Biennial Conference of the Hungrian Society for the Study of English*. Debrecen: University of Debrecen, 2004.182-191; and Kušnír, J. "Time, Metafiction, Intertextuality in Kurt Vonnegut's Novel "Timequake." Stulov, J.V. (ed.). *Problemi identičnosti, etnosa, gendera v kuľture i literaturach starogo i novogo sveta*. Minsk: Minsk Linguistic University, 2004.108-121).

Some other chapters were originally published in the conference proceedings in Slovak, but were translated into English, slightly modified and extended (Kušnír, J. "Od zážitkovosti k postmodernej senzibilite (na texte

Roberta Coovera Červená Čiapočka)". *O zážitkovosti a funkčnosti v literatúre pre deti a mládež*. Prešov: Náuka, 2002. 44-54; "Vnútropriestorové aspekty románu Roberta Coovera Pinocchio v Benátkach." *Zborník materiálov z vedeckej konferencie Vnútropriestorové priestory textu v literatúre pre deti a mládež*, 18.-20.10.2000. Prešov: Náuka, 2001. 252-261).

I would like to express my gratitude to many people who have significantly contributed to the publication of this book, especially to Professor Mark Kulikowski, a historian from Johnson City, USA, for his regular donation of books to our library— both primary and secondary resources without which it would have been much more difficult to write this book (many books, especially by Robert Coover and various literary theorists, donated by Professor Kulikowski, are listed in the Works Cited section); my friend and former colleague Professor Janet Gerba from Arlington, Texas, USA, for her proofreading of several chapters of the book; Professor Stephen Lund from the Arizona Western College at Yuma, Arizona, USA, for his proofreading of Chapter I; Andrew Billingham for his careful proofreading of Chapter II and stimulating suggestions; and other friend David Potts from Manchester, Great Britain, for his proofreading of Chapter III; my friend Professor Richard Betts from The Penn State University, Delaware Campus, USA, for sending me not only several books, but especially scholarly articles, essays and papers related to the topic, but especially for his proofreading of chapter I and several sub-chapters; Professor John Cox, a historian from The Wheeling Jesuit University, West Virginia, USA; Dr. William Webster from The South Georgia College at Douglas, Georgia, USA; and Mr. Glen Huff from Mississippi, USA, for sending other relevant materials quoted in this book; Associate Professor Josef Grmela, CSc. from the Deparment of English Language and Literature, Pedagogical Faculty of Charles University, Prague, the Czech Republic, for supervising, reviewing my work as well as for professional encouragement and stimulating advice; Associate Professor Anna Grmelová, CSc. from the same institution; Associate Professor Ludmila Urbanová, CSc., from the Masaryk University at Brno, the Czech Republic (all my former instructors of English and literary theory from whom I have learned a lot not only about literature); Professor Anna Valcerová, CSc.; Professor Stanislav Rakús, CSc.; Professor Viera Žemberová, CSc. from the Department of Slovak Language and Literature, Faculty of Arts, the University of Prešov, Slovakia; Professor Karol Horák, CSc. from the Department of Aesthetics and Theory of Arts, Faculty of Arts, The University of Prešov at Prešov, Slovakia (all my former instructors and distinguished scholars in Slovak literature and literary theory at the former P. J. Šafárik University at Prešov, Slovakia, who have stimulated my appreciation of literary studies); Professor Nina Vietorová, CSc. from the Pedagogical Faculty of the Comenius University at Bratislava, Slovakia; Associate Professor Štefan Baštín, CSc., from the Faculty of Arts, the Comenius University, Bratislava, Slovakia; Professor Tibor Žilka from the Constantine the Philosopher University at Nitra, Slovakia; Professor Howard Wolf from the State University of New York at Buffalo, USA; Professor Josef Jařab from the Palacký University at Olomouc, the Czech Republic, a former President of the European Association for American Studies; Professor Zuzana Stanislavová, CSc. from the Department of Slovak Language and Literature, Pedagogical Faculty, The University of Prešov at Prešov, Slovakia; and many others for professional encouragement, co-operation and support; PhDr. Mariana Prčíková, PhD., and all my colleagues from The Department of English Language and Literature, Faculty of Humanities and Natural Sciences, The University of Prešov at Prešov, Slovakia, for their help, understanding and patience. In addition, I wish to express my gratitude to my colleague, Ivana Cimermanová, for encouragement and fabulous technical help without which neither my first nor this book could be published.

CHAPTER I
BETWEEN MODERNISM AND POSTMODERNISM: DONALD BARTHELME'S NOVELS *SNOW WHITE* (1965) AND *PARADISE* (1986)

However complicated, ambiguous, and problematic the term modernism may seem, modernist literature is understood as a psychological and subjective response to the external world[1]. This subjective and psychological response mostly manifests itself in the authors' use of the first person narrator often overlapping with other narrative voices as well as in the use of stream-of-consciousness method, which are typical narrative techniques giving modernist psychological and subjective vision of the world. As Randall Stevenson argues

"[...]modernist fiction's most obvious and celebrated innovation lies in its focalization of the novel in the minds or private of its characters. Stream of consciousness and a variety of other devices are used to transcribe an inner mental world at the expense of the external social experience most often favoured in the conventional, realistic forms of earlier fiction"(Stevenson 1991: 19).

These narrative techniques can evoke an effect John Lye calls "perspectivism", which he understands as

"the locating of meaning from the viewpoint of the individual; the use of narrators located within the action of the fiction, experiencing from a personal, particular (as opposed to an omniscient, 'objective') perspective; the use of many voices, contrasts and contestations of perspective; the consequent disappearance of the omniscient narrator"(Lye).

Stephen Spender, as one of the first theorists of modernism, suggested the idea that modernist art seems to understands itself as an aesthetic product representing a way out of the everyday dull and quotidian reality (Spender in Hoffmann,1984:14-17). In Spender's view, modernist literature includes both a destructive and a creative element, destructive when human consciousness is in opposition to the society and creative when manifesting itself in the modernist authors' belief in basic values of aesthetic experience (Spender in Hoffmann, Hornung, Kunow 1984: 14). According to Lye, the meaning of modernist art is "*to create a sense of art as artifact, art as 'other' than diurnal reality (art is seen as 'high', as opposed to popular)*" (Lye).

Also Hoffmann, Hornung and Kunow confirm this idea arguing that "*modernism becomes a matter of a clearly negative evaluation of 'modern' society, which appears as a 'wasteland' from whose suffering one escapes through the aesthetic*"(Hoffmann, Hornung, Kunow 1984:22).

Lye further argues that such an approach to reality stimulates "*The appearance of various typical themes, including: question of the reality of experience itself; the search for a ground of meaning in a world without God; the critique of the traditional values of the culture; the loss of meaning and hope in the modern world and an exploration of how this loss may be faced*"(Lye).

According to Hoffmann, Hornung and Kunow, Modernists believe "*[...] that subjectivity, formal experimentation and the autonomy of art represent the appropriate response to a world that has become so complex as to elude traditional interpretation*"(Hoffmann, Hornung, Kunow 1984: 19).

In connection with the understanding of social reality, modernist literature expresses critical attitudes towards a world because of the presence of violence, destruction, and chaos. The modernist response to such a world is thus detachment, alienation and even nihilism. These feelings manifest themselves in both narrative techniques (the 1st person narration, stream-of-consciousness, multiplicity of narrative voices) and in the depiction of characters, setting and themes. As G. Hoffmann, Alfred Hornung and Rudiger Kunow observe, this results in the subjectivism of the modernist outlook

"*[...] which causes the social context of human life to shrink in importance and ultimately leads to the supposition that all practical action is pointless as well as to a negation of rationality as a means of explaining the world*" (Hoffmann, Hornung, Kunow 1984:17).

Such a modernist outlook and subjective vision of the world developed in a period of considerable technological progress (telephone, aircraft, railway lines) at the beginning of the 20th century. On the one hand, the period was marked by a belief in technical progress but, on the other hand, by skepticism and even nihilism associated with the post-World War I period. The artistic results of this period were the literary works of modernist authors such as Franz Kafka, Marcel Proust, Robert Musil, Thomas Mann, James Joyce,

Virginia Woolf, E. M. Forster as well as the works of such American authors as Gertrude Stein, Ernest Hemingway, F.S. Fitzgerald, John Dos Passos, William Faulkner and others.

In the 1960's there was an evident change in the nature of both American society (influenced by a rapid growth of technology, mass media and the rise of popular culture) and fiction. Realist, naturalist and modernist writers (William Faulkner, Ernest Hemingway, John Dos Passos, but also Southern and Jewish-American authors) had to compete with a new generation of authors whose literary work was based on experimentation with language and form. These works expressed the sensibility of the contemporary period marked by rapid development in technology, especially media and information systems. Especially the media have considerably stimulated a massive interest in popular culture. In her essay *One Culture and the New Sensibility* (1978), characterizing the sensibility of a new period Susan Sontag argues that

"*This new sensibility is rooted, as it must be, in our experience, experiences which are new in the history of humanity—in extreme social and physical mobility; in the crowdedness of the human scene (both people and material commodities multiplying at a dizzying rate); in the availability of new sensations such as speed (physical speed, as in airplane travel; speed of images, as in the cinema); and in the pan-cultural perspective on the arts that is possible through the mass reproduction of art objects*"(Sontag 1978:296).

The work of such authors as John Barth, Thomas Pynchon, Donald Barthelme, Vladimir Nabokov and Kurt Vonnegut was marked by radical experimentation with language and its referential function, by the use of parody, radical irony, pastiche, metafictional and other experimental strategies. All these strategies undermined the poetics of traditional ("exhausted"— Barth, 1967) realist, naturalist and even modernist literary works, but also, in this way, expressed a critique of traditional literary techniques, forms and genres. At the same time, they gave a critique of consumerism, of the worshipping of traditional national icons, of the stupefying effect of popular culture and, last, but not least, a critique of current political and social ideologies and the socio-political situation. This kind of literature has "crossed the borders" (Fiedler, 1975) between serious and popular fiction, between poetry, prose, and drama, between fiction and reality, between literature and visual arts or music, between history and modernity, and between past and present. This literature can be understood as postmodern. Nina Vietorová characterizes it in the following way:

"*In postmodernism there is no obligation to believe any story, on any level. Postmodernism presents us with a sense of infinite possibility. Like story also the idea of personality is often eroded in postmodern fiction. Narrative figure exists but its status is uncertain. This uncertainty is expressed in a shift in narrative voice from first to the third person or through an unexpected use of tense*" (Vietorová 2002:7).

In addition to this, postmodern literature has opened the space for the realization of the diversity of ethnic, regional, feminist, sexually different (gay, lesbian) identities and cultures that had been suppressed before and that represent a diversity of American culture and society. The changing character of fiction, thinking and technologically advanced societies was discussed in such essays as Irving Howe's *Mass Society and Post-Modern Fiction* (1959), John Barth's *Literature of Exhaustion* (1967), Leslie Fiedler's *Cross the Border—Close That Gap* (1967), Jacques Derrida's *Structure, Sign and Play in the Discourse of Human Sciences* (1988), and Francois Lyotard's *Answering the Question: What is Postmodernism?* (1993). Theoretical concepts of Postmodernism and its cultures were explored in Ihab Hassan's, Susan Sontag's, Gerald Graff's, Andreas Huyssen's, Linda Hutcheon's, Brian McHale's, Charles Jencks' and other theorists' works.[2] All these authors have also suggested a difference between modernist and postmodernist societies and literature and have significantly contributed to the understanding of a new social reality, its changed sensibility and culture.

In addition to this, the authors mentioned above have laid the theoretical foundations of postmodernism and postmodernity. In contrast to modernism (and modernity as a cultural and social phenomenon), postmodernism rejects the ability of human mind to perceive the world as a subjective, interiorized entity or as a psychological experience since the vision of the world of a man in this period is distorted by new technology, especially by mass media, television, film, computers, and is replaced by its simulation (Baudrillard, 1993), by the image, and by popular culture. Seen in this context, the world cannot be perceived and known either subjectively or objectively, it can only be faced and absorbed through a diversity of images, forms, and various ontological realities. Such a response to reality means a rejection of the ability of reason to explain the world. This means a rejection not only of reason, but also of the idea of order of any kind modernity (in broader understanding the period since the Enlightenment) represents (by the organization of social life, knowledge, science, human societies, and culture). Francois Lyotard uses the term "grand narratives" to refer to dominant discourses in the particular stage of the development of the society or theories which are, according to Mary Klages, "*stories a culture tells itself about its practises and beliefs*"(Klages) including knowledge, science, ideologies and theories. The grand narratives are characterized by order, rationality, and are part of modernism. On the other hand, as Mary Klages further observes,

"*Postmodernism then is the critique of grand 'narratives'* (Klages) and, *"[...] rejecting grand narratives, favors 'mini-narratives', stories that explain small practises, local events, rather that large-scale universal or global concepts*"(Klages).

According to Klages, these "mini-narratives"
"*[...] are always situational, provisional, contingent, and temporary, making no claim to universality, truth, reason, or stability*"(Klages).

In literature, this postmodernist disbelief in rationality, order, grand narratives and subjectivity manifests itself in the authors' use of language games as a response to the rationalist belief in the ability of language to produce a clear, unitary and logical vision of the world. Logics and rationality are undermined by the subversion of the referential function of language, especially the relation between the signifiers and the signifieds. As Klages argues,

"*In postmodernism [...] there are only signifiers. The idea of any stable or permanent reality disappears, and with it the idea of signifieds that signifiers point to. Rather, for postmodern societies, there are only surfaces, without depth; only signifiers, with no signifieds*"(Klages).

I cannot fully agree with Klages' ideas about the absence of the signifieds. If Klages' ideas were true, this would mean the rejection of any meaning; it would result in linguistic anarchy and nonsense. I do not think the signifieds are absent, but that the relation between the signifiers and the signifieds is different, based on playing with meaning through experimentation with language and the use of language games. The emphasis on the signifiers and experiments with language in literature then means a rejection of deep psychological structures and subjectivity. Formally, psychological structures and subjectivity manifest themselves mostly in interior monologues and stream-of-consciousness narrative techniques. But, referring to the new fiction of the 1960's, Raymond Federman argues that

"[...]the new novel invents its own reality, cuts itself off from referential points with the external world. The new novel affirms its own autonomy by exposing its own lies: it tells false stories, inauthentic stories; it abolishes absolute knowledge and what passes for reality"(Federman in Hoffmann,G., Hornung, A., Kunow, R. 1984: 137).

In postmodern literature, reality is mostly presented as a series of incompatible images, ontological worlds, and surfaces which all struggle for their legitimization none of which is, however, superior to the other. As Federman sees it, in postmodern literature

"Reality (and I mean here daily social reality) is only one possibility among the millions of possibilities whose combinations of elements constitute the world. The world is but the perception one has of it. There is no right or wrong perception; there is no absolute truth. The real world is everywhere [...]"(Federman in Hoffmann 1984:143).

That is also why in postmodern literary works there is often no clear distinction between reality and fantasy, between different ontological worlds and visions of reality. This distinction is blurred especially by the use multiple and overlapping narrative techniques, by the juxtaposition of fiction and reality; by mixing the genres, and especially by metafiction which Patricia Waugh understands as

"[...] a term given to fictional writing which self-consciously and systematically draws attention to its status as an artefact in order to pose questions about the relationship between fiction and reality"(Waugh 1984:2).

The order, chronology or the linear plot (if any) are rejected. Since the characters are mostly rid of their specific identity and psychological background, in postmodern literary work they tend to be derivative from their literary prototypes and their identity is often unclear and ambiguous. According to Raymond Federman, in postmodernist fiction

"Characters inhabit a dimension of structureless being in which their behaviour becomes inexplicably arbitrary and unjudgeable because the fiction itself stands as a metaphor of derangement that is seemingly without provocation and beyond measurement"(Federman in Sim 2001:123).

Anticipating the metafictional character of the future fiction as early as in the 1970's, Federman further argues that

"[...] the primary purpose of fiction will be to unmask its own fictionality, to expose the metaphor of its own fraudulence, and not pretend any longer to pass for reality, for truth, or for beauty. Consequently, fiction will no longer be regarded as a mirror of life, as pseudorealistic document that informs us about life, nor will it be judged on the basis of its social, moral, psychological, metaphysical, commercial value, or whatever, but on the basis of what it is and what it does as an autonomous art form in its own right"(Federman 1975: 8-9).

In postmodernist literary works, both the logical and clear vision of reality and order are further undermined by fragmentation, by the use of parody, irony, and pastiche. These narrative strategies express the instability of both the perception and the position of postmodern man in the contemporary world. On the one hand, parody, irony and pastiche establish a make-believe relationship with reality. On the other, they consequently subvert it. Postmodern literature often parodies popular literary genres to emphasize the "exhaustion" of traditional "grand narratives" and literary forms and thus it acquires a status of an intramural critique of these genres (Barth, 1967) as well as a critique of a simplified, logical and clear vision of the world as represented in these genres. On the other hand, postmodern parodies give a critique of the iconic aspects of particular national identities. The postmodern parodies of the western genre such as, for example, Richard Brautigan's *The Hawkline Monster* (1976), or Robert Coover's *Ghost Town* (1998) imply a critique of both the frontier myth and the American Dream as the manifestations of American cultural identity. In addition to this, as I have mentioned above, in contrast to modernism and modernist literature which tend to understand high art as the possible alternative to chaotic and problematic social reality, using popular genres and popular culture, postmodern literature tends to erase the differences between the high and the low (popular) art and appeals to broader masses.

In his theoretical study on postmodernist literature entitled *Postmodernist Fiction* (1987), Brian McHale both suggested a difference between modernist and postmodernist literary texts and, at the same time, gave an exhausting analysis of the inventory of topics, poetics and textual strategies of postmodernist fiction that he supported by a variety of examples. In contrast to, for example, Ihab Hassan, who suggested oppositional categories to stipulate a difference between modernism and postmodernism[3], Brian McHale has given a more systematic definition of postmodernist literature. Although he understands postmodernist fiction as a "superior construction" (McHale 1987: 5), I will not discuss the term itself, but rather focus on the idea of the basic difference between modernism and postmodernism as understood by McHale. McHale sees this difference in the formal, aesthetic and philosophical approaches of these kinds of literature to the depiction of reality. Drawing on Jakobson's idea of the dominant, McHale argues that

"[...] the dominant of modernist fiction is epistemological. That is, modernist fiction deploys strategies which engage and foreground questions such as "How can I interpret this world of which I am a part? And what am I in it?[...]What is there to be known? Who knows it? How do they know it, and with what degree of certainty? How is knowledge transmitted from one knower to another, and with what degree of reliability? How does the object of knowledge change as it passes from knower to knower? What are the limits of the knowable?" (Mc Hale 1987: 9).

He further identifies characteristic modernist devices that are, in his view,
"the multiplication and juxtaposition of perspectives, the focalization of all the evidence through a single center of consciousness[...]interior monologue[...]" (McHale 1987: 9).

According to McHale, the dominant of postmodernist fiction is, on the other hand, ontological (McHale 1987: 10). In his view,
"[...] postmodernist fiction deploys strategies which engage and foreground questions like 'Which world is this? What is to be done in it? Which of my selves is to do it?" (McHale 1987:10).

McHale further argues that

"*Other typical postmodernist questions bear either on the ontology of the literary text itself or on the ontology of the world which it projects, for instance: "What is a world? What kinds of world are there, how are they constituted, and how do they differ? What happens when different kinds of world are placed in confrontation, or when boundaries between worlds are violated? What is the mode of existence of a text, and what is the mode of existence of the world (or worlds) it projects? How is a projected world structured?[...]"* (McHale 1987:10).

All the theorists and critics I have mentioned above have significantly contributed to the debate on and understanding of what can be characterized as postmodernism. At the very beginning of this story, however, there was a certain misunderstanding. Although Irving Howe had prophetically anticipated the changing character of society and literature even before any coherent treatment of postmodernism and its theory was formed, that is in 1959, his identification of the new authors he qualified as "post-modern" (Saul Bellow, Wright Morris, Bernard Malamud, Jerome David Salinger, Herbert Gold, and Nelson Algren) seems inappropriate in terms of the contemporary understanding of postmodern literature, especially from Brian McHale's (1987), Linda Hutcheon's (1988), and Patricia Waugh's (1984) points of view.[4] The authors Howe mentioned in his essay *Mass Society and Post-Modern Fiction* can be understood as modernist rather than postmodernist, despite the fact that Howe was not dealing with particular aspects of postmodernist poetics in this essay. Characterizing some of the novels[5] by the above authors which he understands as postmodern, he argues that

"*Though vastly different in quality, these novels have in common a certain obliqueness of approach. They do not represent directly the postwar American experience, yet refer to it constantly. They tell us rather little about the surface tone, the manners, the social patterns of recent American life, yet are constantly projecting moral criticism of its essential quality. They approach that experience on the sly, yet are colored and shaped by it throughout. And they gain from it their true subject: the recurrent search—in America, almost a national obsession— for personal identity and freedom. In their distance from fixed social categories and their concern with the metaphysical implications of that distance these novels constitute what I would call 'post-modern' fiction*" (Howe 1979: 137).

In the context of the characteristics of modernism I have given above, moral criticism, a search for freedom and personal identity, and a distance from the fixed social categories may imply a modernist rather than a posmodernist vision of the world and poetics.

Most scholars consider Donald Barthelme to be an exclusively postmodernist author.[6] I think there is one exception in his work, and it is his novel *Paradise* published in 1986. Analyzing Donald Barthelme's novels brings me to the conclusion that this novel is modernist rather than a postmodernist work. I can agree with McHale that

"[...] postmodernism should not be defined so liberally that it covers all modes of contemporary writing, for then it would be of no use in drawing distinctions, but neither should it be defined too narrowly" (McHale 1987: 4).

Through a comparative analysis of this and another novel by Barthelme, *Snow White* (1965), which I find a "classic" example of postmodernist fiction, I would like to point out the modernist character of his novel *Paradise*, as well as differences between modernism and postmodernism. In my view, this difference can be seen more clearly on the examples which represent a typical postmodernist (*Snow White*) and a different, rather modernist poetics (*Paradise*, 1986). Drawing on some of the above characteristics of modernism, but especially on Brain McHale's understanding of the differences between literary modernism and postmodernism, I will focus on the way Barthelme constructs a modernist vision of the world in his novel *Paradise*. This manifests especially itself, in my view, in his depiction of his protagonists and themes, although he uses postmodern narrative techniques and strategies as well.

Paradise

The focus of Donald Barthelme's novel *Paradise* is on the life experience of a well-off divorced aging intellectual (architect) Simon shortly before his retirement. He seems to compensate for his life crisis by his drinking and dallying with three young girls from Colorado, creating a "Paradise" for an aging man as an exchange for his financial sponsoring of them. The actions of Barthelme's protagonists are reduced to satisfying their basic physical needs (eating, sleeping, drinking, sex) and to reflecting on their current condition, which seemingly evokes the author's interest in foregrounding ontological questions. Barthelme's interest in ontological questions can be further supported by the absence of a typical modernist device—stream of consciousness—in this novel. Such seemingly ontological strategy is violated quite radically by "epistemological," rather modernist, narrative techniques, as well as by Barthelme's construction of the characters, their place and time.

Although Barthelme's narrative in his novel *Paradise* does not include typical modernist devices such as interior monologues or the stream-of-consciousness method of manifesting the projection of the outer world in the human mind, in addition to his emphasis on psychology the author uses an even more traditional device—an omniscient narrator; dialogues between Simon, the aging architect, and his girlfriends; and dialogues between entities referred to as Q and A (question, answer), apparently between Simon and a doctor. This narrative section (Q and A dialogues) reminiscent of a therapy session turns out to be a dialogue on the meaning of life. The traditional omniscient narrator reveals both Simon's and the girls' current and past social situations and backgrounds, and both kinds of dialogues (between Simon and the girls, and the Q:A dialogue) fulfill a function similar to a modernist stream-of-consciousness to explore the characters' attitudes to the world and their thinking. Thus the omniscient narrator constitutes a make-believe relationship to reality based on the establishment of the "single center of consciousness" associated with a central protagonist. Although Barthelme's omniscient narrative voice has humorous and ironical undertones to express a critique of Simon and his attitudes to the world as well as of his feelings associated with aging, there is no doubt about the central problem the narrator establishes: the life, emotional and intellectual crisis of an aging intellectual coping with the changing sensibility of the period, its life styles as well as its art, as represented especially by the architecture Simon is an expert in. Simon is described in the following way:

"*Simon was delighted to be fifty-three, lean and aggressive except for his belly which was not lean and aggressive. He was younger than I.M. Pei, younger than Dizzy Gillespie, younger than the Pope. He had more wisdom packed in his little finger than was to be found in the entire Sweets catalog,* with its pages of alluring metal moldings and fire-rated expansion joints" (Barthelme 1986:107).

This passage undermines the seriousness of the narrative tone, but not the belief in reality, and turns out to be a mockery of both Simon's denial of aging, and the uniformity, stupidity and growing impact of commercial culture. Naivistic juxtaposition of incompatible phenomena—aging and fame— make Simon a person unable to cope with aging, but on the other hand also a person worshipping youth as symbolically representing innocence. Youth identified with the contemporary, with free life and sex, with worshipping the popular culture that all three girls appreciate is, however, in contradiction with Simon's understanding of innocence. Thus Simon paradoxically both accepts and rejects contemporary morality and sensibility. On the one hand, he has regular sexual intercourse with the three girls, listens to popular music, and thus is involved in the contemporary life style and sensibility; but on the other he longs for security in family life and in his care for children. This security is paradoxically achieved by his living in a common household and enjoying a free relationship with three young women. Thus he is in the position of a passive receiver of new experience, in the position of clown or jester unable to cope either with his new personal life situation or with the contemporary state of both morality and art:

"When he asked himself what he was doing, living in a bare elegant almost unfurnished New York apartment with three young and beautiful women, Simon had to admit that he did not know what he was doing. He was, he supposed, listening. These women were taciturn as cowboys, spoke only to immediate question, probably did not know in which century the Second World War had taken place[...]what they knew was wildly various, a ragout of Spinoza and Cindy Lauper with a William Buckley sherbet floating in the middle of it. He'd come in one evening to find all three of them kneeling on the dining room table with their rumps pointing at him. Obviously he was supposed to strip off his gentlemanly khakis and attend all three at once[...] One night on his back in bed he'd had six breasts to suck, swaying above him, he was poor tattered Romulus. When they couldn't get a part of him they'd play with each other" (Barthelme 1986: 60-61).

The contradiction between different periods, life styles and cultures represented by Simon on the one hand, and the three girls on the other manifests itself in the girls' ignorance of history and art (World War II, Keith Jarre's music or the Marshall plan), but also in Simon's inability to identify the meaning of references to contemporary popular culture (for example, a T-shirt which reads "Ally Sheedy Lives").

In this novel omniscient narration introducing and commenting on the characters' behaviour overlaps with interior monologues and dialogues. The monologues reveal Simon's and other protagonists' attitudes not only to life, but often to art and culture as manifested in the following monologue:

"New architecture is 'soulless', Simon reads, again and again and again. He has trouble disagreeing when what is being talked about is a seventy-story curtain-wall building on Sixth Avenue. People don't like to live or work above the second floor in any building, the third at the outer extreme. No building should be taller than a ship. People like light; on the other hand, they also like caves. An austere facade pleases architects; people like decoration, a modicum of drama. Embassies are now being designed like banks, with more and more security as one moves deeper and deeper into the building, the most secure space, deep inside, mighty like a vault. Reconcile with the idea of an embassy as a pleasing, friendly presence. Metal detectors set up at the entrances of schools. Gun-toting Wackenhuts in supermarkets [...] Giant concrete flowerpots all around the Capitol which have nothing to do with love of flowers. The messianic-maniacal idea that architecture will make people better, civilize them, central to much 1920's-1930's architectural thought, Corbusier, Gropius, even Wright, abandoned. Although modesty is not what architects do best, there is more restraint now, Simon thinks. I'll do my piece of the problem and you do yours. Not at all soulless, rather more cottage industry, S.O.M. notwithstanding. The image that seems to him really on the mark of the circus" (Barthelme 1986: 69).

This monologue's function is to reveal Simon's reflection on the situation of architecture and his rejection of modernist, pragmatic architectural patterns. At the same time, this monologue reveals the difference between past and contemporary architecture and culture. However, not only this but also other passages in the book avoid showing clearly any preference on Simon's part for contemporary art, culture and way of life. He has quite a critical approach to the girls' ignorance of history and past art, but himself rejects the dominant modernist functionalist ideology in architecture, longs for safety and security, although living an unbalanced free life characteristic of the contemporary period. He listens to old music, but is not familiar with contemporary popular cultural icons. Through these narrative strategies Barthelme emphasizes the idea of hesitation, especially hesitation between the past and contemporary values, between innocence and immorality, between (sexual) freedom and (family) security, between old (modernist) and new (postmodern) art. As Stanley Trachtenberg suggests,

"*Simon's rebellion against form is not so much a reaction against the past as an attempt to prevent his estrangement from the present*" (Trachtenberg 1990: 202).

This estrangement manifests itself in his uncertainty and hesitation which puts him on the trajectory of a displaced, alienated person occupying a blank position between the past and present, personal and public life, "high" and popular art.

Dialogues in this Barthelme novel deal mostly with banal every day topics which often turn out to be, similar to the above and other interior monologues, reflections either on the status of art, culture and the way of life, or self-reflexive passages focusing the reader's attention on the language and its working. This can be seen in the following example:

"*You want to jump the babysitter.*"
"*Where does this word 'jump' come from?*"
"*I know you.*"
"*I don't think I've ever said that to anybody.*"*I know you.*"
"*You're too wrapped up in your own stuff even to try. To know someone.*"
"*The phrase is a bit total.*" As in, "*I totaled the Buick*" (Barthelme 1986: 52).

This narrative technique represents a typical postmodernist narrative strategy, turning the reader's attention to the working of the language and the process of its construction, that is, using McHale's terminology, on ontological issues. On the other hand though, this strategy is not dominant, for multiple narrative techniques (omniscient narration, interior monologues, dialogues) emphasize Simon's epistemological quest for meaning in the contemporary world, and that is a modernist quest. Simon becomes alienated from both modernist and contemporary (postmodern?) culture, from both traditional and modern life experience, but he tries to find the epistemological grounds for his life position both as a human being and as an architect. For him, art, as in

Modernism, can represent a certain way out of quotidian, everyday but inadequate reality (his comments on art, music, and popular culture) and an epistemological ground which is to justify his life experience. Using McHale's terminology, this quest is based on trying to find an answer to such questions as

"*How can I interpret this world of which I am a part? And what am I in it?[...]What is there to be known? Who knows it? How do they know it, and with what degree of certainty?*" (McHale 1987: 9).

Simon tries to see, read, and interpret the world represented by both his life and artistic experience (architecture), despite the ironic distance he has from it. Moreover, the modernist quest is further supported by other dialogic exchange between Q and A, apparently between Simon and a doctor. At the same time, however, these dialogues between (let us say) a questioning and answering person may represent Simon's consciousness, a dialogue within his contradictory and unbalanced personality symbolically represented by two persons (Q states he is a doctor). According to Trachtenberg, these dialogues

"*represent the conflicting voices of the same figure. Though A's preference in the story for frozen dinners is deleted from the novel, he is made to alternate concerns that in the story were cast as a repeated sequence of statements all attributed to Q, each revealing some aspects of his self-questioning uncertainty*" (Trachtenberg 1990: 218).

If we trust Trachtenberg's characterization of a dialogue between Q and A as the representation of conflicting voices, then these voices exchange their roles and questioning Q often becomes an answering person or voice. In addition to this, these "voices" seem to turn out to gain a parodic tone, being both a parody of the psychological consciousness as a typical modernist device and, at the same time a parody on therapy itself. This can be seen from the following exchange between Q and A when women become the subjects:

'"*Q: You mean they fought*".
"*A: They were sisterly most of the time. Once in a while they fought*".
"*Q: Using what means?*"
"*A: Mouth, mostly*".
"*Q: Remarkable*".
"*A: I thought so*".

"*Q: When I first married, when I was twenty, I didn't know where the clitoris was. I didn't know there was such a thing. Shouldn't somebody have told me?*"

"*A: Perhaps your wife?*"

"*Q: Of course she was too shy. In those days people didn't go around saying, This is the clitoris and this is what its proper function is and this what you can do to help out. I finally found it. In a book*".

"*A: German?*"

"*Q: Dutch*'" (Barthelme 1986: 128-129).

Such a narrative strategy used in a dialogue between Q and A, mystifying the roles of both voices as well as "serious discourse"(doctor-patient dialogue) through the use of parody, is seemingly and formally a postmodern attack on the unitary and authoritarian voice, on the "grand narratives", as well as on the modernist consciousness and psychology, but the function of this Q and A dialogue does not exceed the epistemological framework. It expresses Simon's hesitation, his inability to cope with contemporary reality and the state of art, with his personal condition, especially his aging. Simon's hesitation and unbalanced personality— the character of which is revealed also through this dialogue— represent his search for understanding of the world, past and present, private and public, which is an epistemological search. This hesitation is close to a nihilistic approach to the world which *"[...] becomes the central preoccupation, the Inner Demon, at the Heart of Modern Literature"*(Howe in Hoffmann, Hornung, Kunow 1984: 18).

As it was suggested above, through his protagonist Barthelme asks the questions McHale defines as epistemological and modernist:

"*How can I interpret this world of which I am a part? And what am I in it?[...]What is there to be known? Who knows it? How do they know it, and with what degree of certainty?*" (McHale 1987: 9).

The self-reflexive dialogues mentioned above, the parodistic treatment of a modernist self-consciousness (some parts of the Q and A dialogue) are close to postmodernist narrative techniques which tend to foreground ontological questions related to the working of the language and the world, but which, however, do not dominate in this novel. They are only supplements to the epistemological framework of the world Barhelme's novel represents and legitimize the idea of Simon's search for freedom and understanding of the world, his position in it as well as his estrangement from the present. They express the protagonist's modernist alienation from the world which is "*[...] the main theme of modernism*" (Hoffmann, Hornung, Kunow 1984: 23).

Snow White

Narrative techniques used in Barthelme's novel *Snow White* are radically different from those used in his novel *Paradise*. In his *Snow White* Barthelme presents a variety of narrative forms, with very often overlapping, often unidentified voices each struggling for its legitimization, each establishing and at the same time undermining its identity, especially through the author's use of fragmentation, ellipses, irony and parody. The reader can find an inventory of various narrative techniques (omniscient narrator, both first-person singular and plural, interior monologues, dialogues) loosely arranged on a collage-like principle. All these narrative voices do not present any coherent discourse, plot or events, but are rather fragmentary reflections on the protagonists' roles in the story, on the state of art, culture, economy, language and other issues. The coherence of the narrative voices is fragmented and broken up by the inclusion of other narrative "discourses" representing non-literary devices— a letter, questionnaire,

"*boldface chapters consisting of mock subject headings, philosophical or historical commentary, psychological interpretation of the characters, or indications of narrative development*"(Trachtenberg 1990:170).

Barthelme further uses headings reminiscent of film subtitles such as "*The Psychology of Snow White: In the Area of Fears, She Fears Mirrors, Apples, Poisoned Combs*"(Barthelme 1986: 17) or "*What Snow White Remembers: The Huntsman The Forest The Steaming Knife*"(Barthelme 1986: 39); cliché-like slogans or phrases representing political speech, scholarly jargon or phrases used in different discourses. This can be seen from the following example:

"*The revolution of the past generation in the religious sciences has scarcely penetrated popular consciousness and has yet to significantly influence public attitudes that rest upon totally outmoded conceptions*" (Barthelme 1986: 54).

The example above uses a film technique of subtitles anticipating the forthcoming action, commenting on it, or replacing dialogues. In Barthelme's novel it alludes to both the famous story and its popular Walt Disney version, but at the same time it becomes a parody of them, since the conventions of both the famous story and its film version are undermined by the reference to "psychology" which is unacceptable for these genre conventions, as well as by the response to this heading and Snow White's psychology on an earlier page: "*What is Snow White thinking? No one knows*" (Barthelme 1986: 16). In addition to this, Barthelme's parody is further confirmed in the novel by the fact that Snow White is not presented as an innocent mythical figure, but as a contemporary pseudo-intellectual and erotic figure contemplating on and complaining about her position in the contemporary world; reflecting on her role status as a myth and figure. This is also one of the functions of the above headings: to point out a considerable difference between Barthelme's Snow White and the famous fairy tale. Snow White's reflections can be seen in the following passage:

"*Snow White took her head out of the window, and pulled her long black hair which had been dangling down. "No one has come to climb up. That says all. This time is the wrong time for me. I am in the wrong time. There is something wrong with all those people standing there, gaping and gawking. And with all those who did not come and at least try to climb up. To fill the role. And with the very world itself, for not being able to supply a prince. For not being able to at least be civilized enough to supply the correct ending to the story*" (Barthelme 1986: 131-132).

Barthelme's Snow White's reflections are not reflections on the human condition, but on the role and function of a myth in the contemporary period Snow White represents. It is a myth of innocence, but also of the simplified black and white vision of the world represented by the popular genre conventions, especially the fairy story of which Snow White is protagonist. Snow White's dissatisfaction thus becomes Barthelme's dissatisfaction with both contemporary life influenced by a massive influx of popular and consumerist culture and the distorted language which represents it. According to Trachtenberg,

"*The dissatisfaction with reality [...]is grounded in a dissatisfaction with the manner in which it is conceived, that is to say what is wrong is not simply with the world but with the willingness of the world to submit to the formal structure of a story. Snow White, then, does not so much long for the prince as for the 'abstract' notion that, to her, meant 'him'[...]*" (Trachtenberg 1990:170-171).

This narrative strategy focuses the reader's attention not on the real life situation, but on the workings of the language which represents it, which reveals its status of a signifier and a means of construction of the world. The questionnaire, letters and "utterances" representing various discourses fulfil a similar function. Barthelme's narrative voices establish their identities using a particular jargon, a particular way of speech or utterance, but at the same time the author undermines their serious status through his use of parody and irony, distracting the reader's consciousness and attention through these devices, as well as through the commentary following the voice he establishes a realization of the workings of the language he uses. For example, the questionnaire concluding Part One in Barthelme's Snow White asks the reader questions such as:

"*1. Do you like the story so far? 2. Does Snow White resemble the Snow White you remember? 3. Have you understood, in reading to this point, that Paul is the prince-figure?*" (Barthelme 1986:82).

Barthelme establishes a seemingly serious voice and form for this questionnaire, asking readers for their opinions on the book, but its function is deliberately misplaced in this context and has at least a twofold function: to stimulate readers' awareness of the fictitiousness of what they are reading now (and through other questions even to involve them in the plot construction) by asking them to compare the stories they know and what they are reading now. This is to reveal the fictitious character of Barthelme's version of a story creating an autonomous world, that is the world of language which constructs the real world, and, at the same time it becomes a parody on familiar commercial questionnaires when the narrator asks, at the end, such questions as

"*14. Do you stand up when you read? Lie down? Sit? 15. In your opinion, should human beings have more shoulders? Two sets of shoulders? Three?*" (Barthelme 1986:83).

Such strategies used by Barthelme in his questionnaires, self-reflexive passages and other "discourses" in his novel are metafictional strategies *par* excellence, entirely different from the mimetic narrative strategies he used in his novel *Paradise*, which was written, quite paradoxically, some twenty years later. They are strategies which foreground the workings of the language and its ability to construct an autonomous world. Patricia Waugh characterizes metafiction as

"*[...] fictional writing which self-consciously and systematically draws attention to its status as an artefact in order to pose questions about the relationship between fiction and reality*" (Waugh 1984: 2).

I consider metafiction to be one of the most typical postmodern devices, that is, a device foregrounding, in McHale's terms, ontological issues.

A similar narrative strategy of establishing the voice, be it the first person singular or a "collective voice" (e.g. of dwarfs), an omniscient narrator, a modernist stream-of-consciousness—but later undermining it by abandoning the focus, point and "center of consciousness", consequently leading the reader/perceiver to awareness of the workings of the language along with its juxtaposition to various discourses represented by a language typical of them, is a strategy which occurs frequently in Barthelme's novel, as in the following extract:

"*Henry said, "this language thinking and stinking everlastingly of sex, screw, breech, 'part', shaft, nut, male, it is no wonder we are all going round the bend with this language dinning forever into our eyes and ears [...]*'" *"I am not going round the bed", Dan said, "not me". "Round the bend," Henry said, "the bend not the bed, how is it that I said 'bend' and you heard 'bed', you see what I mean, it's inescapable." "You live in a world of your own Henry." "I can certainly improve on what was given", Henry said"* (Barthelme 1986: 30).

The language of conversation, private or public dialogues, formal or informal, scientific or popular language become, in Barthelme's presentation, deprived of their meaning in the contemporary world, when cliché-like phrases and slogans are referred to quite often in the text as objects or trash, as one of his narrators comments:

"*They are 'trash', and what in fact could be more useless or trashlike? It seems that we want to be on the leading edge of this trash phenomenon, the everted sphere of the future, and that's why we pay particular attention, too, to those aspects of language that may be seen as a model of the trash phenomenon. And it's certainly been a pleasure showing you around the plant this afternoon, and meeting you, and talking to you about these things, which are really more important, I believe, than people tend to think. Would you like a cold Coke from the Coke machine now, before you go?"* (Barthelme 1986: 97-98).

Barthelme emhasizes this cliché-like character of language, characteristic of contemporary culture and its "consumerist" nature through his juxtaposition of often absurd, cliché-like language of his protagonists' speech and a consumerist imagery, a vending machine in the above example.

As I have mentioned, the fragmentary narrative flow presents a contemporary and parodical version of the famous story figure. Snow White and the Seven Dwarfs (named Kevin, Edward, Hubert, Henry, Clem, Bill and Dan) live in a contemporary world, drink beer, and enjoy sex and contemporary culture. They also have "modern" jobs, that is, washing the buildings and tending the vats.Barthelme's novel is not a simple traditional mocking parody of a famous fairy tale, but, as Stanley Trachtenberg suggests,

"[...]more central to the Barthelme version is the value of the story itself, recovering the surprise available in the linguistic vitality of popular oral forms, a vitality, the novel suggests, that had been lost through self-conscious substitution of language for either feeling or understanding and through the consequent continuing need for novelty to insure interest" (Trachtenberg 1990:167).

Thus it can be said that Barthelme's narrative strategies, his use of metafiction, of fragmentary and often unfinished multiple narrative voices which establish and then undermine their "serious" status (their function of a signifier) and meaning too through the use of irony and parody, as well as his inclusion of various discourses representing different jargons of private and public, scientific and popular, artistic and commercial culture, all these are the strategies of the ontological dominant through which the author interrogates the principles of construction of real and fictional worlds. At the same time, Barthelme reveals the ability of language to construct an autonomous world, as well as the relation between the real and the fictional, present and past worlds. Parody and irony show a distance from the past and from seriousness, and, at the same time, along with metafiction reveal the fictitiousness of the presented reality. In addition to this, referring to the artificial, non-physical world (language in general, different styles and genres, different artistic and literary works), parody and metafiction both point out and reveal the nature of representation by using artistic (literary) language through which they challenge the ability of language to represent the world rationally and objectively. Along with McHale, Barthelme is asking questions such as

"*What is a world? What kinds of world are there, how are they constituted, and how do they differ? What happens when different kinds of world are placed in confrontation, or when boundaries between worlds are violated? What is the mode of existence of a text, and what is the mode of existence of the world (or worlds) it projects? How is a projected world structured?*" (McHale 1987: 10).

Since Barthelme's focus in *Snow White*, in contrast to his novel *Paradise,* is not on the epistemological but on the ontological questions mentioned above, his use of narrative techniques in *Snow White* confirm the ontological dominant of this novel, that is its postmodern character *par excellence*. Thus the difference between the novels *Paradise* and *Snow White* shows also the difference between literary modernism and postmodernism. In Barthelme's novel *Paradise* the author uses more coherent and traditional narrative techniques which, despite the parallel use of some postmodernist literary devices (irony, some metafictional elements, juxtaposition of several narrative voices), seen in the context of McHale's theory, these narrative strategies construct modernist rather than postmodernist vision of the world. Typical of these narrative strategies is the depiction of hesitation, alienation or even nihilistic approach to the world. In contrast to this novel, Barthelme's novel *Snow White*, using such narrative strategies and literary means as metafiction, juxtaposition of fragmentary and elliptic voices, postmodern parody, irony, and mixing of the genres shows the artificiality of our construction of the world and reveals its ontological status by drawing a reader into the process of construction of its meaning. This creates what Brian McHale calls "ontological dominant."

The main aim of this chapter was to show the difference between modernist and postmodernist literary techniques to show a difference between different approaches to the literary representation of reality. It cannot be said, however, that anything experimental can be understood as "postmodern", just as Umberto Eco argues:

"Unfortunately, 'postmodern' is a term bon á tout faire. I have the impression that it is applied today to anything the user happens to like. Further, there seems to be an attempt to make it increasingly retroactive: first it was apparently applied to certain writers or artists active in the last twenty years, then gradually it reached the beginning of the century, then still further back. And this reverse procedure continues; soon the postmodern category will include Homer" (Eco in Hutcheon 1988: 42).

Although very often there are not clear boundaries between Modernism and Postmodernism in the arts, my conviction is that the analysis of narrative strategies modernist and postmodernist arts use can help us distinguish different sensibilities and constructions of the world both kinds of art create.

CHAPTER II
POSTMODERNISM AND POPULAR CULTURE

In technologically advanced areas such as the USA, Great Britain and other Western European countries, rapid advance in technological progress, especially in mass media such as television, cinema and video has contributed considerably to changing the nature of both society and culture since World War II. New media, able to appeal to the broad masses, have significantly influenced the formation of a unitary mass society influenced and manipulated by these media. This was a mass society Irving Howe characterized as

"[...] a relatively comfortable, half welfare and half garrison society in which the population grows passive, indifferent, and atomized; in which traditional loyalties, ties, and associations become lax or dissolve entirely; in which coherent publics based on definite interests and opinions fall apart; and in which man becomes a consumer, himself mass-produced like the products, diversions, and values that he absorbs"(Howe 1979:130).

According to Irving Howe, it is passivity, indifference and consumerism, but also a crisis and relativization of traditional values and a lack of the "firsthand experience" which are the typical features of such society (Howe 1979:131-132).

Television, video and movie theatre programs have acquired the character of a commodity (Jameson, 1991), a product the main aim of which is to gain financial profit. With rising living standards and increasing passivity of the population as well as with growing influence of the media, direct contact with reality has been replaced with its imitation or simulation, that is by its image. This has contributed to the inability of the broad mass of people— influenced by these mass media and the new technology - to distinguish between fact and fiction, between good and evil, between the natural and the artificial. In his comments on the power of digital images and media, Jean Baudrillard argues that

"[...] from the fact that images ultimately have no finality and proceed by total contiguity, infinitely multiplying themselves according to an irresistible epidemic process which no one today can control, our world has become truly infinite, or rather exponential by means of images. It is caught in a mad

pursuit of images, in an ever greater fascination which is only accentuated by video and digital images. We have thus come to the paradox that these images describe the equal impossibility of the real and of the imaginary"(Baudrillard 1993:194).

The rapid growth in advanced technologies including the mass media has considerably stimulated the popularity of popular culture as well. Using Marxism-inspired terminology, Jameson argues that popular culture has become a "commodified product of the late capitalist production"(Jameson, 1991). Popular literature as part of popular culture thus becomes an advantageous and profitable product, a marketable commodity. Popular literature using schematic narrative conventions understandable by the broad masses gives a simplified and unproblematic, black-and-white vision of reality. At the same time, popular culture has changed in its character. It has become a product of visual rather than oral or written culture, and this is a change that expresses the sensibility of the contemporary (post-modern) period (Sontag, 1978). This postmodern period is characterized by Lloyd Spencer as

"[...] one in which cultural activity is dominated by media industries capable of appealing directly to a public (itself the beneficiary of mass education) over the heads of any cultural elite. Mass media and the culture industries, informatics and cybernetics, virtual reality and an obsession with 'image'— postmodernists and their detractors map the changes in the increasingly synthetic fabric of social life in very similar ways"(Spencer 2001: 159).

Leslie Fiedler sees the nature of this age as

"[...] apocalyptic, anti-rational, blatantly romantic and sentimental; an age dedicated to joyous misology and prophetic irresponsibility; one, at any rate, distrustful of self-protective irony and too great self-awareness"(Fiedler 1977: 330).

Juxtaposing incompatible images, commercial television in particular, as Grenz comments on it, relativizes both the difference between fact and fiction and the hierarchy of aesthetic and ethical values. In Grenz's view,

"A typical evening newscast, for example, will bombard the viewer with a series of unrelated images in quick succession—a war in a remote country, a murder closer to home, a sound bite from a political speech, the latest on a

sex scandal, a new scientific discovery, highlights from a sporting event. This collage is interspersed with advertisements for better batteries, better soap, better cereal, and better vacations. By giving all these varied images - news stories and commercials alike - roughly equal treatment, the broadcast leaves the impression that they are all of roughly equal importance"(Grenz 1996: 34).

In their attempt to earn more profit through commercial programmes, popular films, soap operas or cartoons, especially commercial television and popular films which flatter and attract the mass audience, turn the viewers into consumers and are thus able to capture them. Popular culture including not only popular films and TV programmes, but also music and popular fiction such as spy, pornographic, detective, horror and other stories or science-fiction have become an inseparable part of the postmodern culture. Science fiction especially, appealing to a technologically competent audience, has become extremely popular lately. As Bohuslav Mánek observes, it

"[...] has gradually become one of the basic components of contemporary Anglo-American popular culture"(Mánek 2000: 16).

Paul Maltby argues that

"The cultural space of late capitalism is suffused with the representations of commodity aesthetics and mass-media entertainment. These are understood to supply the dominant forms of cognition and imagination. Hence the postmodernist preoccupation with artifice, spectacle, dreck and kitsch. These features of a 'debased', commercial mass culture become the materials of an art whose relationship to (high) modernism is, in consequence, rendered ambivalent"(Maltby 1991: 4).

Postmodern culture has "crossed the borders and closed the gaps" (Fiedler, 1975) between high and low (popular) culture, between the academic and vernacular audience. In his essay *Cross the Border—Close That Gap*, Leslie Fiedler anticipated the popularity of this popular culture, especially the popular literary genres such as western, thriller, detective stories, pornography and fairy tales. He also anticipated their role in both the creation of a new sensibility and a new kind of writing, a writing parodically and playfully re-writing these genres. Such a re-writing then transg resses the boundaries between the high and popular culture. According to Fiedler, as suggested above, postmodern literature has often used and, at the same time, parodied the narrative conventions of popular literature. Popular culture dominates especially in the USA. Moreover Tomáš Pospíšil argues that

"*Popular culture is an integral part of the American reality. Much of what the United States is now—its values, attitudes, lifestyles, perception of the world—is in one way or another informed by its popular culture*"(Pospíšil 1998:28).

Through the use of parody, irony, metafiction and other narrative strategies, the aim of these tropes and literary devices was not the undermining of traditional narrative conventions for its own sake, but through the subversion of traditional narrative techniques to make a critique of the traditional "objective", unitary vision of reality mostly used in popular genres which tend to evoke a make-believe, mimetic representation of reality. In addition, the other aim of postmodernist literature is to make a critique of popular culture as a product of consumerism; and last but not least, through the use of intertextual and metafictional strategies, to point out a sensibility of contemporary postmodernist culture influenced by visual and popular culture. As suggested above, this sensibility is based on a perception of reality influenced mostly by technological progress, especially the new media and the popular culture including popular fiction. The use of narrative techniques of traditional genres shows one of the basic aesthetic tenets of postmodernist literature.

In contrast to modernism, which tended to emphasize the separatedness of art as a way out of chaos and disillusion, postmodernist art does not claim its originality and separatedness, but a belonging to particular cultures, and the connection to the conventions and myths creating crucial aspects of particular cultural identities.

Various narrative strategies, conventions and myths are re-considered, transformed and recycled to show the inevitable connection between cultural (and commercial) products (including popular culture), the mass consumers and social reality. Such a transformation breaks the illusion of newness, since reality is perceived and understood as a copy, as a collection of images which have already been used in the past. As Alan Bilton argues,

"*Images seem to be breeding in a wild state, a copy of a copy of a copy, until the original source eventually disappears; this then is where the originality of the Postmodern lies, in reproduction rather than production, dissemination rather than creation"*(Bilton 2002: 3).

In postmodern literature, the language and narrative conventions of popular literature are often parodied to present a critique of linguistic representation of the forms and genres producing a simplified image of reality. This is not a traditional parody with a mocking intent, but a neutral postmodern parody showing differences between the past and present, between past and contemporary representations of reality (Hutcheon 1978: 202). It is especially parody and irony which are the means the authors use to make their critique of consumerist culture—a simplified vision of reality conveyed through media and popular culture - as well as of the linguistic representation itself. On the one hand, using the narrative strategies of popular cultural forms, postmodernist literature can appeal to a broader audience and can thus stimulate its interest in reading. On the other hand, many postmodernist works, quite paradoxically, do not overcome the gap between popular and high cultures, but tend to be either highly intellectual or naively popular and kitschy. Postmodern parodies of popular literary genres thus become double-coded. According to Theo D'haen, who refers to Charles Jencks' notion of double-codedness,

"On the one hand, by using subject material and techniques from the popular level of the culture they form part of, postmodern artefacts and texts have a direct appeal as consumer articles to all, even the least artistically or literarily trained, contemporary Americans. On the other hand, by its parodistic use of earlier— and predominantly Modernist—works of art and literature, and by its ironizing of its popular material and techniques, it also appeals to the artistically and literarily sophisticated"(D'haen 1986: 226).

In his study of popular genres, John Cawelti understands each popular literary form as *"a structure of narrative or dramatic conventions"* and as both *"a conventional way of treating some specific thing or person"*, as *"larger plot types"*(Cawelti 1976: 5), and as genres which use fixed narrative conventions; which are mostly escapist; which fulfill an entertainment function; and which give a schematic vision of reality. In his view,

"[...] formulas are ways in which specific cultural themes and stereotypes become embodied in more universal story archetypes"(Cawelti 1976: 6),

which he further understands as

"[...] *a combination or synthesis of a number of specific cultural conventions with a more universal story form or archetype"*(Cawelti 1976: 6).

It follows from the above, according to Cawelti, that these formulas represent certain aspects of particular cultures' identities. This chapter deals with the way such authors as Robert Coover, Donald Barthelme, Edgar Lawrence Doctorow, and Richard Brautigan use postmodern narrative strategies, techniques and tropes, especially postmodern parody, irony, metafiction, fragmentation and juxtaposition of reality and fantasy, to undermine traditional formulas, genres and kinds of writing such as westerns, Gothic novels, pornography, fairy tales, popular autobiographies (travel books), cartoons and science-fiction, and at the same time to demonstrate the way they create new postmodern works appealing to contemporary sensibility. In addition, this chapter will attempt to show how these authors, by parodying traditional narrative conventions and formulas, provide a critique of the stereotypical image of reality and particular cultural identies constructed and manipulated by the media and popular culture. However eclectic the selection of authors and genres may seem, they are all connected with popular culture, and these postmodernist authors use the genres in their own way to undermine traditional narrative patterns, simplified, schematic visions of reality and the construction of the stereotypical image of American cultural identity presented through the media and popular culture.

II.1 The Western

II.1.1 Parody of the Western in American Literature (E. L. Doctorow's *Welcome to Hard Times*, 1960; and Robert Coover's *The Ghost Town*, 1998)

According to many critics (e.g. Poirier 1968; Bradbury 1980), parody is one of the most important forms and tropes of 20th century literature. As mentioned above, both parody and irony used in popular genres on the one hand point out the "exhaustion" of traditional forms and genres and on the other both express a critique of some "myths" creating particular cultural traditions. This does not mean traditional ancient myths, but modern myths that are produced by particular nations and cultural contexts to emphasize the distinctiveness of cultural identity of these nations and their cultural contexts. The genre of the western is one of the most traditional and genuine American genres expressing the specificity of American cultural experience (Smith 1950; Turner 1938). Leslie Fiedler considers the western along with pornography and science fiction to be one of the most typical genres of popular culture (Fiedler, 1975). In his study of popular culture entitled *Adventure, Mystery and Romance: Formula Stories as Art and Popular Culture* (Chicago and London: 1976), John Cawelti calls popular literary forms "literary formulas", which he understands as

"[...] *archetypal story patterns embodied in the images, symbols, themes and myths of a particular culture. As shaped by the imperatives of the experience of escape, these formulaic worlds are constructions that can be described as moral fantasies constituting an imaginary world in which the audience can encounter a maximum of excitement without being confronted with an overpowering sense of the insecurity and danger that accompany such forms of excitement in reality*"(Cawelti 1976:16).

In addition to this, Cawelti considers the western to be one of the major formulas (Cawelti 1978:16), and emphasizes their cultural contexts. In his view, these formulas "have some sort of influence on culture because they become conventional ways of representing and relating certain images, symbols, themes, and myths" (Cawelti 1976:20).

It is especially the ideas of the frontier, harsh life, violence, outlawed gun fights, a symbolic landscape (Cawelti 1976:193) as well as the inventory of characters such as gunslingers, villains, beautiful ladies and prostitutes that have not only formed specific aspects of the genre of the western, but also shaped the myth of American cultural identity. From this point of view, by undermining the myths a particular culture generates, postmodern parodies could be understood as a kind of cultural criticism but also as a critique of idealization of the iconography through which particular cultures emphasize their cultural values and experience.

In their parodies of the western genres, then, Edgar L. Doctorow and R. Coover undermine not only the traditional structure of this genre, but also some aspects of American cultural identity. These authors' use of parody and irony in their novels *Welcome to Hard Times* (Doctorow, 1960) and *Ghost Town* (Coover, 1998) shows, speaking in Linda Hutcheon's terms, both distance and difference between the past and present, between past and present sensibilities (Hutcheon 1985: 32). She argues that

"There is nothing in parodia that necessitates the inclusion of a concept of ridicule, as there is, for instance, in the joke or burla of burlesque. Parody, then, in its ironic 'trans-contextualization' and inversion, is repetition with difference. A critical distance is implied between the backgrounded text being parodied and the new incorporating work, a distance usually signalled by irony"(Hutcheon 1985: 32).

As already mentioned, the use of parody shows up differences between traditional and contemporary literary forms, and, at the same time, exposes them to critique. According to McHale,

"Parody [...] is a form of self-reflection and self-critique, a genre's way of thinking critically about itself"(McHale 1987:145).

In a similar vein, Poirier observes that

"The literature of self-parody continues, then, the critical function that parody has always assumed, but with a difference[...] parody has traditionally been anxious to suggest that life or history or reality has made certain literary styles outmoded"(Poirier 1968:339).

In this section, the above authors' narrative and textual strategies will be analyzed to show not only the diversity of parody of the western genre, but also the way these authors undermine traditional myths and icons forming American cultural identity. The main focus will be on studying the setting and partly the characters, although both authors' parody manifests itself even more apparently in their narrative techniques and the depiction of the plot. But comparative study putting emphasis on the setting and partly the characters can better show a postmodern playful, parodic and ironic reconsideration of both the generic conventions and cultural myths of the USA associated with both the genre and the myth it generates. In addition, the intention is to show the way in which both authors' parodic and ironic distortion of the traditional western setting and partly the characters represents not only a new kind of writing but also an instance of cultural criticism. It must be emphasized, however, that both Doctorow's and Coover's works were written in a time span of more than 30 years (Doctorow's *Welcome to Hard Times* was written in 1960, while Coover's novel *Ghost Town* appeared in 1998).

Setting/Landscapes

It might be considered self-evident to observe that the western is a genre of fiction *"associated with the western states of the U S A"* (Cuddon 1991:1042). From the very beginning of their novels, however, both authors emphasize the role of the landscape and depict it as the archetype used in traditional western genres—as a desolate, dry, harsh but majestic geographical territory associated with the western states of the United States. According to Theo D'haen,

"[...] the postmodern western employs setting to express the mood of its characters, the wider import of their actions, and the importance of the issues at stake" (D'haen 1987:170) and landscapes *"[...]illustrate the magnitude of the principles pitted against one another involved: good versus evil, law and justice versus lawlessness order versus anarchy"*(D'Haen 1987:166).

In both novels the depiction of setting (landscape) dominates and plays a symbolic role, although in connection with other components of these novels (characters, narrative techniques, plot) the function of the landscape evokes different connotations. In Doctorow's novel *Welcome to Hard Times*, the western city as part of the landscape is depicted as situated in

"[...] the Dakota Territory, and on three sides—east, south, west—there is nothing but miles of flats[...] Most times the dust of the horizon moved east to west—wagon trains nicking the edge of the flats with their wheels and leaving a long dust turd lying on the rim of the earth[...] To the north were hills of rock and that was where the lodes were which gave an excuse for the town, although not a good one"(Doctorow 1960:3-4).

Not only flatness, dryness, dirt and hard living conditions, but also the roughness and violence associated with them are emphasized in Doctorow's novel. Doctorow's depiction of characters corresponds to his depiction of the landscape and setting and gains a symbolic function. His characters are mostly presented as poor, dirty and rough; the main street is covered with manure, and general hygiene in the desert city is inadequate because of the lack of water. Blue, narrator and later unofficial mayor and record-keeper of the city at the same time, observes that

"[...] people would throw their slops into the alleys. Some didn't care where they did their business and it got so you were hard put to walk in the street without putting your boot down in a mess. One morning Molly found a drunken man peeing against the door"(Doctorow 1960: 169).

This harsh, dirty and rough setting plays a symbolic role in Doctorow's novel. The attempts to get rid of dirt (Blue's shaving his beard, women's bathing in a tub) symbolize the anticipation of both the city's progressing prosperity and its inhabitants' attempt to restore civilized order and life after the former city's destruction by the Bad Man from Bodie. This anticipated prosperity manifests itself in the fact that Blue wants to continue with keeping his records and establishes his business with water; that Isaac Maple establishes his shop and Zar his public house and a saloon. In addition to this, the harsh and rough landscape and dirt symbolize evil, hard life and violent lawlessness, and a certain anarchy as depicted in traditional westerns. In addition to this, in Doctorow's novel *Welcome to Hard Times* the landscape and the setting represent a certain enclosure and microcosm of the (frontier) society—poor farmers, workers, unsuccessful gold-diggers, whores, small entrepreneurs (Maple), artisans, villains, mysterious Native inhabitants—

Indians (John the Bear), an illegal Russian businessman, a calm Swedish farmer and settler, and a Chinese prostitute.

Similarly, in Coover's novel *Ghost Town* the landscape around the town is depicted as *"Bleak horizon under a glazed sky, flat desert, clumps of sage, scrub, distant butte[...] a land of sand, dry rocks, and dead things. Buzzard country[...] A space there and not there, like a monumental void, dreadful and ordinary all at once"*(Coover 1998:1,4).

The town itself is characterized as

"a plain town that comes past, empty and silent, made of the desert itself with a few ramshackle false-fronted frame structures lined up to conjure a street out of the desolation. Nothing moves in it[...] the sign over the saloon door hangs heavy in the noontime sun as the blade of an ax"(Coover 1998:6).

In contrast to Doctorow, who puts emphasis on the social observation of city life in his *Welcome to Hard Times*, this element is suppressed in Coover's novel. His city represents an iconic city of the western, but it is a city where almost no progress or purposeful activity, but only violence can be observed. The reduction of the social observation is replaced by Coover's emphasis on the wild cruelty and violence which dominates the city, and which the main character, an unknown intruder and cruel gunslinger and later, albeit undesirably, a sheriff coming to the city, is unable to remove. This unnamed narrator becomes both the subject and object of violence. The violence becomes everyday reality in the city, as can be seen from the following scene:

"[...] the fat man's smile is widened from ear to ear, his stiffened handlebars snicked to a brush, and his belly's so punctured his guts start to spill out; but neither man gives an inch. Whuck, whuck, whuck, the knives go, and nothing he can do but watch, both men blinded now by blood and injury, taking blow after blow after blow, the other men of the posse cheering them on, laying bets on the side, pushing the antagonists back into it if they chance to stagger apart. Finally, the butcher knife breaks off in the mestizo's ribs and, as the disarmed fat man slumps to his knees, the mestizo finishes him off in the slaughterhouse manner by stabbing him two-fisted in the back of the neck"(Coover 1998:63).

In Coover's novel *Ghost Town*, the juxtaposition of the ghost and town evokes not only a feeling of ambiguity between the real and the imaginary, but especially of decay, mystery and fear. The eponymous ghost town of the novel is associated with the cultural fringe or periphery, with the unimportance of being located outside all cultural centres. The main character of the novel, an indefinite gunslinger, visitor and later part-time sheriff *"[...] doesn't know what it's rightly called, nor feels any need to know. It's just the place he is going to"* (Coover 1998: 5). The town is also threatening:

"Nothing moves in it. In an open window, a lace curtain droops limply, ropes dangle lifelessly from the gallows and hitching posts, the sign over the saloon door hangs heavy in the noon-time sun as the blade of an ax" (Coover 1998: 6).

Emptiness, silence, desolation, lifelessness and the gallows are all the imagery of death and decay Coover juxtaposes to the natural imagery, the meaning and connotations of which are altered. Nature does not evoke positive feelings, physical and spiritual regeneration, but represents fear, threat and decay in the same way that the town does. The desert itself represents flatness, nothingness and plainness; it is the *"[...] land of sand, dry rocks, and dead things. Buzzard country"* (Coover 1998: 3). The sun is juxtaposed to an ax, and plain objects referring to the family life and community become threatening (gallows) and desolate. All this threatening atmosphere established at the very beginning of Coover's novel is further developed as it progresses through Coover's use of the imagery of violence. Violence is inextricably associated with the rough life of this remote desert town on the frontier. Coover depicts it as the legendary, iconic town known from western literature and film. It is not, however, only violence and rough, remote and desolate country, but especially gunslingers, cowboys, popular saloon singers, prostitutes and killers, the saloon, bank, horses and murders all forming the inventory of the western genre, an authentic American product/genre associated with both the idea of the frontier as part of the American cultural identity and violence as part of this cultural heritage associated with western expansion. In addition to the depiction of the country given above, there is also the character of the rough horseman, cowboy, gunslinger and mysterious stranger coming to the city, who is introduced at the very beginning of the novel in the following way:

"His lean face is shaded from the sun overhead by a round felt hat with a wide brim, dun-colored like the land around, old and crumpled. A

neckerchief, probably once red, knotted around his throat, collects what sweat, in his parched saddle-sore state, he sweats[...]A soft tattered vest, gray shirt, trail-worn cowhide chaps over dark jeans tucked into dust-caked boots with with pointed toes, all of it busted up and threadbare and rained on, dried out by sun and wind and grimed with dust, that's the picture he makes, forlorn horseman on the desert plain[...]He wears a wooden-butted six-shooter just under his ribs, a bowie knife with a staghorn handle in his belt, and a rifle dangles[...]He is leathery and sunburnt and old as the hills[...](Coover 1998:3).

With the imagery and characters mentioned above, Coover establishes the narrative conventions of the western genre in which the city represents both a physical and a mental space giving an iconic picture of the frontier life, a life with natural, spontaneous but brutal rather than officially, legally authorized rules. According to J. A. Cuddon, the western is the exclusive fiction of the Wild West, in which:

"*White pioneer settlers[...]created a folklore of the regions. This in turn produced frontier stories and sketches about hunting, trapping, ranching, cowboys, conflicts with Indians, cattle-rustling, sheriffs, gun-law, prospecting, brigandage and so forth[...]*" (Cuddon 1991:1042).

In addition to this, Theo D'haen observes,

"*The typical western plot pits a hero—the good guy—[...] against a villain, with a number of subsidiary characters[...]having a stake in the action[...]The conflict between the hero and the villain is not simply a personal one. The villain disturbs the established order in the world of the western: he is a gambler, a rustler, a bank robber, or a killer. In the lawless West, only few men (or women) dare stand up against him, as he is ruthless and quick on the draw[...]*"(D'haen 1987:166).

As has been mentioned, Coover invokes the narrative conventions of the western genre at the very beginning of his novel. A mysterious stranger, a killer and gunslinger comes to the desolated city, and in confrontation with the local gunman establishes his reputation as a brutal killer, even becoming a temporary sheriff who is confronted with other local gunslingers, rascals and killers in series of narrative events. Violence becomes a part of the natural order in *Ghost Town* and can be responded to only by violence. It often becomes violence for violence's sake, portrayed by Coover through a series of graphic, naturalistic scenes, almost revelling in their goriness, as in the knife/fight between the fat man and the mestizo (Coover 1998:63).

Thus the landscape in Coover's novel symbolically emphasizes the function of the city as a representative of violence, cruelty, brutality and lawlessness. Cruelty is, however, glorified through the depiction of a series of unmotivated murders and violence. In this way the conventions of the traditional western are invoked, but the naturalistic depiction of violence which forms a dominant image in the novel undermines the western genre conventions, becoming a certain glorification of it, although further undermined by Coover's depiction of characters, his use of parody and grotesque. In contrast to traditional westerns, there are no clear connections or relationships among the characters. Moving between the city and the desert they appear and disappear, meet and depart randomly. As Bill Marx argues, *"The herky-jerky story line could be written on flash cards flickering in and out of the cowboy's view"*(Marx 1998:3). The characters' background is ambiguous and unclear, identity depicted only as the identity of iconic representatives of the western genre—a horse rider, the gruff barkeep, the saloon bawd, the grizzled drunk, Indian, Mestizo, singer, sheriff and sheriff's deputy. Thus in contrast to Doctorow's emphasis on social observation, in Coover's novel *Ghost Town*, chaotic behavior rather than purposeful action of the characters dominates and suppresses the function of other compositional elements of the traditional western, especially the plot and the western's romantic and adventurous nature.

Parody/Undermining the Western

The landscape and setting in both novels seems to be reminiscent of the setting of the traditional western genres. They have a symbolic function, but both authors first invoking the traditional inventory of the western genre subsequently undermine it by emphasizing other elements and other symbolic connotations associated with the narrative strategies they use. The title of Doctorow's novel itself evokes negative connotations, but at the same time it becomes an untraditional name for the western city. It is thus at variance with traditional western genre expectations involving a positive resolution of the situation and the establishment of order, for the title itself suggests skepticism and pessimism, and is in contradiction with both readers' and city inhabitants' expectations. The city is finally destroyed by the Bad Man from Bodie again, and order, law and prosperity are not restored, goodness and love go missing (Blue's love for Molly, for example), and the characters' hopes are dashed. In addition to this, the title has ironic connotations. Paradoxically, it does not correspond to the optimism associated with both westward expansion and gold-digging in the USA, but creates a metaphor of pessimism, difficulties and possible failure of the protagonists' dreams. As Christopher Morris suggests, the title of Doctorow's novel is *"a paradox: for who would want to welcome or to be welcomed to hard times?"*(Morris 1991:26). Morris further comments on other meanings of the title as possibly alluding to Charles Dickens'novel Hard Times (and thus evoking the idea of social criticism, and a critique of capitalist exploitation), or evoking metafictional associations (Morris 1991:27)[1]. Thus the landscape, setting and their names invoke and subsequently undermine both their original function in the western genre and traditional western conventions. These conventions are further undermined by Doctorow's emphasis on social observation, partly on psychology through his reduction of the plot and through his depiction of the almost apocalyptic final tragic destruction of the city when evil is only partly destroyed (the boy Jimmy Fee seems to anticipate a future follower of the Bad Man from Bodie, thus also future destruction).

As suggested above, also in Coover's novel Ghost Town the landscape and its symbolic function are reminiscent of traditional western genre conventions. At the same time, both the name of the city and the title of the novel indicate its sinister character, desolation, emptiness and purposelessness, which are in contradiction both with the names of the real cities and optimistic expectations of their settlers. Similarly, in Doctorow's novel Welcome to Hard Times, the name of the city becomes an iconic name evoking the atmosphere of disillusion, lawlessness and anarchy that further develops into violence as the dominant image not only of this novel, but also of the western culture and frontier life. The idea of violence is evoked at the very beginning of the novel. Coover uses the imagery of death, dreadfulness and danger, with the saloon sign compared to "the blade of an ax" (Coover 1998:6). This imagery dominates, either literally or symbolically, in the whole novel. The novel teems with deaths, blood and violence, but also with chaos and anarchy that the unnamed and tough gunslinger along with his deputy are unable and perhaps often unwilling to remove. They become a part of the violent and brutal circus ending in itself and creating a metaphor of the frontier life and its culture. It is a metaphor of cruelty and aimless violence as a representation of frontier culture that is associated with a mythical role of the idea of the American frontier as an important part of American cultural identity. This violence results in an almost apocalyptic ending where the town becomes destroyed, abandoned and dead:

"Nothing but a dark cobwebbed and dusty murk in there. Busted furniture strewn about, broken lamps and bottles, the old grand piano fallen face forward as if to bite the floor with its sad scatter of chipped teeth[...] The only sign of life is his hat in the middle of the empty street[...] The town's been abandoned. He's all alone"(Coover 1998:146).

The optimism of the American myth of westward expansion and possible fulfillment of the American Dream are subverted by Coover's glorification of violence leading to pessimism and almost nihilism. In addition to this, and in contrast to Doctorow, Coover suggests the possible illusory, imaginary character of the city and thus symbolically of the whole idea of the frontier myth. His main character has doubts about the existence of the city, as it

"[...] disappears behind a slight rise, then reappears when that rise is reached, often as not even further away to the naked eye, his naked eye, than when last seen, like a receding mirage, which it likely is. Sometimes there's no horizon at all, burned away by the sun's glare or night's sudden erasure, so no town either[...]" (Coover 1998:5).

This evokes a doubt about the real existence of the city and about the gunslinger's perception of reality, which is further supported by Coover's depiction of his visions, dreams and imagination. More radically than in Doctorow's novel, the imagery of violence and absence may stand for a metaphor of doubt, doubt about the importance of this myth in American cultural tradition. At the end of the novel, the gunslinger's survival becomes a purposeless fact since the town is destroyed, his enemies and loves lost, and his function of a restorer of order unfulfilled. What remains, however damaged, is the inventory of both the western genre and the frontier life, that is a horse, the saloon, jailhouse, claims office, steepled church, store, the landscape, and death (Coover 1998:146-147). This destruction and absence imagery ironically highlights both the conventions of the western genre and the myth of the frontier life. As Jeff Yanc observes,

"Coover remains steadfast in his goal to continually knock the reader off balance by trotting out an endless series of Western clichés—the trusted horse, the limping old codger as Sheriff, the good-time saloon gal[...]—then brutally twisting them into nightmarish caricatures to illuminate the staleness of such conventions"(Yanc 1998:1).

Such depiction of the landscape in connection with other compositional elements evokes a parodic effect. It is not a traditional parody; it is a parody that does not necessarily stick to the structural pattern of the parodied genre, but a parody that distorts not necessarily all, but only some compositional elements and narrative strategies of the parodied genre; a parody which lacks a ridiculing effect but which points out the "exhaustion" of traditional genres.

According to Linda Hutcheon, such parody

"[...] implies a distance between the backgrounded text being parodied and the new work, a distance usually signaled by irony. But the irony is more playful than ridiculing, more critical than destructive"(Hutcheon 1978: 202).

In both Doctorow's and Coover's novels, the depiction of the landscape is used first to establish the genre conventions of the western and then to undermine them. In Doctorow's novel, the parodic undermining is done through the author's emphasis on other elements of the novel (social observation, partly psychology, an apocalyptic ending evoking a resemblance to the ancient tragedies); in Coover's novel, it is done mainly through the mythologization of the violence associated with the symbolic function of the rough setting and through the juxtaposition of the imagery evoking the real western landscape (and present in the traditional western genre) and the imagery of dreams, visions, absence and doubt. Such a distortion of the function of the landscape in its own way evokes a parodic effect. In addition to this, by undermining the western genre conventions both authors call into question the importance of the cultural value of the western and frontier myths and their importance for the formation of American cultural identity. Parody in both novels serves as a form of intramural critique of the traditional genres, but without a ridiculing effect. At the same time, this intramural critique suggests a possibility of a new kind of writing using and distorting (through parody, irony, pastiche) traditional forms and genres. In addition to this, Doctorow's novel can be read in different ways, not only as a parody of the western, but also as a story of evil, as a story of the failure of the frontier setting; as a story of the negative effects of violence (Vilikovský 1989:186). In Coover's case, the mythologization of violence ends in itself and thus becomes purposeless. The acts and aims of the main character and violence associated with him lose all purpose and result in absence. There are no winners, no happy ending, and no resolution. What remains, as suggested above, are the remains of the inventory of the western genre through which Coover has constructed a different story that could be read as story on the power of evil or, more importantly for this argument, as a postmodern parody of the western.

As a form of cultural criticism, radical distortion of the western genre conventions means also a radical attack on the genre that represents one of the most important aspects of American cultural mythology, suggesting that the myth of the American frontier is only an illusion, a myth with negative rather than positive connotations.

II.1.2 Reconsideration of Nature, Myths and Narrative Conventions of Popular Literature in Richard Brautigan's Novel *The Hawkline Monster: A Gothic Western* (1976), or Gothic Novel and Western in One

In his book entitled *Waiting for the End* (1964), Leslie Fiedler argues that

"Not only in our literature but in our lives, we have shuttled back and forth between a romantic nature cult and a Philistine anti-nature religion: on the one hand, becoming enthusiastic advocates of nudism and the world's warmest supporters of Freudian psychology; on the other, joining movement after movement against whatever pleasures of the flesh; alcohol, meat, tobacco, drugs. In fact, we maintain these two polar attitudes not alternately but simultaneously, choosing duplicity rather than compromise; and this, indeed, is the essence of the American way" (Fiedler 1964: 140).

This results, according to Fiedler, in contradictory policies simultaneously corresponding to each attitude, one to

"[...] stamp out nature: chop down trees, kill off buffalo, slaughter whales, rape and ruin the wilderness, join the Christian Science Church" (Fiedler 1964:140),

and the other to

"[...] disappear into Nature: preserve our primitive areas, guard our natural resources, provide summer camping grounds with real live bears, strip to the buff and lie in the sun" (Fiedler 1964: 140).

After a certain celebration of the power of nature, spirituality and imagination in his essay *Nature*, Ralph Waldo Emerson gives rather a pessimistic vision of nature in his other essay *Experience*. In most of his novels, Richard Brautigan favours idealistic and romantic nature characterized above as the Rousseauesque or Emersonian kind (Fiedler 1964:140). It manifests itself especially in his novels *A Confederate General from Big Sur* (1964) or *In Watermelon Sugar* (1968). According to Manfred Pütz,

"[...] in Brautigan's fiction, locale and setting—as significant materializations of the fictional counterfield in the sujet movement of pastoral identity stories—take on decisive importance. It is here that Brautigan interconnects a wide range of topoi, motifs and codified elements from various literary traditions falling within the circumference of pastoralism" (Pütz 1979:111).

For most of Brautigan's protagonists, society represents danger and threat and is in opposition to nature and imagination. However, in his novel *The Hawkline Monster* (1974) *the Gothic Western,* Brautigan does not use idealized natural pastoral imagery. In this novel he employs several conventions of popular literature genres, especially the western, the Gothic novel, fantasy or even science-fiction. Gordon E. Slethaug identifies the exact sections and number of pages devoted to particular genres in this book. In his view,

"*Book 1 (59 pages) depends upon a western format, Book 2 (18 pages) upon the Gothic, and book 3 (113) upon a combination of fantasy, science fiction, and then the detective story, concluding with a turn to realism*" (Slethaug 1985:139).

In contrast to other Brautigan novels, in *The Hawkline Monster* nature and landscape represent terrifying, threatening and destructive forces, ultimately turning both into objects of parody. This paper analyzes the way Brautigan undermines the traditional symbolic meaning of nature as a positive force. At the same time, it attempts to show the way Brautigan distorts the traditional narrative conventions of popular literature (the western and the Gothic novel) in order to make a critique of some issues associated with American cultural identity (the idea of success; the American Dream; and the belief in technological progress).

In Book I, entitled *Hawaii,* the landscape evokes a romantic or pastoral atmosphere. The narrator gives a description of harmony among people, nature and culture in a place generally evoking the image of a tourist paradise:

"*The man and boy and the horse were in the front yard of a big white house shaded by coconut trees. It was like a shining island in the pineapple fields. There was piano music coming from the house. It drifted lazily across the warm afternoon*" (Brautigan 1976:10).

This atmosphere is, however, at odds with the function and roles of the cowboys named Greer and Cameron. Hired to kill the family acting as typical cowboy characters, they in fact refuse to spoil the idealistic natural atmosphere. In this way they become only parodic versions of their western prototypes. Nature functions here only as a background for Brautigan's parodic intentions. In addition, the cowboys are geographically, spiritually and emotionally displaced; they are far removed from the context of the western setting and characters. The narrator portrays this displacement in the following way:

"*Greer and Cameron were not at home in the pineapple field. They looked out of place in Hawaii. They were both dressed in cowboy clothes, clothes that belonged to Eastern Oregon*" (Brautigan 1976: 9).

This depiction of the natural landscape is in contradiction with the landscape typical for the western genre. On the other hand, the journey of the cowboys back to the western cities of Portland, Oregon; Gompville; Brooks; Billy; Central County and Dead Hills means a return to the typical setting of the western genre. This setting involves a version of nature which is not a positive force, but rather rough and threatening. At the same time, nature creates a symbolic background for the "roughness" and cruelty of the cowboys' nature. The final destination of their journey where they are hired to kill "the indefinite monster" is near the Dead Hills, a landscape characterized as mountainous and rough:

"*There were thousands of hills out there: yellow and barren in the summer with lots of juniper brush in the draws and a few pine trees here and there, acting as if they had wandered away like sheep from the mountains and out into the Dead Hills and had gotten lost and had never been able to find their way back [...]*" (Brautigan 1976: 24).

Brautigan's depiction of nature is presented here, on the one hand, in keeping with the conventions of the western genre. On the other hand, the rough landscape is not reflected in the otherwise expected rough nature of Greer and Cameron. These characters are only parodied versions of killers, indulging in sex, alcohol and the meaningless counting of different objects (Cameron). The depiction of nature gradually gains a terrifying, threatening character and Gothic atmosphere that culminates in Book III. With the physical movement of the two protagonists approaching the Dead Hills and the city of Billy to which the murder hirer's (Miss Hawkline's) house and the monster are situated, the reader is gradually prepared for tension evoked by this atmosphere. The landscape shortly before the protagonists meet Miss Hawkline is without life, barren and desolate:

"The road was very bleak, wandering like the hand-writing of a dying person over the hills. There were no houses, no barns, no fences, no signs that human life had ever made its way this far except for the road which was barely legible" (Brautigan 1976: 52).

While Brautigan heightens tension as the protagonists (Greer, Cameron, Magic Child) approach the Dead Hills, this atmosphere is weakened on the other hand by the author's depiction of the seemingly typical western tough characters/gunfighters. These characters are hired to kill people for money, but they indulge in sensual and sexual experience with Magic Child, a double of Miss Hawkline. The cowboys become only parodic versions of the typical western characters. Narrative conventions of both the western and the Gothic novel are undermined not only in this way, but also through Brautigan's use of irony. The narrator comments on the protagonists' observation of the country in the following way:

"Finally they came across something human. It was a grave. The grave was right beside the road. It was simply a pile of bleak rocks covered with vulture shit. There was a wooden cross at one end of the rocks" (Brautigan 1976:54).

Brautigan's use of irony passes into parodic imagery expressing the banality of the typical icons of western literature and film, such as desolate graves for example. The grave standing for violence and death supported by the image of vultures becomes only a banal icon and an unimportant detail when Brautigan uses the expression "shit". Here the Gothic landscape and atmosphere are similar to those known from the traditional Gothic novels depicting castles, manor houses and mysteries. This atmosphere culminates at the end of Book II and continues to the end. The final, fatal destination of Greer, Cameron, and Magic Child— Miss Hawkline's double—at her house, is described as

" [...] a huge three-storey yellow house about a quarter of a mile away in the center of a small meadow that was the same color as the house[...] There were no fences or outbuildings or anything human or trees near the house. It just stood there alone in the center of the meadow with white stuff piled close in around it and more white stuff on the ground around it [...]" (Brautigan 1976:5).

Brautigan gradually draws the reader's attention to the geographical and topographical imagery associated with the East (New England) and West (Oregon), the USA and Europe, culture and primitivism (nature). The Hawkline manor house is further referred to as

"[...] a classic Victorian with great gables and stained glass across the tops of the windows and turrets and balconies and red brick fireplaces and a huge porch all around the house [...]" (Brautigan 1976: 58).

This Victorian Gothic setting is supported by the interior of the house referred to as "[...]filled with beautiful Victorian furniture and very cold"(69)[...] The parlor was exquisitely furnished in an expensive and tasteful manner" (86).

This all represents the imagery of the Gothic novel, which is further supported by Brautigan's depiction of characters and events typical for this genre: an old faithful butler; a desolate house and mystery (the monster). The depiction of such setting and characters refer to European (British) tradition and its "refined culture". Fowler argues that

"The word gothic initially conjured up visions of a medieval world, of dark passions enacted against the massive and sinister architecture of the gothic castle [...] The gothic is characterized by a setting which consists of castles, monasteries, ruined houses or suitably picturesque surroundings, by characters who are, or seem to be, the quintessence of good or evil [...] irrational and evil forces threaten both individual integrity and the material order of society" (Fowler 1987: 105).

Although the Gothic "landscape" and atmosphere in Book II and further on is in keeping with the conventions of the Gothic novels (the house, the terrifying landscape and setting, *"irrational and evil forces threaten both individual integrity and the material order of society"*), Brautigan alters the function of both the Gothic novel and the western. The Gothic writers' typical landscape of the British kind seems to be geographically, topographically, emotionally and spiritually incompatible with the American setting. In a broader sense, it is incompatible with American culture represented by Brautigan's use of the conventions of the western genre as well as of natural imagery. This natural imagery intensifies the incompatibility of the British Gothic tradition and culture with the American cultural context. The narrator says that

"[...] the house [...] did not belong out there in the Dead Hills [...] the house belonged [...] any place other than where it was now [...] the house looked like a fugitive from a dream" (Brautigan 1976: 59).

The whole Victorian Hawkline manor becomes a "melting pot" of different genre conventions, rationality and irrationality, reality and fantasy, seriousness and humour, past, present and future. The house becomes a symbol of traditionally optimistic cultural expectations and its incompatibility with reality itself. The vision of a house in an isolated area is reminiscent of John Winthrop's vision of "a city upon a hill" alluding to the idea of a cultural experiment in a new country (Willis 1981-82: 37), which is further supported by Brautigan's depiction of the mysterious and absent character of Professor Hawkline and his chemical experiments. The result of this experiment is a monster representing an evil and destroying force acting against its creator. Not only the chemical, but also the cultural experiment of the Puritans and consequently the New Englanders (symbolically represented by educated Professor Hawkline and, for example, Magic Child/Miss Hawkline who accom-panies the cowboys) seems to fail in the cultural environment of America. The narrator argues about Magic Child/Miss Hawkline that

"She was a member of a prominent New England family that dated back to the Mayflower. Her family had been one of the contributing lights that led to the flowering of New England society and culture" (Brautigan 1976: 56).

Brautigan symbolically shows that a rationalistic understanding of and approach to life and society can be only partly successful. It can bring some technological progress, whose result is, however, unsure (Professor Hawkline and his product, the monster). Rationality represented by Greer and Cameron can temporarily destroy the life-threatening forces, but it cannot definitely bring happiness. Greer and Cameron, representing parodied versions of gunfighters and therefore the rationalistic approach to life, must face the irrational world of fantasy at Hawkline Manor and are unable to transcend its boundaries. The only weapon they want to use to destroy it is typical for the western characters— guns, violence and a rationalistic, however parodic, handling of the situation. The world of fantasy and imagination, as well as the symbolic, spiritual and intuitive approach to life, is strange to them:

"What does supernatural mean?" Cameron said [...] "It means out of the ordinary," Miss Hawkline said.

"That's good to know," Cameron said. He did not say it in a pleasant way" (Brautigan 1976: 89).

Although their rationalistic, commonsensical and pragmatic ways help the cowboys to destroy the monster (by pouring alcohol on it), it does not bring them happiness and makes of them the parodic clichés of the Hollywood films of the 20th century. Professor Hawkline is saved, but nature, and symbolically the past, present and especially the future are still terrifying. This is expressed in the final apocalyptic situation, reminiscent of Edgar Alan Poe's short story *The Fall of the House of Usher* (1839). Hawkline Manor is destroyed in an almost ritualistic way:

"The flames roared high into the sky. They were so bright that everybody had shadows (181) [...] By the light of the morning sun the house was gone and in its place was a small lake floating with burned things [...]" (Brautigan 1976: 183).

The narrator characterizes this situation as "the end of a scientific dream" (182) and continues: *"It was almost like something out of Hieronymus Bosch if he had been into Western landscapes"*(183). According to Lonnie Willis,

"Brautigan reveals his theories about America's apocalyptic future, to be wrought by a national inability to distinguish between illusion and reality" (Willis 1981-2: 44).

Here nature is not a source of Emersonian inspiration known from his earlier essays, but represents a force of destruction, a symbol of failed ideals and failure of the American Dream represented by the cultural expectations associated with a new land and its possibilities. The Gothic landscape turns out to consist of ordinary, plain soil of no importance at the very end of the novel. It turns into a park,

"[...] but being in a fairly remote area of Oregon with very poor roads, the lake never developed into a popular recreational site and doesn't get many visitors" (Brautigan 1976:188).

According to Willis

"The Hawkline Monster investigates the failure of the American experience to harmonize expectation and reality, and it calls attention to illusions that have distorted the national vision" (Willis 1981-82: 37).

Willis goes on to argue that

"The Professor's idealism to the contrary, the novel fails to provide anything but a sense of doom for the American experiment [...] the dream and the myth beckoned Americans into the big white house of illusion: the reality of America is to be revealed back in the Hawkline mansion" (Willis 1981-82: 37).

Brautigan's novel here becomes a symbolic expression of scepticism and a negative vision of the future. With one exception— Cameron, the typical representative of a success story— the protagonists end tragically at the conclusion of the novel, unable to adapt to the new technological and commercial conditions of the forthcoming (20th) century. They become anachronisms and clichés belonging in Hollywood films rather than to 20th century reality. According to Pütz, in Brautigan's fiction

"[...] the corporate state and technocracy obviously comprise the mechanisms of urban life, the pressures of an all-pervading economic machine, a society which defines its objectives as the circuitous structure of efficient producing and affluent consuming, the degra-dation of everything to a commodity, and the functional utility of individual life" (Pütz 1979: 126).

For Brautigan, nature in this novel is not idealized, it is not a source of inspiration or a place of escape known from his earlier novels (*A Confederate General from Big Sur* (1964), *Troutfishing in America* (1967), and *In Watermelon Sugar* (1968). While in most Brautigan novels his protagonists' imagination represents a renewed unity of nature and man (Pütz, 1979), in this novel, as Pütz further argues, *"[...] nature and divine primitivism have lost their symbolic qualities"* (Pütz 1979: 128). In this novel, in line with Thoreau, Brautigan rejects the materialistic and commercial character of society, but unlike Thoreau he presents nature not as a place of escape and inspiration, but only as a cliché-like icon. At the same time, through his treatment and depiction of nature, Brautigan presents a critique of some American myths related to American cultural identity (the heroism of frontier cowboys, a retreat into nature). Through his parodic use of the conventions of popular literature (the western, the Gothic novel, the sci-fi novel), he expresses a critique of materialistic and consumerist culture. In addition to this, Brautigan criticizes the commodification of national symbols and myths thus challenging the illusory vision of national cultural identity, its history and alleged success. At the same time, Brautigan's parody of the typical American genres of popular culture expresses a critique of American cultural symbols, especially the idea of the success story and the American Dream.

II.1.3 Parody of the Western (Film): Robert Coover's *Adventure! Shootout at Gentry's Junction* (1987)

As mentioned in the previous sections, the genre of the Western represents both a kind of popular literary genre and at the same time a genre which is representative of the most iconic aspects of American cultural identity. In his famous essay *Cross the Border—Close That Gap*, Leslie Fiedler ranked this genre, along with science-fiction and pornographic literature,[1] among the most typical genres of popular literature of the postmodern period. Analyzing westerns along with such popular literary genres as romances and detective stories in his study of popular culture in the book entitled *Adventure, Mystery and Romance* (1976), John Cawelti calls these genres formulas, considering them to be representatives of some aspects of particular cultural experience. He argues that

"[...] popular story patterns are embodiments of archetypal story forms in terms of specific cultural materials. To create a western involves not only some understanding of how to construct an exciting adventure story, but also how to use certain nineteenth- and twentieth-century images and symbols such as cowboys, pioneers, outlaws, frontier towns and saloons, along with appropriate cultural themes or myths—such as nature vs. civilization, the code of the West, or law and order vs. outlawry—to support and give significance to the action. Thus formulas are ways in which specific cultural themes and stereotypes become embodied in more universal story archetypes" (Cawelti 1976: 6).

It can be argued that the western thus points out the specific nature and distinctiveness of the American experience, and creates a myth on American cultural identity both Frederick Jackson Turner and Henry Nash Smyth tried to define in their seminal studies on American history and culture. Turner argues that

"European men, institutions and ideas were lodged in the American wilderness, and this great American West took them to her bosom, taught them a new way of looking upon the destiny of the common man, trained them in adaptation to the conditions of the New World, to the creation of new institutions to meet new needs; and ever as society on her eastern border grew to resemble the Old World in its social forms and its industry, ever as it

began to lose faith in the real ideal of democracy, she opened new provinces, and dowered new democracies in her most distant domains with her material treasures and with the ennobling influence that the fierce love of freedom[...] furnished to the pioneer"* (Turner in Smith 1999: 353-354).

Turner further argues that

"This perennial rebirth, this fluidity of American life, this expansion westward with its new opportunities, its continuous touch with the simplicity of primitive society furnish the forces dominating the American character"(ibid.).

In addition to this, Marsden and Nachbar argue that

"Over the last seven decades the American Western story has fulfilled more social and cultural functions for its audience than has any other American story form. Indeed, the Western can be seen as a record of America's national self-awareness" (Marsden, Nachbar 1980: 1).

The idea of the West and the frontier as both the literal and symbolic expression of American optimism, hope and a new beginning, but also a disappointment with unfulfilled desires associated with the frontier, is emphasized by Dean McWilliams. He argues that

"From the beginning of American culture, the open land lying just beyond the civilized settlements has been a unique focus for American aspirations. We have seen that frontier encourage the hope of a new beginning, and then we have seen that hope sour into disappointment[...] The fact that the frontier still survives as a vital, if ironic, theme in contemporary literature suggests something important about America's hope for renewal" (McWilliams 1979:131).

The distinctiveness of the West is often linked with the idea of the American Dream (new settling and business opportunities, success, freedom, democracy), a romantic landscape, man's co-existence and struggle with nature, but also with harsh frontier life and uninstitutionalized rules where the ever-present battles of good versus evil, law versus outlawry, optimism versus pessimism and fair play versus treachery take place. The idea of the American Dream is described by Howard Nixon quite clearly:

"American values over the past few decades have shown that Americans tend to care a great deal about achievement, success, material comfort and 'getting ahead'. The combination of these values with others concerning equality of opportunity, ambitiousness and hard work forms a

complex of values regarding success and the means of attaining it that might be referred to as the 'American Dream'"(Nixon 1984:10).

In his *Lectures on American Literature* (Prague, 2002), Martin Procházka finds the idea of the American Dream manifested in Jefferson's *Declaration of Independence,* which forms, in his (and Jefferson's) view, the distinctiveness of the American experience and cultural tradition often associated with the new land and the idea of the frontier. Procházka argues that

"[...] the utopian dream inherent in the Declaration consists in the superimposition of the general 'natural right'—the 'pursuit of happiness' unrestricted by any geographical limits— on the otherness of American nature. It also includes a belief in the unlimited possibilities of the appropriation of land and wealth.

In this way, the frontier as the limit of 'civil society' and the boundary between nature, 'the virgin land' and civilization becomes a privileged locus of American utopias" (Procházka 2002: 50).

Summarizing the basic characteristics of the western, Cawelti finds that *"the most significant aspects of the western is its representation of the relationship between the hero and the contending forces of civilization and wilderness"* (Cawelti 1976: 194).
This conflict is, in his view, *"basic to American thought and feeling"*(Cawelti 1976:194). He further emphasizes the symbolic role of the landscape in the western which

"[...] is a field of action that centers upon the point of encounter between civilization and wilderness, East and West, settled society and lawless openness"(Cawelti 1976:193).

He also points out the diversity of plot variations of the western (revenge stories, chase and pursuit, conflict of different groups) which are different from more or less stable detective story conventions (Cawelti 1976:193), but he emphasizes the hero-antagonist confrontation as one of the most significant features of the western plot (Cawelti 1976: 193). Cawelti's ideas about the importance of the hero versus antagonist(s) conflict are further and more specifically developed by D'haen, who argues that

"The typical western plots pits a hero—the good guy, whether he be a young cowhand[...] or an aging gunfighter such as Gary Cooper in High

Noon—against a villain, with a number of subsidiary characters both looking on and having a stake in the action[...] The conflict between the hero and the villain is not simply a personal one. The villain disturbs the established order in the world of the western: he is a gambler, a rustler,a bank robber, or a killer. In the lawless West, only few men (or women) dare stand up against him, as he is ruthless and quick on the draw[...] The hero[...] often stands alone in his altruistic pursuit of justice or while carrying out what he considers his duty[...] In the end, the hero succeeds, at the risk of his life, and often of his love, to reestablish order by resorting to the very violence the villain disturbs that order with[...] This also condemns him to leave the very same society (village, town) he has defended and safeguarded: he rides off into the setting sun"(D'haen 1987:166).

As can be seen from the above, these characteristic features of the western are dominated especially by the struggle of the hero against a villain and the associated violence, and by the symbolic function of the region and landscape. In his short story *Adventure!: Shootout at Gentry's Junction* (1987), part of the collection *A Night at the Movies or You Must Remember This* (1987), in which mostly film genres such as comedies, cartoons, romances, travellogues and westerns are imitated, transformed, but also reconsidered and parodied, Robert Coover uses the basic inventory of the western (be it film or book), especially the Sheriff as an archetypal hero trying to keep order; a Mexican villain who wants to disturb the city's order with his violence, vulgarity and gun; a saloon, a bank, a schoolmarm, and the terrified inhabitants of the city unwilling to join the Sheriff in his fight against the Mexican villain. This set of characters forms the basic inventory of the western genre.[2] To emphasize the conflict of good versus evil, law versus lawlessness, as well as the basic characteristics of the western genre, Coover depicts an iconic western situation—the townspeople's expectation of the villain's arrival and the Sheriff's preparation for the meeting with him. Thus two protagonists representing the conflicting forces of good and evil, law and lawlessness, violence and peace stand in the centre of Coover's short story— they are Henry Harmon, or Hank, the Sheriff, and a Mexican gunslinger called simply Mex. Similarly as in Fred Zinnemann's film western *High Noon* (1952), where the basic narrative situation culminates in the meeting between protagonist and antagonist, good and evil symbolically at high noon, in this short story Coover anticipates this climax scene, depicting the representatives of lawfulness and villainy whose actions and behavior are contrasted in the story. Peter Homans even considers such final scene and its anticipation to be one of the typical features of the action of western films. He argues that

"The action of the screen-image western takes place in three phases: the opening, the action, and closing phases; or everything before the fight, the fight, and everything after the fights"(Homans 1972:103).

Characters

The Sheriff symbolically represents power, order and goodness. This is emphasized by Coover's depiction of the Sheriff's physical strength, which symbolizes not just power but especially law and order:

"He was a big man with bullish shoulders, a tall man who stooped through doorways, peered down with severe blue eyes over lean cheekbones[...] A tough honest man with clear speech and powerful hands, fast hands, fair hands and sure"(Coover 1992: 53-54).

The narrator comments on the Sheriff's status: *"Hank knew for whom law and order in this town came natural"*(Coover 1992: 58). On the other hand, the Mexican villain the sheriff is supposed to meet and fight against to keep order in the city is presented as an iconic villain disturbing the order in the western city. The city inhabitants' fear of him derives from his actions rather than from his appearance. The Mexican gunslinger is presented as fast in the draw, obscene and cruel, as a violent murderer, robber and rapist, and is renowned *for*

"[...] burning the prairies and stealing the cattle and derailing the foolish trains"(Coover 1992:61).

As the narrator comments on the Mexican: *"[...] all the womans die beneath the Mexican later or sooner. It is the, how you say? the legend"*(Coover 1992:55).

The Mexican's cruelty and perversity especially manifest themselves in his obscene drawings and urinating on the papers in the Sheriff's room; in his burning of places in the city and in his treatment of its inhabitants. One example of his cruelty in this respect could be his treatment of the banker mourning over the death of his wife (which happened shortly before he encounters the Mexican), because he refuses to join in the laughter with the other people in the bar:

"*The Mexican from behind the sad old man he is twisting on the ears of him so until they are bleeding. "Eh, amigo! Why you no laugh, eh? We all happy here! You laugh!" But still the man sits himself there, pallid and miserable, as though he no hears nothing or even feels his ears not coming away now from his head[...] The soft brown fingers of the Mexican bandit they insert in the sides of the mouth of the melancholic widower[...] The weeping man with the prodigious grin he is a most very funny man to see! Ah...! The flesh she is breaking. She is cracking down across the face from the white hair to the white throat and then away she is tearing from the skull with a peculiar very sucking sound*"(Coover 1992: 58).

Coover's portrayal of the Mexican's violence and Sheriff's attempt to establish order create the basic narrative conventions of the genre of the western, and the expected final meeting of both protagonists evokes the feeling of expectation of the symbolic meeting of good and evil, law and outlawry. In addition to this, the Sheriff's vain attempt to recruit volunteers from the city inhabitants to fight the Mexican recalls the situation in *High Noon*, but is also reminiscent of Yul Brynner's frustration with the villagers in John Sturges' film *The Magnificent Seven* (1960). The Sheriff's inability to convince the inhabitants to resist the Mexican reveals their cowardice and hypocrisy in this short story as in the classic Western films. In Coover's story, the inhabitants' cowardice is shown to be based on hypocrisy and selfishness through his depiction of their unwillingness to fight for the whole community. Perhaps the most significant example of cowardice hidden behind the pretended commitment to religious belief is Coover's portrayal of the highest moral authority in the city, the Reverend Slough. Slough's religious belief does not allow him to support violence, or to respond to violence with violence, and he refuses to help Sheriff and the community to rid themselves of evil. On the other hand, unusual and rough conditions have always required some participation and a special treatment of reality, morality and religion even from the representatives of religious and therefore moral authorities as well. The Reverend's exaggerated emotionality (weeping), however, shows his attempt to protect only his, not the whole community's life and freedom. The conflict between the institutionalized execution of law (morality) on the one hand, which treats reality from the secular perspective and which is represented by Sheriff, and the religious thinking incompatible with the special conditions (life in the west, the frontier) on the other hand, which turns out to be only a pretext for the pursuing of individualistic and selfish ends (Reverend Slough's attempt to save his own life) can be seen in the dialogue between the Sheriff and the Reverend in the church:

"The wee wet eyes of the preacher peered dolefully down on the Sheriff. "Seek your salvation, Henry," he snuffled solemnly, leaning forward, "while there is still time!"

Harmon fidgeted[...] "Well, I mean t'seek the salvation, as you put it, Rev'rend, of all of Gentry's Junction. [...] I'm going after the Mex in just twenty minutes. I want you there. I need you, Rev'rend."
"There is no question, Henry," sighed the preacher, straightening up and gripping the pulpit, "to which violence is the answer."

"Now wait a minute, Rev'rend. We all know what the story is here. That Mex is the cause of this town's trouble. I mean t'get rid of the cause. It's as simple as that."

"[...] I tell you, if there be chaos and evil in this corral of sorrows, my son, it is by God's— "
"Don't call me son, Slough! Remember who you're talking to!"
"We are all sons of the one Father, Henry. We must live by the laws not of man but of God Almighty. Our duty is to get a rope on our wayward souls, to throw them and brand them for the Lord![...]"
"Cut the horseshit Slough! I want you down at— "
"Henry Harmon! This is the camping place of the Lord! In the name of all that's holy—!"
"Shut up and listen, goddamn it![...] I want you in Flem's general store at twelve noon." (Coover 1992:63-64).

Sheriff Henry Harmon's thinking and speaking shows a common-sense, rational treatment of reality aimed at finding a solution to the problem (getting rid of evil), while the Reverend's speech reveals his attempt to justify his cowardice by religion and belief which seems to be an inappropriate response to violence and the western way of life. Thus depicting two central characters representing essentially conflicting forces, Coover seemingly follows the basic narrative situation of *High Noon*, but at the same time he uses the palimpsestic technique of *imitation* and *rewriting* not only of this film western, but also of the narrative conventions of westerns in general. This rewriting is achieved through the undermining of these narrative conventions, especially by his use of parody and irony, and alteration of the motifs and characters known from the film *High Noon*. In this undermining of the western genre conventions, parody dominates. It is a parody which, according to Bradbury,

"[...] by accepting the truth of the monument, but also by probing and questioning the artifice used in its construction, both perpetuates and destroys, becomes a form of mysterious translation, often but not always in the same language as the original, which explores the mystery of institutionalisation and the paradox of the classic art-object or text. It exaggerates a process basic to literature and art, which oscillate between the extremes of mimesis and artifice, insisting on both the force and the emptiness of a prior object"(Bradbury 1980:46).

In keeping with Bradbury's understanding of parody, Coover's own becomes a "form of mysterious translation", partly using the language and style of the original, but also partly using language which distorts and rewrites the motifs and narrative conventions of the western genre. Although the Mexican is firstly depicted as a threat to the community living in the city, and as a typical western villain, a representative of evil and outlawry (McWilliams, 1979), but also of freedom and individuality as suggested above, once this identity is established by Coover, it is later undermined especially through his use of parody. First of all, it is Mex's physical appearance which undermines his mythical power and his status as a threat to and violator of law and order. He is presented as

"short to the extremity, nor is he lean. Squat[...] dark with brown eyes like liquid. No severe. No honest[...] He carries his pants and his belt of the gun low, under his marvelous world of the bouncing belly, and when he laughs he reveals teeth of the purest gold"(Coover 1992:54).

Such a depiction is close to caricature and grotesque, manifested further in the narrator's comments on him:

"He laughs in himself and his ground balloon of a belly she shakes and shakes. Ay! How comic is she the grand balloon of a belly of the Mexican! Laughing and laughing! Hee hee hee!" (Coover 1992: 59)[...] Don Pedo the *grand terrible Mexican he is raising up the bandanna on his fat nose, concealing his gold-tooth smile"*(Coover 1992: 69).

In addition to these references to the Mexican's physical appearance undermining the readers' tendency to admire the anti-heroic villain and representative of evil (he is short and fat, with gold teeth), the juxtaposition of poetic imagery with ordinary and even ugly things evokes an ironic contrast. Thus the marvellous world, or a grand balloon are juxtaposed to a bouncing belly, which evokes not only irony about the anti-heroic status of the villain, but it also creates a grotesque effect. The Mexican really represents a threat to the community with his gambling, raping and killing, but the idea of his strength and the threat he represents are derived from the city inhabitants' fear of him and their cowardice rather than from his real physical power or his ability to use his guns perfectly. In addition to this, not only his physical appearance but also the narrator's comments imitating Mex's language create an ironic effect. The Mexican's pidgin English with distorted vocabulary, grammar and the inclusion of Spanish words create a grotesque dimension in this character. This can be seen in the following example:

"More than nothing, the Mexican he tells of two things: of calentitas and putitas. Calentitas—how you say? little hot ones, no?—and putitas comprehend all the womans he knows. An the Mexican, Don Pedo the Mexican bandit, he knows very much womans. Sí, señores!"(Coover 1992 :54)*[...]Don Pedo the Mexican bandit he is famoso for many talents, but none has attracted more notices than that for which his dear mama bruja named him. No importance the occasion, the Mexican is prepared[...]His bowels intricately reply wrath with wrath, love with love, but always with a spice of obscene humor[...]Ay de mí! Such are our happy perplexities, no? Well, come then, Pedo! That we may be friends!"*(Coover 1992:67).

Such a depiction of the Mexican does not characterize him from the outer perspective, but through the mocking imitation of the Mexican's speech and thinking Coover emphasizes this character's negative qualities. This imitation creates a distance from the possible identification of the readers with the Mexican as a serious character through the creation of ironic, parodic and even grotesque effect. Irony manifests itself in the depiction of the false idealization of this character (his knowing many women, his bravery, humor and roughness, which evokes the opposite effect); and this depiction further passes into parody manifesting itself in the portrayal of the Mexican's physical appearance and distorted language, evoking a grotesque effect (the Mexican's physical features are distorted and exaggerated, just like his language and behavior). As Philip Thomson argues,

"*It has always been generally agreed that the grotesque is extravagant, that it has a marked element of exaggeration, of extremeness, about it*"(Thomson).

He cites further features of the grotesque which are, in his view, the comic, disharmony, and vulgar humor. He goes on to observe:

"*Writers on the grotesque have always tended to associate the grotesque with either the comic or the terrifying. Those who see it as a sub-form of the comic class the grotesque, broadly, with the burlesque and the vulgarly funny. The most consistently distinguished characteristic of the grotesque has been the fundamental element of disharmony, whether this is referred to as conflict, clash, mixture of the heterogeneous, or conflation of disparates*" (Thomson).

In his short story *Adventure! Shootout at Gentry's Junction*, Coover's Mexican is both comic and vulgar (he urinates on the Sheriff's papers, for example, and vulgarly mistreats both men and women); he uses vulgar humor; he is extravagant and both his physical features and behavior are vulgarly exaggerated. Thus in contrast to the Sheriff, who is presented as a serious, commonsensical but also rough defender of law, order and the city community, the Mexican is an ironically comic and parodic character. Coover's Mexican thus disturbs and undermines not only the order in the city as in the traditional western novels and movies, but especially the genre conventions of the western. This disorder and subversion of the western genre is further intensified by Coover's presentation and development of the plot.

Plot—Action

Coover's presentation of the plot in his *Shootout at Gentry's Junction* imitates the narrative pattern of the western film *High Noon,* and is partly reminiscent of film techniques, especially the fast sequence of scenes and the suppression of the psychological, social and other characteristics of the characters. Two pictures of reality and two scenes dominate in this short story—one is the scene depicting Sheriff Hank Harmon preparing for the encounter with the Mexican villain and trying to recruit some helpers, and the final scene in which the Mexican and his destruction of the city culminate. In these scenes the characters' function is symbolic and represents either order and good (Sheriff) or destruction and evil (Mexican). This is why these contrasting characters' identities have a more universal function, and also why these characters' social or psychological dimensions are suppressed. These characters are rather types (Homans 1972:101). Although Coover establishes these and other characters as typical representatives of both the western genre and a particular western film (*High Noon*), both the western genre and particular film conventions are subverted also through the alteration of the plot and the motifs known from *High Noon*. Similarly as in this film, the whole narrative situation in Coover's story centers around the evocation of tension caused by the expectation of the encounter between the two conflicting forces in the final scene, as well as around the depiction of cowardice among the local inhabitants. This results in a certain glorification of individualism(s) represented by these two different and conflicting forces. But in contrast to *High Noon*, in his short story Coover alters the motifs, plot and meaning of both the original story and the whole western genre. First of all, there is the idea of a meeting which is supposed to take place in a hot wild-western setting at high noon, as known from Zinnemann's film. High noon evokes the image of the typical hot and dry western landscape but, at the same time, heat is the symbolic expression of the expectation of the tension and climax stemming from it. In addition to this, noon represents a balance between two halves of the day (the same length, including day and night), and thus symbolically a balance between the two conflicting forces, one of which is supposed to win. Coover, however, subverts the idea of balance and equality by postponing the meeting of the conflicting forces until 12.10 p.m.

which introduces the idea of belatedness into this encounter, and symbolically suggests the belatedness of all heroic fights. Both protagonists as representatives of American cultural experience within the genre of the western seem unaware of the significance of coming late to the scene. This makes their fight, in other words the fight for the values they represent, questionable, and both their heroism and villainity outdated. This belatedness of heroism and the protagonists' attempt to represent a mythical part of American cultural identity represented by the genre of the western is further undermined by the degradation of the status of the hero represented by the Sheriff, since his papers are urinated on and his lover raped by the Mexican during his final meeting with him. In addition to this, other representatives of law and order are likewise humiliated and degraded (the judge's daughter is raped, the marshall's wife kidnapped by the Mexican, and the judge and marshall travelling in a stagecoach are robbed by him in the meantime). Such subversion of heroism and the mythical glorification of law, order and individuality through Coover's depiction of evil and outlawry represented by the Mexican is further intensified in the final scene of the story, which is supposed, if we follow the narrative line of *High Noon*, to be a direct gun fight between the two individuals representing two different sets of values. In contrast to the film, the final scene of Coover's story is unheroic, no fight takes place, and the action is short and quick:

"*Pedo the notorious Mexican bandit sat on old overturned bucket[...] the Sheriff approached the Mexican. The Mex had something in his hands. Something that shone in the sun. Knife? Gun? A Watch![...] Henry recognized it. It was his own[...] He reached down toward the Mexican to disarm him[...] Still, the bastard offered no resistance. Harmon drew the Mex's six-shooters out of their moldly holsters. Rusty old relics[...]He pitched them away. Easy as that[...]He turned to signal for Flem and the others to bring the rope. Heard a soft click. Hand flicked: holster was empty! Henry Harmon the Sheriff of Gentry's Junction spun and met the silver bullet from his own gun square in his handsome suntanned face*" (Coover 1992: 72).

Following the narrative conventions of the western film and literature, good and the law should ultimately win. As Peter Homans suggests, in the western film:

"With the destruction of the evil one, the action phase is completed. In the closing phase the town and its hero return to their previous ways" (Homans 1972:105).

As in many westerns, Coover also suggests the idea of the survival of the fittest, but on the other hand in this final scene he lets goodness, law, order and at the same time the myth of the American Dream be punished and subverted at least twice. The Mexican's stealing of the Sheriff's watch indicates the symbolic tardiness and inadequacy of both Sheriff's fight and the mission he is supposed to fulfill as a representative of goodness, a character in the western genre, and at the same time one of the myths of American cultural identity. Moreover, in contrast to western film and novel conventions it is not goodness and order which are restored, but evil and villainy represented by the Mexican which win. The Mexican's victory evokes ironic connotations associated with both the western genre and the American values creating the myths of American cultural identity (the American Dream, individuality, freedom), since it is not the symbolic and triumphant victory of an iconic cowboy or sheriff, but a mocking victory of evil that the Mexican represents in the final scene:

"Don Pedo the grand Mexican bandit away he is riding on his little pinto into the setting sun, the silver star of the Sheriff pinned on his bouncing barriga like a jewel, his saddlebags full to the top, his gold teeth capturing the last gleams of the dying red sun. Clop clop clop clop. Adiós to Gentry's Junction![...]But these are the things of the life, no? Pues—hee hee!—adiós! Clop clop clop.Red red gleams the little five-pointed star in the ultimate light of the western sun"(Coover 1992:72-73).

In this final scene Coover accumulates the motifs and imagery and creates a mockery and the sharpest parody of Zinnemann's film *High Noon*, the genre of the western in general, and through this parody also the myth this genre represents (the mythical status of the American dream creating some of the most significant aspects of American cultural identity). Violence, vulgarity, outlawry, evil and perversity as represented by the Mexican win out over order, justice and law as represented by the Sheriff and the city inhabitants. In addition, this victory means degradation of all the values the this character symbolically represents in both real life and in the genre of the western, which is alluded to not only through the Mexican's triumphant appropriation of the Sheriff's star, but also by another "little five-pointed star" juxtaposed to the image of the mythical American landscape of the west. This juxtaposition of a star apparently from the American flag and the "western sun" creates iconic symbolism associated with American cultural identity—a star representing the United States, and both the western genre and the typical western landscape. This cumulation of imagery representing iconic aspects of American cultural identity is, however, put in an ironic context because of the reasons given above, especially because of the victory of evil, outlawry, violence, destruction and vulgarity over law, order and justice. Thus the Mexican's laughter and mockery turns out to be a mockery of the American Dream and other aspects of American identity such as freedom, individualism, optimism and courage represented by the western genre. At the same time, through such parodic and ironic rewriting of the western genre conventions, Coover points out the exhaustion (Barth, 1967) of traditional forms of writing represented in his short story *Adventure! Shootout at Gentry's Junction*. Through the western setting, he provides an intramural critique of the traditional literary forms and genres, but at the same time he suggests a postmodern playful and pluralistic rewriting of the western genre offering the readers a new poetics. In this way he shows how the traditional forms of art can be used playfully to create a new style compatible with the postmodern sensibility and perception of the world. On the other hand, the Mexican's triumph may allude to the victory of extreme individuality. Coover's letting an ethnically and culturally different protoganist win might seemingly point to his critique of multiculturalism and his nationalistic concerns (the Mexican is a negative, rough, violent and vulgar antagonist who wins the fight with the blue-eyed, apparently WASP-origin Sheriff), but it would too simplistic to claim this. Coover continues in his subversion of the genre, and his mocking and triumphant victory by the Mexican villain may be a warning against the exclusion of ethnically and culturally different people from the myth of the American West and the American Dream, as a critique of the fear of white (WASP) inhabitants of the USA of otherness represented by these people (the city inhabitants' cowardice) as well as an evocation of the awareness of ethnic and cultural diversity. Thomas Kennedy suggests that this story

"[...] is a parody, a satire of the classic western film plot embodying the core myth of popular American culture: the triumph of law over chaos, of courage over cowardice, of good over evil. As with any satire, however, the familiar is reversed. 'Evil' triumphs[...]" (Kennedy 1992:81).

Conclusion

As suggested above, by his use of parody, irony and the grotesque, and by his transformation of the plot, characters, motifs and meaning of both Zinnemann's western film *High Noon* in particular and of the whole tradition of western literature and films in general, in his short story *Adventure! Shootout at Gentry's Junction* Robert Coover undermines these traditions, by which he presents an extramural critique of traditional narrative techniques and suggests new possibilities for the creative rewriting of these genres, which is compatible with the new sensibility and character of the postmodern period where media and popular culture dominate and are able to influence broad masses of people, and thus create a simplified image of reality. Moreover, Coover calls into question the simplifed and unitary vision of reality caused by the influence of popular culture including the westerns, and their potential to create a mythologized picture of some aspects of cultural identity, by offering a new poetics which undermines this image and by subverting the mythologized aspects of American cultural identity such as the American Dream, optimism, individualism and heroism in the fight against the wilderness (Cawelti, 1976; Homans, 1972). Transforming and playfully rewriting the motifs, imagery, characters, situations and plots of well-known western films and the western genre in general, Coover questions the false heroism and glorification of national mythology associated with American cultural identity. In this parodic and playful rewriting of the famous western film, it is not the ideal of beauty, power, order and civilization represented by the Sheriff, but violence, vulgarity, destruction, disorder and anarchy represented by the Mexican that triumph, which at the same time offers a plurality of vision of the world and national character, and a playful alternative to life, culture and art.

II.2 Pornography
II.2.1 Pornography, Western Myths and Violence in R. Coover's *Spanking the Maid* (1982)

Violence

Violence can be understood as a manifestation of both evil and the misuse of power of any kind. The application of power is a result of the socio-political and economic development of particular societies. These societies, based on certain social, religious and ideological models of organization, have always tried to use power in order to influence the social behavior of people and their relationships. In the history of western cultures, the application of institutionalized political power mediated by the Judeo-Christian tradition has considerably influenced especially the relationships between men and women. In many societies even today women are considered as inferior to men, and as a certain derivation and "supplement" to men and their allegedly privileged position in the universe. In the Judeo-Christian tradition, the understanding of woman as an inferior being is derived from the idea that woman was created by God only after, and from part of the first Man, Adam, and because of her sinfulness and inability to resist temptation, which is derived from the interpretation of the Bible.

In his novella *Spanking the Maid* (1982), Robert Coover portrays the relationship between an unidentified aristocratic and eccentric master and his maid. The ordinary and routine relationship between these characters turns out to be not only a ritualistic one between superior and inferior characters, but at the same time this relationship becomes the central metaphor of the novella. Through this metaphor Coover explores relationships between men and women, the powerful and the powerless, the superior and the inferior. In this chapter Coover's imagery of violence (physical and sexual) and the literary techniques he uses to make a critique of the use and misuse of power in the tradition of Western cultural discourse will be analyzed. In this novella Coover depicts a situation of constant coming and going by both protagonists (the male as aristocratic master, and the female as maid), reminiscent of false beginnings which are repeated, altered and modified. Such repetition expresses not only boredom and routine work, but at the same time stiffness and stereotypy in relationships.

The very beginning of the novella suggests both the universal status of the characters representing men and women as well as their relationships, since the characters are referred to only as "she" and "he". Thus they are rid of their individual, unique, specific identities and become models, symbols and iconic representatives of both gender and class differences, as well as the difference between men and women in the discourse of western cultural tradition. "She" is presented not only in a socially inferior position, as a maid whose duty is to serve and to be "professionally" inferior, but also as a hesitating, polite, humble and obedient person:

"She hesitates. No. Again. She enters. Deliberately and gravely, without affectation, not stamping too loud, nor dragging her legs after her, not marching as if leading a dance, nor keeping time with her head and hands, nor staring or turning her head either one way or the other, but advancing sedately and discreetly through the door[...] As she's been taught. Now, with a humble and yet authoritative gesture, she draws the curtains open..." (Coover 1982: 9).

The woman's hesitation is not an expression of her personal qualities and character, but of fear motivated socially rather than emotionally. The woman's fear becomes the fear of both servant and of a woman of 'betraying' the roles allotted to her, the roles to be played, and the roles which represent her inferior position. The above passage presenting the woman's fear of breaking the walking conventions symbolically represents the stereotypical gender relationships in patriarchal society in which the woman must stick to the behavioral conventions and roles imposed on her in such a social and class structure. On the other hand, the man referred to as 'he' is presented in a clearly dominant, superior position. The woman's role of serfdom is contrasted to the man's role of a person being served, a receiver of services. In contrast to the maid's hesitation, fear, stress and socially inferior position, the man is presented as socially superior (having a servant), as a person enjoying this superior position with its comfort and leisure. The narrator introduces him in the following way:

"He pushes the bedcovers back and sits up groggily, pushes his feet into slippers, rubs his face, stretches, wonders what new blunders the maid

(where is she?) will commit today. Well, I should at least give her a chance[...]" (Coover 1982:12).

In this extract the man's dominant, superior position and power are emphasized by his authoritarian role of a commander and ruler whose role is to give orders, expect obedience and execute power. Such power and gender relationships are further mythologized, but on the other hand also ironized and parodied by Coover's juxtaposition of the imagery of authority and obedience, the low and the high. The woman is presented as having an almost absolute sense of devotion, obedience and inferiority. She knows she must be

"[...] always diligent in endeavoring to please him, silent when he is angry except to beg his pardon, and ever faithful, honest, submissive, and of good disposition[...] The trivial round, the common task, she knows as she sets about her morning's duties, will furnish all she needs to ask, room to deny herself, a road...to bring her daily nearer God" (Coover 1982: 12-13).

Coover plays with the imagery of the ordinary and the aristocratic, and alters its traditional meaning by a mocking juxtaposition not only of low and high, but also the spiritual and the physical. In this novella, belief in God traditionally representing devotion to an emotional and spiritual ideal, is not associated with spiritual regeneration and purification, but with the devotion to a man, to a physical being, and to duties to be done for him. Man as God and as the highest object of emotional and spiritual devotion thus gains mythological power. As can be seen from the following extract, this mythologized power manifests itself in Coover's depiction of the man as an object of worship, prayer and meditation—an unachievable ideal similar to God. The woman meditates:

"Yet: virtue is made for difficulties, she reminds herself, and grows stronger and brighter for such trials."Oh, teach me, my God and King, in all things thee to see, and what I do in any thing, to do it as for thee!" she sings out to the garden and to the room, feeling her heart lift like a sponge in a bucket"(Coover 1982: 14).

Female subordination thus becomes almost mythological subordination to male power, and the maid's passive acceptance of violence becomes an act of almost spiritual purification, since the narrator argues as follows:

"That God has ordained bodily punishment (and Mother Nature designed the proper lace of martyrdom) is beyond doubt[...] Every state and condition of life has its particular duties, and each is subject to the divine government of pain, nothing could be more obvious, and looked on this way, his chastisements are not merely necessary, they might even be beautiful"(Coover 1982: 63-64).

Such meditation is the expression of a wish for dependence, for perfectness in women's humbleness, obedience and duty, which become the woman's ideal and ambition in this novella. This ironic contrast between male and female ambitions represents a critique of the female subordination to males, subordination of the poor to the rich, and spiritual subordination to the physical. According to Jerry A. Varsava, in this novella

"Emotionally and professionally committed to servitude, the maid acknowledges her master's niggling criticisms; she identifies him not as a petty tyrant, not as a morbid solipsist, but as one capable of bringing about her moral improvement, perhaps even moral perfection—because it is perfection she strives for even as she understands the futility of her efforts" (Varsava 1990 :115-116).

As has been mentioned above, the critique of subordination is intensified by Coover's further juxtaposition of the imagery of the high and low, the spiritual and physical. The male's symbolic patriarchal power, however, is undermined by Coover's imagery of the low, ordinary and physical, which all counteract the seriousness, nobility and authority of both spiritual and male powers. The low, physical and ordinary is represented by the strange items found on and under the man's bed, items such as a broken glass or a blood-stained leather belt; by caricatured physicality (the man's farting); and by his sexual desires resulting in the unintentional discovery of his erect penis by the maid. The maid's unexpected revelation of the man's erection represents the revelation of his imperfection, of his physicality, suppressed complexes and poorness. At the same time, this revelation becomes an act of demystification through which Coover undermines the mythological role of male power. This manifests itself, for example, in the following scene:

"She takes a deep breath of the clean warm air blowing in from the garden and, fearing the worst, turns upon the bed, hurls the covers back, and *screams. But it is only the master. "Oh! I beg your pardon, sir!" "A...a dream," he explains huskily, as his erection withdraws into his pajamas like a worm caught out in the sun, burrowing for shade"* (Coover 1982: 55-56).

The master's sexual organ is compared to a worm hiding from the sun, which evokes the male's shyness and imperfection, an unpleasant physicality undermining the male's self-confidence. At the same time, it evokes both comic and parodic effect, which also question the male's superiority.

The banality of bodily functions revealing the artificiality of both the male character and his gender role also manifests itself in Coover's depiction of the man's deviant sexual practices with his maid, as can be seen from the following example:

"Oh well, he envies her, even as that seat chosen by Mother Nature for such interventions quivers and reddens under the whistling strokes of the birch rod in his hand. "Again!" "Be...be diligent in endeavoring to please your master—be faithful and...and..." Swish—SNAP! "Oh, sir!" "Honest!" "Yes, sir!" Does she—CRACK!—think he enjoys this?" "Well?" "Be...be faithful, honest and submissive to him, sir, and— Whish—SLASH!—and—gasp!—do not incline to be slothful! Or— THWOCK!—Ow! Please, sir!" Hiss—WHAP! She groans, quivers, starts...The two raised hemispheres upon which the blows from the birch rod have fallen begin (predictably) to make involuntary motions both vertically and horizontally, the constrictor muscle being hard at work[...] She shows no tears, but her face pressed against the bedding is flushed, her lips trembling, and she breathes heavily as though she's been running, confirming the quality of the rod which is his own construction[...] (Coover 1982: 41-43).

Coover's play with gender relations culminates in his depiction of these sexual practices. On the other hand, however, deviant sexual practices in which man dominates paradoxically mostly do not lead to sexual excitement, orgasm and climax, but are the expression of the male's debauchery and indulgence in power. They represent the totality of female subordination and humility. The male's act of sexual domination becomes an act of patriarchal domination:

"[...]then she hears the master turn the taps off, step out of the shower. Oh no...! She lowers her drawers to her knees, lifts her dress, and bends over the unmade bed. "These towels are damp!" he blusters, storming out of

the bathroom, wielding the fearsome rod, that stout engine of duty, still wet from the shower[...] Sometimes he uses a rod, sometimes his hand, his belt, sometimes a whip, a cane, a cat-o'-nine-tails, a bull's pizzle, a hickory switch[...] (Coover 1982: 45).

In addition, the male's sadism turns out paradoxically to be a manifestation of his desire to punish his maid, not of his sexuality. Sexuality is suppressed in exchange for violence, as expressed in the following extract:

"But then the master emerges from the bathroom, his hair wild, fumbles through the clothes[...] "What's this doing here?!" he demands, holding up his comb. "I-I'm sorry, sir! It wasn't there when I—" "What? What?!" He seizes her by the elbow, drags her to the foot of the bed, forces her to bend over it. "I have been very indulgent to you up to now, but now I am going to punish you severely, to cure you of your insolent clumsiness once and for all! So pull up your skirt—come! pull it up!" (Coover 1982: 47-48).

Such a forced, deviant and superficial sexuality suppressing its primary biological nature becomes an ironic metaphor representing the misuse of male power. The man thus becomes only a caricature of male patriarchal power, a parodic version of mythologized authority. Parody along with irony become the main means of Coover's critique not only of gender relationships, but also of pornographic literature, Victorian manuals, stereotyped and prescribed conventions in moral behavior in patriarchal society as well as of American captivity narrative's myth of regeneration through violence, as exemplified by Mary Rowlandson's *A Narrative of the Captivity and Restoration of Mrs. Mary Rowlandson* (1682). In contrast to Mary Rowlandson, who after suffering returns to her social background spiritually regenerated, Coover's maid wishes violence for violence's sake, which does not bring any spiritual satisfaction. "She" in Coover's novella accepts her subordinate position and the associated violence fatalistically, as can be seen from the following extract:

"[...] her punishments [were] serving her as a road, loosely speaking, to bring her daily nearer God" (Coover 1982:51),

and she understands her punishment in similar terms:

"That God has ordained bodily punishment (and Mother Nature designed the proper place of martyrdom) is beyond doubt"(63).

At the same time, however, *"she does not enjoy the discipline of the rod"* (50).

Violence, physical punishment and sexual tyranny become ends in themselves, and ultimately meaningless acts, since the man is never satisfied with his maid's fulfillment of her duties, and thus she can never achieve perfection. Violence does not mean a purifying process, but consists of pointless, self-motivated acts, which undermines Rowlandson's idea of regeneration through violence as part of the American literary tradition.

Pornography

According to Christopher Baldick, pornography is

"[...] a kind of fictional writing composed so as to arouse sexual excitement in its readers, usually by the repeated and explicit description of sexual acts in abstraction from their emotional and other interpersonal contexts" (Baldick 1990:174).

J. A. Cuddon gives a similar definition, but he identifies two kinds of pornography— *erotica*, which *"concentrates on the physical aspects of heterosexual love"* (Cuddon 1991:729), and *exotica*, which

"[...] concentrates on what are known as abnormal or deviationist sexual activities[...] sadism, masochism, fetishism, transvestism, voyeurism[...] (Cuddon 1991:729).

In addition to this, Roger Fowler emphasizes a subversive and critical function of pornography, criticism associated with the critique of society (Fowler 1995:190).

In his novella Coover uses the conventions of pornographic novels of the exotica type, but the absence of orgasm means that the sexual act becomes only the male's physical endulgement in power which, in addition to Coover's depiction of the male's imperfection (suddenly-revealed erection, farting), evokes a parodic effect. The repetition of the unfinished and fragmentary scenes, images, dressing and undressing is never finished, close description of any sexual acts and sexual organs interrupted or avoided, and orgasm is absent, which all undermine the basic function of pornographic literature, which is the stimulation of sexual excitement. This all creates a parody, but of a type which is not simply a parody of sadomasochistic and pornographic novels for its own sake. In fact, through his undermining of the conventions of pornography Coover produces a critique of the implementation of male power, as signaled by his use of irony. According to Varsava,

"*Spanking the Maid is indeed a parody of literary forms, but its parody is ultimately rooted in human behaviour and human attitudes and not merely in literature and 'literalness'"*(Varsava 1990:110).

Using Hutcheon's words, Coover's "playful irony" produces a distance between pornographic, popular works and high art, and expresses a critique of gender relationships. At the same time, the female's constant fear of misbehaving, of violating the rules of behavior required from her (as in the Victorian manuals), along with the man's authoritarian position and his insistence on such female behaviour, becomes a parody of Victorian morality, conventions and the gender roles required from both sexes. Coover does not develop either plot or psychology of his characters in this novella, but introduces the reader to fragmented and interrupted scenes consisting of two basic situations; the maid's constant coming to the room, attempting to become a perfect maid and woman, and the man lying in his bed, mumbling, dreaming or complaining about his maid. This narrative situation remains static and with minor variations is repeated throughout the novel. As Sarah E. Lauzen argues,

"*Robert Coover's Spanking the Maid (1981) achieves a sense of progress within this technique, not through the illusion of passing time, but rather through variations of emotional tone. The reader cannot consistently account for the repetition as entirely being a matter of successive days or as entirely being a matter of a character's fantasy-expectations or mental replayings of a one-time event*" (Lauzen 1986:103).

Such a static situation in which no activity, whether tidying up, cleaning, talking or sexual act is ever completed, becomes a ritual of repetition evoking the weariness of everyday routine behavior and reveals the stereotypical character of social and gender relationships. The imagery of imperfection and incompleteness (of dialogues, dreams, sexual acts) becomes a metaphor which undermines the fulfillment of both female and male roles, and which points to the impossibility of achievement of perfection in human behavior. In addition to this, Coover blurs the difference between fact and fantasy, reality and dream, especially through his use of the imagery of the man's inconsistent dreaming. This raises a doubt whether the man's domination and sexuality is reality or only his dream, and with this both the clarity and convincingness of male domination and power are subverted. Thus the man's sadism and treatment of his maid may be only his imaginary application of sexual desires and power, the application of roles he would like to play in his relationship with women, since Coover's male protagonist often has a dream about what seemed to be, earlier in Coover's book, a reality:

"*He sighs ruefully, recalling a dream he was having when the maid arrived (when was that?), something about a woman, bloody morning glories (or perhaps in the dream they were 'mourning' glories: there was also something about a Paphian grave[...]*" (Coover 1982:85).

The imagery in this dreaming represents a final destruction of the male's superior position in the history of Western discourse and in the Judeo-Christian religious tradition. Coover's constant degradation of the man through his depiction of low physicality (farting), unfulfilled sexual desires (erection) and deviant sexual practices (spanking), as well as of the woman's banal, naive subordination to male authority and social conventions evoke a parodic effect. This parody along with Coover's use of irony, playful imagery and juxtaposition of high and low, physical and spiritual, social and biological, all contribute towards our understanding of this novella as a critique not only of the misuse of power in male-female relationships, but also of the application of evil of any kind.

II.2.2 Pornography, Artificiality and Technology: R. Coover: *Lucky Pierre in the Doctor's Office* (1994)

Pornography, and especially pornographic literature have mostly been understood as a kind of popular and kitschy literature, the main aim of which is to arouse sexual pleasure. As Christopher Baldick argues, pornography is

"[...]a kind of fictional writing composed so as to arouse sexual excitement in its readers, usually by the repeated and explicit description of sexual acts in abstraction from their emotional and other impersonal contexts"(Baldick 1990:174).

This is further supported by Roger Fowler, who observes that *"Pornography[...] has no aim beyond sexual stimulation"* (Fowler 1995:189). Moreover, in her study on pornography entitled *The Pornographic Imagination,* Susan Sontag argues that

"[...] pornography is rarely seen as anything more interesting than texts which illustrate a deplorable arrest in normal adult sexual development. In this view, all pornography amounts to is the representation of the fantasies of infantile sexual life, these fantasies having been edited by the more skilled, less innocent consciousness of the masturbatory adolescent, for purchase by so-called adults" (Sontag 1982:206).

In contrast to some other critics' views, Sontag emphasizes the reactionary function of pornography, and in her view it

"[...] becomes a group pathology, the disease of a whole culture, about whose cause everyone is pretty well agreed"(Sontag 1982:207).

In Sontag's view, this reactionary function is mostly apparent in strictly religious societies in which sexuality is suppressed, and this suppression leads to the creation of pornography as an alternative to strict morality and dogmatically-controlled sexual life. With its obscenity and immorality, pornography stands in opposition to Christian models of the exemplary moral life and represents a distortion of the cultures in which it is written. On the other hand, with the rise and establishment of permissive and technologically-advanced societies, especially in Western Europe and the USA in the 1960's, pornography became associated with alternative culture, and at the same time became a highly popular and marketable product which could reach its audience especially through technologically-advanced media such as film, television, video, CDs and the Internet. Such societies, characterized by free flow of capital, free markets and free access to goods, offer free access to pornography, but its effect is, quite paradoxically, the suppression of any subversive function it might be considered to have. Thus pornography becomes a part of popular culture accessible to the broadest audiences through the mass media. As Russell Nye argues,

"[...]popular art is folk art aimed at a wider audience, in a somewhat more self-conscious attempt to fill that audience's expectations, an art more aware of the need for selling the product, more consciously adjusted to the median taste[...]Popular art must be adaptable to mass production, and to diffusion through the mass media"(Nye 1972:10)

The above characteristics of pornography refer mostly to its commercial version, the main aim of which is to arouse sexual excitement and to make profit from it for the companies offering it as a commercial product. On the other hand, Susan Sontag distinguishes different kinds of pornographic works which, while still being clearly of a pornographic nature, are more than simple, commercial pornography and have an undeniable artistic quality, because the nature of these works goes beyond mere depiction of sexual acts, and their significance is deeper. Sontag considers such works as Pierre Louys' *Trois Filles de leur Mère*, George Bataille's *Histoire de l'Oeil* and *Madam Edwarda*, the anonymous *Story of O*, or John Cleland's *Fanny Hill*, to be representatives of her "artistic pornography" (Sontag 1982:205).

In many of his works such as *Spanking the Maid* (1982), *Pinocchio in Venice* (1991) and *Lucky Pierre in the Doctor's Office* (1994), Robert Coover uses sexual, erotic and pornographic elements whose primary intention is not to evoke sexual pleasure as in commercial pornography, but through the establishment of the pornographic atmosphere and imagination (Sontag, 1982) and their subsequent subversion to give a postmodern, playful and parodic vision of reality which evokes a critique of commercialism, consumerism and the traditional conservative, unitary vision of reality. Thus pornographic elements and some genre conventions of commercial pornography become only the means through which Coover develops his postmodern play, and through which he points out the distortion of values in consumerist societies. In contrast to his *Spanking the Maid*, which has a static and circular structure with the repetition of the motifs evoking an atmosphere of preparation for a sexual act, the narrative situation in his short story *Lucky Pierre in the Doctor's Office* is much more dynamic. While in the former novella Coover's depiction of sexuality, perversion and pornographic elements are further developed into metaphors of male-female relationships, power and submission, his aims are different in the latter short story. The basic situation in Coover's short story *Lucky Pierre in the Doctor's Office* centers on the doctor-patient relationship in the doctor's office, and on the doctor's medical examination of the patient. The depiction of the procedure of a complex medical examination of a patient resulting in a sexual act between patient and doctor is reminiscent of the narrative patterns of pornographic literature, but these are, however, undermined and further developed into a different meaning from the very beginning of this short story. The doctor and her office evoke a metaphor of cleanness, sterility and illness. The office is antiseptic and sterile, which is supported by Coover's depiction of the doctor herself. The doctor

"[...] is glowing with well-being, her silvery-blonde hair pulled back in a tight bun at the neck, her teeth sparkling, her complexion radiant, her bright uniform clean and fragrant[...]She picks through an array of instruments, her metallic nails clicking, selects an otoscope and a sensitometer"(Coover 1994: 553).

This antiseptic, sterile imagery is at odds with the patient's situation. Patient Pierre's role of pornographic movie star is undermined by his status as a patient. He is depicted as

"[...] a livid mass of welts, bruises, abrasions and deep discontents, wearing only a short hospital gown tied at the back and laid out on an examining table like raw stock[...]"(Coover 1994:553).

From the beginning of the story Coover juxtaposes the seriousness of the medical survey and treatment of the patient to the vulgarity and even perversion of the subsequent sexual act between doctor and patient, which produces a grotesque situation and an ironic contrast. A close medical survey of all the patient's organs is commented on by the doctor in the professional medical language she normally uses to comment on all her patients' illnesses. This language is not a common, but a highly professional variety understandable to professionals but not to ordinary people. Thus the sterility of the atmosphere evokes an image of artificiality enhanced by the use of this highly professional language, which loses its communicative function and thus itself becomes artificial. The doctor comments on her patient's illnesses in the following way:

"'Looks like a bad case of advanced misentropy!' she chuckles, winking at her colleagues. She is encircled by the glint of stainless steel and the glaze of lights, by wall charts and diplomas, by the hum of apparatus and the soft, hushing movement of nurses and production assistants. She peers under his eyelids, into his ears and nostrils, down his throat, dictating to an aide: 'Signs of hypopraxia, idiodynamic delusions, hot lips and circadian decubitus'"(Coover 1994: 553-554).

The sterility passing into artificiality evoked by both the imagery of the office and the language the doctor uses contrasts starkly with the common, even vulgar words and behavior associated with sexual excitement and the sexual act:

"Deglutition and exteroceptors normal. More or less. There are cunt hairs between his teeth: Query cohort relationships"(Coover 1994: 554).

In addition to this, the professional medical terminology is gradually distorted and becomes only a pseudo-medical jargon, since the combination of the Latin (medical and also distorted) terms and ordinary language create an effect of bathos. This evokes a parodic effect associated with both the artificiality of the language of science, and the atmosphere this language produces along with the technically-advanced medical technology. This artificiality in the inappropriate use of language and, in a wider sense, in contemporary society's sensibility is further contrasted to and subverted by the doctor's attempts to achieve sexual excitement:

"'Aha!' She smiles. 'Feeling better?'
She peeks under his gown.
'My goodness! I guess you are!'[...]
THE END, he means, but she just laughs and stuffs his awakening hand up her skirt[...]Her mound is warm and wet, thickly padded with with wiry little curls. Her labia seem to reach out, grip his fingers, count them, twist his knuckles, read the palm[...] As they pull his hand away to roll him over, her cunt sucks up his fingers...then—fffffpop!—lets them go"(Coover 1994:554).

This graphic description of reality as a contrasting image to the artificiality of the doctor's appearance and use of language evokes a critique of contemporary sensibility and inappropriate use of language, as well as a call for authenticity associated with sensual, bodily, physical pleasure as an alternative to the artificiality of the language, whose referential function is weakened by its improper use (not only by the doctor, but generally in the media, for example). The improper use of language thus stands as a metaphor for the whole cultural situation of contemporary, technologically-advanced societies, which produces a manner of thinking that widens the gap between the natural and artifical, between words and the objects they refer to, and which drives human beings away from all natural connection with perceived reality. As suggested above, Coover first offers an alternative to artificial reality (i.e. the sterility of the doctor's office and the language she uses) which is a direct, physical and more authentic contact with reality represented by real sexual pleasure in the depiction of sexual scenes and acts in this short story. This alternative, while it evokes a sharp contrast to the artificiality of medical treatment by including pornographic elements, goes on to undermine the meaning of these pornographic elements and develops connotations associated with male-female relationships. The doctor's medical examination of Pierre and his bodily parts is a simulation of sexual foreplay resulting in a sexual act itself (preparation, excitement, sexual act and orgasm). Coover, however, modifies and alters the motifs and structure of the narrative conventions of pornographic literature. This structure simulating the phases of the sexual act results in orgasm just as in pornographic literature, but it also represents the phases of doctor-patient, ill-healthy, natural-artificial and male-female relationships. In these relationships the woman takes the dominant role, and the phases of the sexual act become the phases of her gradual gaining dominance over the man through her role (not only symbolic) of a curer, but also of a punisher of the man. Her role as dominant person and punisher manifests itself in her

1) role as a doctor using professional jargon that is inaccessible to Pierre;
2) physical punishment and degradation of Pierre as a man and as a porn star;
3) turning Pierre into an object of scientific observation, a mere thing.

To expand on these points:
1) Pierre's inability to understand his ailment(s) because of the language the doctor uses creates a gap between him and the doctor and places him in

a subordinate position, putting her in a position to manipulate the situation;

2) the doctor's degradation and tormenting of Pierre manifests itself, for example, in the following extract:

"She spreads his cheeks, sniffs about critically, squeezes a pimple, pokes a proctoscope into his rectum[...]

"Not a pretty picture, I'm afraid. Some evidence of diathetic dysteology, as well as time-orientation compulsions, possibly due to a faulty diet. Better stick an exposimeter up there, while I take a look at his tail. What's left of it"[...]

She probes the base of his spine, finds a raw nerve, sending him bucking off the table.

"Yowww! Damn it, Clara, take it easy! That hurt! "

"There it is, girls, that's where the old caudal appendage got broken off. The original hypostatic disunion; he's been looking for it ever since. Thus, the first phase of hominization: the quest motive. Which in the present instance has degenerated into a kind of sacral eschatology—you can see the open sore here—confused by the dysgnostic assumption that woman was created from that severed tail and to this day, as the doggerel goes, must serve his will and solace his posteriors still!"(Coover 1994: 555).

This degradation of Pierre is an attack on male dominance. The degradation culminates in a grotesque and parodic scene in which preparation for medical examination, observation and treatment of the patient are reminiscent of sadomasochistic practises known from pornographic literature and film:

"Rig him up for stress analysis," she says to her assistants.

His feet are bound together in ankle cuffs, and Lucky Pierre, last of the great pornographic-film icons, is hoisted upside down and hung from a gambrel stick. The gown is stripped away and he is smeared over with a photoelastic covering. Weights are suspended from his arms, neck, mustache, penis and navel, and a stereoscope is fitted to his eyes. He is subjected to a sequence of 3-D images—body parts, falling buildings, circus acts, snowstorms, genteel sodomies, worm fucking, electrocutions and the like—while the doctor studies the isochromatic patterns got by bombarding him with polarized light"(Coover 1994:555).

In this scene, however, the seemingly sadomasochist and perverse sexual act is replaced by a different kind of perversion—the perversion of the obsession with scientific-rational understanding of the world and reality. Pierre becomes an object of scientific observation and loses his quality of a human being. He is exposed to "polarized light" (555) and three-dimensional images of *"body parts, falling buildings, circus acts, snowstorms, genteel sodomies, worm fucking, electrocutions and the like[...]"* (555), and his reactions are passionately studied by both the doctor and her female assistants. This tormenting of the patient (a man) is further intensified by the images on the ceiling portraying a doctor castrating a man, which seems to be a visual projection of Pierre's situation, as if reality was being simulated:

"On the ceiling, the doctor has grown fangs and scowling brows and is stealing up on the patient with a gleaming scalpel[...] The doctor, grinning evilly, has slashed off the patient's genitals and is going for his heart, his head, but he pulls himself together. The doctor withdraws, cowering in a dark corner, her eyes gleaming like burning coals. Perhaps she has not yet struck the first blow. Perhaps she is naked[...]

The doctor has discovered his throbbing cock. The scalpel falls from her trembling hand. Her fangs recede, her eyes glaze over with exicitement. Cautiously, she approaches, her heart thumping visibly in the walls of her steaming cunt" (Coover 1994: 559).

Thus Pierre's degraded body evoking sexual perversion and lust turns out to be a degraded version of not just one male, pornographic film-star, or patriarchal authority itself, but at the same time also of technology and the rational, logical approach to reality based on belief in the ability of reason to understand and explain the world. Pierre's upside-down vertical position implies a reversal of values referring to such a rationalistic understanding of reality, and such a depiction of man and his patriarchal power. This position evokes a parodic mockery on both the belief in the positive effects of technological progress and its ability to improve the human condition.

3) During the doctor's medical examination of Pierre, he becomes an object of observation, an item of training material (the doctor reports on her findings and Pierre's illness to the assistants observing the whole procedure) and a mere object of scientific experiment (in the final scene with the cameras). Thus the erotic, sexual and pornographic scenes are undermined by Coover's

transformation of sexuality and the sexual act into a rational, verifiable and controllable phenomenon, the subject of scientific research which evokes artificiality rather than sexual pleasure. Pierre becomes a victim of his sexuality, of his being understood by females as a representative of male power and patriarchal authority, and is degraded through the affront to his sexual organs and sexuality. Pierre's position as a victim of scientific research and a doctor's obsession with the belief in rational and empirical verification of the effects of the sexual act culminate in three scenes in which the effects of Pierre's stimulated orgasm are tested and "measured"; in which the doctor comments on the nymphomania of a mad doctor from the film projection on the wall watched by Pierre in the doctor's office; and in the scene in which the sexual act between Pierre and the doctor is filmed, screened and its effects on the human body finally evaluated on a computer. In all these scenes reminiscent of pornographic films, real sex genuinely takes place, but none of the persons involved enjoys it fully, as should happen either authentically in reality or in a simulated way as in pornographic films. The effects of the pornographic scenes are undermined by Coover's juxtaposition of these scenes and the doctor's comments on them. These comments become an interpretation of reality and a manifestation of the doctor's belief in the potential of scientific, logical, rational experiments to explain reality. Thus emotionality and physical pleasure are juxtaposed with rationality and control, which evokes a parodic effect undermining both discourses, both realities – the emotional, sexual and physical and the rational, logical and verifiable. During the first situation mentioned above, the doctor

"[...] nips at his glans with her feet, stretches his prepuce, clucking her tongue ominously, separates the lips of his penis, peers down the urethra" (557)

in an attempt to do a medical survey. But although an orgasm is stimulated within Pierre, it is not "as good as most orgasms" (558). In the other scene, the doctor considers the mad doctor from the film as schizophrenic and comments that:

"Behind the mad-doctor sequence, you will discover the indifferent doctor, the heroic doctor, the incompetent doctor, the corrupt and the distracted doctor"(559).

This whole parodic and grotesque situation culminates in the last scene depicting the sexual act between Pierre and the doctor. This scene is clearly reminiscent of pornographic imagination:

"*Slowly, methodically, she lowers herself, and he feels her clitoris probe the length of his penis, feels the lips caress, suck, nibble, taste, pucker, blow, nip, feels her pubes thud softly, springily against his own*" (559-560).

The imagery of sexual act and orgasm alluding to the climax is reversed, and the climax turns out to be one of perversion, of the distorted version of the world typified by the belief in rationality, technology and all the ideologies and discourses supporting it. The doctor does not become an equal sexual partner for Pierre, but a machine, a representative of rational and calculative thinking and obsession with technology and science. These characteristics manifest themselves in the technical equipment for measuring the effects of sexual orgasm, and in the doctor's comments on the sexual act during the act itself. Thus

"*Before mounting him, the hovering doctor inserts an endoscopic camera in her womb to photograph the attitude during entry and exit and shoves an extensometer up her ass to measure him through the separating membrane. Her golden body is as sleek and hard as a mannequin's—yet it's rumored she may be more than three hundred years old! The wonders of science!*" (559).

In addition to this, commenting on the sexual act, the doctor says that

"*There is an associative rhythm to all these projections, which will become more evident as coitus proceeds, but it is clear that the projections are not any freer from the influence of the primary and secondary sense organs than our so-called rational operations are from the influence of the gonads*" (560).

Moreover, after the sexual act,

"*The doctor, in her immaculate white uniform, is taking read-outs from her computers. Her assistants are dismantling and storing apparatus, preparing flow charts, admiring the splotch of dripping sperm on the ceiling high above*"(560).

After this sexual act the doctor does not feel any pleasure, for she is in the same position as before and partly during the sexual act, which is the position of an observer, a scientist, a rational rather than emotional being.

Thus the technical equipment, the antiseptic environment of the doctor's office and the white color all evoke the atmosphere of artificiality. This concerns the doctor's position both as scientist and sexual partner. The imagery of artificiality thus evokes a critique and represents a subversion of both these roles. The doctor as a representative of both roles does not fulfill the expectations of either of them and becomes a parodic and caricaturesque version of the roles she is supposed to represent. Her position as a representative of authority and dignity as doctor and scientist is subverted by her use of pseudo-scientific medical jargon, as can be seen in her final comments on Pierre's illness:

"You are suffering from hypotyposis compounded by severe parabologyny. I predict an episode of feverish protocunnicide, but this should be for the best[...]"(561);

it is also subverted by her practising a sexual act with a patient; by her remarks reminiscent of comments during scientific observation, which evokes an exaggerated grotesque and parodic situation. Through this subversion of the doctor's roles and through parodic caricature Coover makes a critique of westen rationality and its obsession with belief in the capability of human reason to understand and explain the world; through subversion of the narrative conventions of pornographic literature and film (Pierre depicted as a caricaturesque version of the pornographic film-star) he also provides a critique of the result of this rationality leading to commercialism and consumerism, the manifestation of which is pornography as a commercial product, a marketable commodity. This critique manifests itself also in the narrative structure of this short story which is reminiscent of a theatre, film or a circus show, whose main characters are a doctor and a patient with the assistants being the audience. This is, however, a sadotechnological rather than a pornographic show which turns out to be only a delusion. This idea of delusion regarding perceived reality manifests itself in the narrative structure of the story, reminiscent of a screenplay for a pornogrpahic film; the doctor seems to be in the position of a director manipulating and directing the actors (herself and Pierre) and the audience (the doctor's assistants); the narrative sequence is reminiscent of scenes from a film; a metacommentary built into the short story often concerns filming; and, finally, the last sentence of the short story: *"and he is wheeled out of the office and off the screen[...]"* (561)

shows that everything the reader has read was a film rather than reality, that is a mediated image of reality. It is a reality not reminiscent of

"*the natural world, but rather a cultural reality, a reality structured by the patterns of social desire, discourse and ideology which manifest themselves throughout the environment and the characters' lives*"(Russell 1984:209).

The doctor becomes a product of this cultural reality and the ideologies shaping her. As mentioned above, Coover further offers an intramural critique of popular genre conventions (pornography) which try to reach the broadest audience by producing a two-dimensional, simplified and pleasurable image of reality accessible to the broad masses. As Russell Nye argues:

"*Popular art, aimed at the majority, is neither abtruse, complicated, or profound. To understand and appreciate it should require neither specialized, technical, nor professional knowledge*"(Nye 1972: 10).

In addition to this, Coover criticizes some feminist ideologies and theories attacking the dominance of men and the patriarchal character of Western societies and culture. Prominent feminist scholars Susan Gubar and Sandra Gilbert argue that

"*Male sexuality[...] is not just analogically but actually the essence of literary power. The poet's pen is in some sense (even more than figuratively) a penis* (Gilbert, Gubar 1984:4)*[...] In patriarchal Western culture, therefore, the text's author is a father, a progenitor, a procreator, an aesthetic patriarch whose pen is an instrument of generative power like his penis*"(Gilbert, Gubar 1984: 6).

In this short story, through the depiction of Pierre's degradation and subordinate position, Coover subverts feminist discourse and shows Pierre as a victim of female dominance. Thus reversing the meaning of feminist discourse, Coover questions the feminist theories operating with sexuality and the image of the pen/penis as a symbol of male and patriarchal power. Pierre is in a submissive position as a patient, a caricaturic and grotesque version of a man and a pornographic star, far away from being a representative of power executed through sexuality and physical strength. Thus such a depiction evokes parodic connotations and refers to the eccentricity of some feminist theories. The doctor represents an eccentric feminist reminiscent of the nature of some feminist theories, which also manifest themselves in her comments:

"[...] that woman was created from that severed tail and to this day, as the doggerel goes, must serve his will and solace his posteriors still!"

The nurses hoot mockingly at that and beat his nates with stethoscopes and clipboards, artificial limbs, leather traction belts and rubber blood-pressure tubes, wagging their own tails excitedly and scratching their fleas"(Coover 1994: 555).

In addition to this, with the woman doctor being a tormentor and degrader, but also acting as a manipulator, mockery of male dominance and rationality becomes an extreme and eccentric version of the qualities attributed mostly to men. Such a reversal of roles suggests that the doctor becomes a victim of her own vision of the world, practising the actions in a way mostly attributed to the subject of her critique—the man. Ironically, then, Coover shows that in trying to emphasize the otherness and difference of their female identity, the feminists and their theories paradoxically emphasize their sameness and similarity, for in emphasizing their difference they use the methods attributed mostly to men. Thus the object of feminist theories disappear, vanishes and nullifies itself. In other words, Coover shows the uselessness of such theories.

Conclusion

Using the narrative conventions of pornographic literature in his short story *Lucky Pierre in the Doctor's Office*, Robert Coover evokes feelings of similarity of this story with popular and commercial pornographic literature. Coover's further use of parody, irony, grotesque and caricature in his depiction of the characters, scenes and composition of this short story, however, undermines the narrative pattern of this kind of writing as well as of mimetic representation of reality. Through this undermining Coover makes a critique not only of the narrative conventions of popular literature and mimetic genres, but especially of the kind of consumerism pornographic literature represents. In addition to this, Coover's portrayal of male-female relationships through his depiction of patient and porn star Lucky Pierre and his lover, the doctor, represents a critique of some feminist theories and the technological, technocratic and rationalistic approach to life, sex and reality, which turns out moreover to be a critique of Western rationalism. Coover's critique, however, is not pragmatic and serious; it is a playful, parodic pluralistic postmodern critique offering the reader both participation in completion of the meaning of the short story and realization of the negative effects of contemporary civilization and the vision of the world manipulated by popular culture and the media.

II.3 Fairy Tales as Popular Culture

II.3.1 Subversion of Myths: High and Low Cultures in Robert Coover's *Briar Rose* (1996)

Oral myths, legends, songs, fairy tales and other genres stem from and are part of diverse oral and folk traditions. The fairy and folk tales popularized through Charles Perrault's fairy tale collection *Contes de Ma Mére l'Oye* (1697), and collections by other French and German authors such as Lady d'Aulnoy and, later, the Brothers Grimm, were understood as genres sending a strong moral and didactic message during Romanticism. This was in keeping with a contemporary belief in the educational and moralistic function of fairy tales as well as with a belief in the ability of folk traditions to express the national identity of different nations. Especially in the 19th and 20th centuries the fairy tale genre used its stable narrative conventions to flatter audiences of children. According to J. A. Cuddon,

"In its written form the fairy tale tends to be a narrative in prose about the fortunes and misfortunes of a hero or heroine who, having experienced various adventures of a more or less supernatural kind, lives happily ever after"(Cuddon 1991: 324).

According to Cuddon's definition, magic, supernatural elements and happy endings provide the basic structure and narrative conventions of this genre. At the same time, fairy tales as a sub-genre of folk-tales and as a part of children's literature can be understood as a specific form of popular culture.[1] Since the narrative conventions of fairy tales tend to be schematic, they give a simplistic vision of reality and are aimed at evoking pleasure. They usually bear a strong and often simplistic didactic and moral message, and they use the narrative conventions of popular literature. They are specific as they are a part of the oral folk tradition[2] and because they have not only a moral and didactic function, but often also an educational one as well.

At the same time, fairy tales and other forms of popular culture have changed in their character. They have become the products of visual rather than oral or written culture, a change which expresses "the sensibility" of the contemporary (post-modern) period.[3] Visual images produced on television, in videos and in movies have replaced the written word and sound and have become a considerably influential means through which people's vision of reality is not only filtered, but also manipulated. Popular culture presented especially through television, video and film uses the technical inventory of visual culture to evoke a simplified and uncomplicated image of the world that blurs the distinction between reality and its visual image, between fact and fiction. According to Lloyd Spencer:

"*The postmodern age is one in which cultural activity is dominated by media industries capable of appealing directly to a public (itself the beneficiary of mass education) over the heads of any cultural elite. Mass media and the culture industries, informatics and cybernetics, virtual reality and an obsession with 'image'—postmodernists and their detractors map the changes in the increasingly synthetic fabric of social life in very similar ways*"(Spencer 2001:159).

Stanley J. Grenz further observers that

"*Filmmaking technology fits the postmodern ethos in that its products-films-give the illusion of being what they are not. The film may appear to be a unified narrative presented by a specific group of performers, but in fact it is a technological artifact assembled by a variety of specialists[. . .] In this sense, the unity of a film is largely an illusion*"(Grenz 1996:31).

Grenz further argues that television has a unique power since it

"*[...] has the ability to juxtapose 'truth' (what the public perceives as actual events) with 'fiction' (what the public perceives as never having actually happened in the 'real' world) in ways that film cannot*"(Grenz 1996: 34).

Commercial television and popular films especially, in their attempt to earn more profit through commercial programs, soap operas or cartoons, transform viewers into consumers and are able to attract mass audiences. Popular culture including not only popular films and TV programs, but also music and popular fiction such as science-fiction, spy, pornographic, detective, horror and other stories, has become an inseparable part of postmodern culture. This culture has "crossed the borders and closed the gaps"(Fiedler, 1993) between high and low (popular) culture, between academic and vernacular audiences. Famous stories, myths and legends, but especially fairy tales have become popular pre-texts for their cinematic and television adaptations, popularized especially through Walt Disney's cartoon series, popular films and TV serials. Not only because of the world audience's familiarity with famous fairy tales, but especially because of the considerable impact of the contemporary (tele)visual versions of the traditional fairy tales, these have become models influencing children's imaginations in a global televisual village.

These images, copies and reproductions are mostly conveyed through mass media and popular cultural forms. They distort people's vision of reality and relativize the difference between fact and fiction, between morality and immorality. Mass media and popular culture become the products of consumerism and the consumer society, their power being derived from and supported by the mass consumers' acceptance of them. Popular fiction genres, including fairy tales as part of popular culture, become suitable pre-texts that postmodernist authors draw on to point out the negative aspects of consumerism and consumer culture, and at the same time the postmodern vision of reality is influenced by a new sensibility generated through mass media and popular culture. Parody and irony, especially, are the means the authors use to criticize consumer culture, the simplified vision of reality conveyed through the media and popular culture, and its linguistic representation. On the one hand, using the narrative strategies of popular cultural forms, postmodernist literature can appeal to a broader audience; it can reach a mass audience and thus stimulate its interest in reading. On the other hand, many postmodernist works, quite paradoxically, do not overcome the gap between the popular and high culture, but tend to be either highly intellectual or naively popular and kitsch.

In his postmodern novel *Briar Rose* (1996), Coover intends to undermine the traditional narrative conventions of fairy tales, but at the same time to present a critique of both traditional representation and contemporary popular (and consumerist) culture. This chapter will focus on the narrative strategies Coover uses to undermine and re(de)construct a famous fairy tale in order to construct a postmodern vision of the world. The main emphasis will be on the author's use of metafictional strategies and parody, and the function of these devices in both undermining these myths and in constructing a postmodern vision of the world. Postmodern parody, irony and metafiction are understood as important means, narrative strategies and tropes which have a subversive function and which provide a critique of both the linguistic representation of traditional and popular genres and the vision of the world these genres convey. Popular culture represents certain aspects of particular cultural identities. In this analysis of Coover's *Briar Rose*, the emphasis will be on the analysis of the function of the image of dreams (representing some aspects of Freudian theory) and the way Coover's use of metafictional strategies undermine Freudian theory and the psychological vision as representative of a modernist vision of the world. The readers' familiarity with the famous fairy tale, which has gained an almost mythical position in children's imaginations, enables Coover to address the global audience and to re-write the traditional icons forming children's innocent imagination.

In his *Briar Rose,* Robert Coover uses a palimpsestic technique of rewriting the pre-text, although he keeps to the narrative conventions of the fairy tale and motifs. Coover pretends to stick to the traditional development of the story and its motifs known from Perrault's or the Grimm brothers' versions of the tale. At the very beginning, Coover introduces the inventory of motifs and protagonists known from the original fairy tale—a Prince, a Princess (Briar Rose), a castle, an ogre and a witch. However, Coover replaces the chronological development of the original tale with direct action *in medias res*, which sees the Prince going to save Sleeping Beauty from her thorny imprisonment. A situation requiring further development ends in itself, although it enables Coover to develop a variety of different connotations associated not only with the traditional fairy tale, but also with the innocence myth and its function in a contemporary sense; with the relationship between the past and present; with the fulfilment of the ideals associated with the idea of the American Dream; and with the power of the imagination. Coover lets his protagonists begin the action as the fairy tale protagonists, but he never enables or allows them to finish it. The action begins with the Prince's progress through the rose briars to save the Princess, but the Princess's and castle staff's sleeping and dreaming never finish; instead, they form a basis for the Coover protagonists' contemplation of their roles and their formerly mythical status. The action dissolves in a cyclical motion returning to the initial situation, that is, either to the Prince's entrapment in the briar rose bushes, or to the Princess's sleep. The static nature of such situations is compensated by Coover's use of metafictional strategies which alter the course of both the chronological narrative development and the original story itself. Coover develops two dominant motifs— the sleeping Princess and the approaching Prince—using two basic strategies: these characters' self-reflexive contemplation and the alteration of the meaning of their roles. These new roles are associated with a contemporary, postmodernist sensibility rather than with the sensibility of the innocent past. Thus Princess/Sleeping Beauty/Briar Rose, confused by her status and role at present, asks: "*Who am I?[...]What am I?*"(Coover 1996: 17).

In addition to this, the crone suggests a different story to dreaming Briar Rose, in which the Princess is a prostitute, "*a kind of wayside chapel for royal hunting parties*"(18), then a mother to undesired children, ending eventually as a cannibal, since she

"*[...] cooked up all her children in a hundred different dishes, including a kind of hash, sauced with shredded onions, stewed in butter until golden, with wine, salt, pepper, rosemary, and a little mustard added*"(19).

Through these strategies Coover offers a variety of possibilities which alter not only the meaning of the original fairy tale, but also its impact on the contemporary reading audience. This alteration takes place as the Prince and Princess become the centers of Coover's self-conscious and metafictional linguistic play. It is not the burden of either briar roses or disobedience which prevent both protagonists from the fulfillment of their roles, but rather it is the burden of tradition, traditional expectations and values, as well as the symbolic burden of language and its traditionally clear referential status which they have to overcome to fulfil their roles. These characters struggle with what is a "*series of patent fictions, sign systems, hidden messages, obscure codes, familiar myths, pop images*"(Russell 1984: 209). Thus the Prince's attempt to cut through the briar roses and the Princess's constantly failing effort to wake up become symbolic expressions of an attempt on the one hand to vivify and establish their mythical role, but on the other, on a more general level and in an allegorical way, to fulfil the idealized expectations of whatever kind, to achieve the unachievable. Some of Coover's narrative strategies are revealed at the very beginning of his novel:

"*He is surprised to discover how easy it is. The branches part like thighs, the silky petals caress his cheeks. His drawn sword is stained, not with blood, but with dew and pollen. Yet another inflated legend. He has* undertaken this great adventure, not for the supposed reward—what is another lonely bedridden princess?—but in order to provoke a confrontation with the awful powers of enchantment itself. To tame mystery. To make, at least, his name [...] Yet he knows what it has cost others who have gone before him, he can smell their bodies caught in the thicket, can glimpse the pallor of their moon-bleached bones[...](Coover 1996:1).

Through such an inter— and hypertextual operation, requiring a familiarity with the Sleeping Beauty story, Coover invades the original story in one of its key moments—in the situation depicting the savior coming to rescue the Princess. In this way Coover immediately alters the nature and course of the story. He establishes the identity of the Prince not as a living person but as "legend", as one in a series of Princes, that is, as an allegorical representative not of living persons, but of all connotations of the figure the Prince evokes. As a representative of a model of goodness, authority and salvation, his task is to fulfil the roles he has gained in the history of artistic and linguistic representations. But the role of Coover's distorted version of the Prince is to overcome the sterility of idealized innocence and to 'tame mystery' of physical, non-artificial experience, to break the illusion of any possibility of the idealization of any values and thus to appeal to contemporary sensibility. This symbolic role of the Prince is confirmed by the narrator, who gives an inventory of possible objects of the Princes' heroic quest, which include *"Honor. Knowledge. The exercise of his magical powers. Also love of course"*(Coover 1996: 4).

Coover's erotic allusions from the very beginning of the story suggest a different, physical-erotic, bodily experience as an alternative to the idealized and sentimental fairy tale imagination. For example, the Prince's attempts to muddle through the bushes and his approach to the Princess evoke connotations associated with the sexual act and an expectation of orgasm. This is another image in the series of symbolic representations of the idea of fulfillment of desires of whatever kind. The imagery of eroticism extends even to sexual and vulgar perversity:

"Once[...] she has been visited by her own father, couched speculatively between her thighs[...] but here in sleep[...]he rests lightly on her and softens her cracked lips and nipples with his tears or else his moist paternal tongue,

whilst he attends her mother, standing at the bedside with cloths and lotions at his service and offering her advice"(Coover 1996: 11).

Coover's Princess is also introduced in the middle of a situation reminiscent of the original story, not as a simple fairy tale figure but as a legend, as a model representing all connotations of the figure a Princess evokes. She is presented as

"[...] the daughter of a mother embraced by a frog[...] the most beautiful creature in the world, both fair and good, musically gifted, delicate, virtuous and graceful and with the gentle disposition of an angel[...] innocent and yielding[...] symbolic object of his quest"(4).

The image of dreaming and sleep become central metaphors which construct the transspatial and transtemporal allegorical identity of the Princess. Dreaming becomes a symbolic expression of unfulfilled desires of any kind, one of the most important of which is the desire for physical, sexual love—that is, a desire to live a real, not a symbolic life:

"She dreams, as she has often dreamt, of abandonment and betrayal, of lost hope, of the self gone astray from the body, the body forsaking the unlikely self"(2).

In a chain of constantly arriving and leaving Princes, appearing in the bushes and the castle and disappearing in them or in a dream again, the Prince's meeting with sleeping Briar Rose represents the fulfillment of her desires:

"She sleeps still, eyes closed, and yet she sees him as he bends toward her, brushing her breast with one paw-hand, rather—and easing her things apart with the other[...]It's happening! It's really happening! She thinks as he lowers his subtle weight upon her as a fur coverlet might be laid upon a featherbed. The only thing unusual about her awakening is that it is taking place in the family chapel and she is stretched out in her silken chemise on the wooden altar[...]"(16).

Coover, however, drives the readers further into his intertextual net of imagination and lets them doubt about the truthfulness of the presented action. The Prince is not actually arriving in person; he seems to be only an illusion, or a dream within a dream, a fictional representative of the Princess's desire:

"His mouth approaches hers and she is filled with his presence, it is as though he is melting into her body or she into his, but when in joy[...] she opens her eyes he is nowhere to be found" (17).

Briar Rose's dreams represent her unfulfilled desires and, at the same time, her dissatisfaction with her role as both an innocent child and embodiment of goodness, purity and sentimentality. Her dissatisfaction with her traditional role of fairy tale character and with the traditional writing/language she represents is a dissatisfaction with traditional past sensibility. The Princess's expectation of the Prince represents a symbolic expectation of a change. This change is characterized on the one hand by the desire to have a closer connection with real life experience (symbolically alluded to and emphasized by the imagery of physical and sexual experience), and on the other hand by the new sensibility which a new textual representation of any kind is able to produce. This new sensibility is characterized by people's awareness of past traditional representations, by "textuality" of any kind. Coover alludes to such awareness through his use of self-reflexive, metafictional strategies and through the imagery of experience. Experience symbolically represents all the characters' self-awareness of their past roles and meanings. Briar Rose reveals both her traditional role as well as her desire to change it, since she has a *"perverse dream of love-struck princes"*(7), and because she knows

"[...] about the bewitching power of desire, knows that, in the realm of first kisses, and this first kiss foremost, she is beautiful, must be[...] must freshen her flesh and wipe her bum[...]"(7).

In this way Coover uses a metafictional strategy characterized in previous chapters (Waugh 1984: 2).

As mentioned above, in Freudian terms dreams represent unfulfilled desires expelled/repressed/relegated to the unconscious realms of the mind, as Freud explained especially in his *The Intepretations of Dreams*. According to Mary Klages, in Freudian understanding dreams

"[...]are symbolic fulfillment of wishes that can't be fulfilled because they've been repressed. Often these wishes can't even be expressed directly in consciousness, because they are forbidden, so they come out in dreams— but in strange ways, in ways that often hide or disguise the true wish behind the dream"(Klages).

In his novel *Briar Rose,* Coover re-considers not only the Freudian idea of a dream as a representation of wish fulfillment, but also other important aspects of his theory, especially the libido, incest, the pleasure principle, death, and Oedipus and the castration complex. In the novel, Briar Rose's dreams represent fulfillment of a wish which is repressed in reality, a desire to achieve sexual pleasure. Since her motives are seemingly primarily sexual, her dreams also represent the realization of her libido which motivates her behavior. Since Briar Rose's motivation is primarily sexual, to achieve sexual pleasure she suppresses both Freud's "reality principle" and the sublimation he described in his *Civilization and its Discontents* and *Beyond the Pleasure Principle.* Briar Rose thus represents the domination of the pleasure principle in contemporary culture and the subversion of the Freudian idea of sublimation. In Freud's theory, the father is a symbol of patriarchal authority and

"*he stands in the position of the originator of culture and of sexual difference, of what is male and female, allowable and forgiven*"(Freud in Fonda).

According to Fonda,

"*[...] the castration complex is the culmination of the Oedipus complex—i.e., where the symbolic violence of the father is internalized by the child as part of a new series of identifications that are brought into play by the castration complex. In this two aggressive forces are combined here: [1] the aggression with which the child feels her or himself threatened: violence of the castrating father; [2] the aggression that the child feels against the father which is generated by the paternal prohibition and repressed because of the child's fear of retaliation and because of the ambivalent feelings that the child has for the father*"(Fonda).

Describing the Freudian theory of castration, Fonda argues that the girl's

"*[...] desire for the penis must itself be renounced and replaced by the desire for a baby—from the father. Here we have a further instance of Freud's misogyny—he assumes that the means to the fulfillment of a woman is through the obtainment of a penis, as symbolized by a child*"(Fonda).

Briar Rose's wish to have children seems to be a realization of the Freudian castration complex, representing a girl's (Princess's) resistance to patriarchal authority and her fulfilment as a woman through a sexual act or perhaps even incest ("perhaps"—because it is not quite clear if her father is the father of her children as well). This realization of the castration complex is, however, undermined by Briar Rose's murdering her own children in a dream which represents a rejection of both the Freudian castration complex and her role as a mother, an authority. The death of Briar Rose's children in a dream further alludes to the Freudian idea of death as a return to the original state, relieving the human body from tension. Thus, Briar Rose's dream about her murdering her own children may represent a wish to return to the original state, relieved of tension. In Coover's novel, however, this could symbolically mean a return to the original meaning of the myth of Briar Rose, to innocence, which is undermined by Coover's use of other narrative techniques throughout the novel. His Briar Rose does not want to get back to her original state, to her original meaning, innocence and simplicity. She and her dreams represent a wish to be mature and un-innocent (physically, sexually), complicated rather than simple, sexual and experiential rather than platonic, corrupted rather than innocent. In this way, as a representative of an untraditional and parodied fairy tale figure, she represents a rejection of the simplified vision of reality that is common throughout popular literature, including fairy tales. At the same time, through her depiction Coover proposes a new postmodern poetics, pointing out both the exhaustion (Barth, 1984) of traditional narrative conventions and the character of postmodern culture based on an understanding and perception of reality as imitation, simulation (Baudrillard, 1988), and a copy. Coover's play with and subversion of key aspects of Freudian dreams and complexes through his use of parody and metafiction means a subversion and rejection of the possibility of a psychological understanding of the world, that is, a belief in the possibility of a psychological perception and explanation of it. Since emphasis on a psychological approach to the world is characteristic of modernist fiction, Coover's use of narrative techniques in this novel also means a rejection of modernism and the modernist approach to the world.

At the same time, a dream produces the effect of the fantastic. Coover plays with the meaning of words, myths, traditional stories, and the connotations they create, using, in Rosemary Jackson's words, "a linguistic fantasy"(Jackson, 1984) based on the characters' awareness of the referential function of language and its manipulative power. According to Rosemary Jackson,

"In expressing desire, fantasy can operate in two ways[...] it can tell of, manifest or show desire (expression in the sense of portrayal, representation, manifestation, linguistic utterance, mention, description), or it can expel desire, when this desire is a disturbing element which threatens cultural order and continuity (expression in the sense of pressing out, squeezing, expulsion, getting rid of something by force)"(Jackson 1984: 3-4).

Coover's postmodern fantasy works both ways—it expresses a desire to overcome the traditional, old sensibility represented by old narrative forms; and at the same time it establishes a new sensibility and new approach to reality and its representation. This new sensibility and a desire for a closer contact with natural experience are expressed in Princess's words at the end of the novel:

"She closes her eyes to such a cruel fate, but, as always, it is as if she has opened them again, and now to yet another prince arriving, bloodied but exultant, at her bedside. She welcomes him, cannot do other, ready as always for come what may. He leans toward her, blows her desiccated gown away. Yes, yes, that's right, my prince! And now, tenderly if you can, toothily if need be, take this spindled pain away[...]"(Coover 1996: 86).

The Princess does not want an imaginary, but real physical and bodily Prince who could fulfil her erotic desires, which contradicts the original fairy tale's intent and meaning. Thus Briar Rose becomes a parodied version of her original prototype.

On the other hand, Coover's fantasy expels desire in a different way, that is, in the way through which it expels a new order, a new sensibility established by the new artistic form. This is a sensibility of a (post) modern popular culture and media, of which fantasy is a critique. Coover's *Briar Rose* is a postmodern fantasy, in which he plays with literature as

"manifestly unreal, as fabrication, as lie[...] taking pleasure in their manifest unreality by presenting only a series of reversible representations"(Jackson 1981: 164).

Conclusion

Robert Coover's postmodern novel *Briar Rose* sticks to the pattern and narrative conventions of its pre-text more closely, but his use of hypertextual and metafictional narrative techniques, as well as parody, enable him to reconsider the pre-text's mythical status at present. Coover undermines the narrative order and meaning through metafictional play as well, and this play enables his protagonists to meditate and reconsider directly their roles as fairy tale characters as well as their function in the present. Such meditations are both literal and symbolic expressions of the desire to change the old narrative conventions and old forms of experience. The imagery of dreams, desire, innocence and experience evokes the contradiction between dream and reality, between the past and the present. Such a contradiction represents a desire to change the situation in both real experience and in its artistic representation. Thus the novel rejects traditional, exhausted forms of representation (idealized, romantic, realistic, and modernist psychological) and offers a new poetics, giving a pluralistic vision of the world. At the same time, metafictional strategies and parodies of the traditional genres and narrative techniques provide a critique of popular culture's distorting influence on our vision and understanding of the world.

II.3.2 Parody in Robert Coover's *Pinocchio in Venice* (1991)

Parody, which had originally been considered to be a derivative and imitative genre and a mode of writing (Rose, 1993; Hutcheon, 1985), has become one of the most important modes of writing of the past century (Bradbury, 1980). While from Aristotelian times at least the intent of parody was, through the imitation of the parodied works, to evoke a mocking effect, the nature and intent of parody considerably changed in the 20th century. Using parody both modernist and postmodernist authors reveal the process of creation of fiction, and especially postmodernist parodists draw the readers' attention to the fictitiousness of a literary work. In this way parody undermines the traditional model of mimetic representation. According to Malcolm Bradbury, this "new" parody

"[...] has an antithetical impulse, to substantiate the nature of fiction as self-making, forgery or falsehood"(Bradbury 1980: 46).

While modernist parody is mostly used rather within the mimetic and psychological framework of a particular literary work, postmodernist parody is mostly used within a metafictional framework. In this way it becomes part of a newly-created, non-mimetic world of fiction and is used to emphasize the linguistic autonomy of non-mimetic artistic representation of reality. At the same time, losing its mocking intent it becomes more neutral to the parodied style, genre, author or discourse, but on the other hand more critical towards the forms of the past representations it parodies. Postmodern parody thus establishes a new relationship between the parodied text or discourse and the new work which uses parody. As Linda Hutcheon suggests, the postmodernist concept of parody is not simply a purely formalistic concept aimed at producing a ridiculing effect (Hutcheon 1978: 202). According to Margaret Rose,

"[...] the attribution of the comic effect to parody has misled many literary historians into seeing the parodist as merely a mocker of the other texts, and to condemning parody on moral grounds"(Rose 1993: 21).

Drawing on and referring to various styles, works, myths and discourses, a postmodern parody expresses the complex problems of understanding reality, of artistic representation, and of representation of basic aspects of particular cultural identities. It represents a postmodern sensibility marked by the growing impact of media, high technology and popular culture on people's vision of the world. This sub-chapter focuses on the difference in narrative, but especially the postmodern strategies and the function of parody which Robert Coover uses in his novel *Pinocchio in Venice,* as well as on the way Coover, re-writing the original pre-text, creates new meaning and points out contemporary sensibility. Pre-text is used here to mean the original text that the post-modern novelist rewrites or refers to. In this case the pre-text is Collodi's famous children's story of *Pinocchio.* The familiarity of most Transatlantic audiences with this pre-text enables Coover to draw on the original, but also to develop a different story which playfully, but in its overall impact not ridiculously, undermines not only the original story, but in particular its original meaning, its role in contemporary times and all the connotations it has evoked in the course of history of both social experience and literary representation. Coover's *Pinocchio in Venice* is associated with the original Collodi story less explicitly. In contrast to his *Briar Rose* (1996), where the protagonists' identities are mostly relatively stable (with the exception of the playful Sleeping Beauty-Briar Rose connection), the identity of the protagonists in *Pinocchio in Venice* is "double coded" (Jencks, 1986) in the past and present by becoming realistic characters living in a contemporary modern world, as well as fairy tale characters living in a fantastic world.

Like in *Briar Rose,* in his novel *Pinocchio in Venice* Coover both uses and abuses the famous "myth", the kind of popular literature that is Collodi's original story of *Pinocchio.* But in contrast to *Briar Rose,* his *Pinocchio in Venice* is only very loosely associated with the motifs known from the original story. Using hypertextual strategies of developing several lines of his story, Coover offers a postmodern story of an American intellectual, a professor at an American university who is an art historian, aesthetician and literary scholar, but also a former Hollywood script writer,

"*the author of intellectual works of a tougher order such as Sacred Sins or Art and High Spirit* (Coover 1991: 41)[...]*The Wretch, Blue Repose; Politics of the Soul, The Transformation of the Beast, Astringent Truth, and other classics of Western letters"* (47)

who is trying to cope with reality as well as the artistic expression representing it. Juxtaposing the traditionally highly cultural European context represented by the city of Venice, and the American cultural context represented by the Professor's American (new cultural) tradition, Coover not only contrasts both cultures, but on a more general level on the one hand presents a critique of the outmodedness and bigotry of high culture and traditional cultural values as well as their artistic representation (especially through his use of parody, irony and grotesque), while at the same time he expresses a critique of popular culture in the contemporary world. According to Judith Seaboyer, Coover's Pinocchio

"[...] parodies as it joins a tradition of adaptation and interpretation that includes popular and academic culture"(Seaboyer 1999: 246).

Coover's novel, based on exuberant linguistic play, deals with the relationships between art and life, spiritual and physical beauty, frankness and hypocrisy, "[...] ideas about art, divinity, moral value, ontology"(McGrath 1991: 1).

In addition to this, McGrath argues that

"[...]conflation of high and low, sacred and profane, is quite deliberately executed: the point is to elevate the grossly physical and to ridicule sublimity, transcendence, humanism and academic pretension"(McGrath 1991:1).

In contrast to the novel *Briar Rose*, the narrative strategy in Coover's *Pinocchio in Venice* is based on mystification of the protagonists' identities; on his use of intertextual elements; and, in addition to parody, on his use of grotesque and allegory. While in *Briar Rose* Coover lets his characters realize their past identities and roles within the fairy tale genre through his use of a mockingly contemplative style, self-reflexivity and metafiction, the identity of characters in his *Pinocchio in Venice* is changeable, transmutable and schizophrenic. The characters in this novel travel between the present and the past, between the fairy tale, modern and postmodern novels, between physicality and spirituality. Once their identity is established, it is soon undermined and re-established in a different form and genre again. Through this strategy Coover compromises the narrative and semantic stability of his novel as well as the narrative conventions of children's stories, and in addition to this he alters all the traditional connotations Collodi's story originally evoked. The identity of Coover's protagonists changes suddenly, they immediately break from the contemporary world to the past world without any logical connection between them. Professor Pinenut having been deceived at the hotel and humiliated by the police is revealed in his other (fairy tale) identity by a police dog which turns out to be Alidoro, a dog known from Collodi's story *Pinocchio:*

"*He says his name is Pinenut, Lido! Professor Pinenut! Haha! There's a tidbit for you!*"

"*Pinocchio—? Does my nose tell me true, is it really you?*"

"*Alidoro—?!*"

"*Ah, Pinocchio! My old friend!"cries the dog[...]*"(Coover 1991:52).

The American Professor Pinenut establishes his identity as a serious intellectual and academic in the contemporary world, but as soon his intellectual (high, dignified, respectful) position is established, it is attacked by the intrusion of physical, low, ruthless and mocking elements. After establishing his dignified position, the Professor finds himself immediately in a different, fantastic, fairy tale world, and the distance between these incompatible worlds is indicated by Coover's use not only of parody, but also the grotesque. The main features of grotesque are, according to Fowler, exeggeration and distortion (Fowler 1987:107). The narrator presents the established American professor in a seemingly "serious" way at the very beginning:

"*On a winter evening of the year 19—, after arduous travels across two continents and as many centuries, pursued by harsh weather and threatened with worse, an aging emeritus professor from an American university, burdened with illness, jet lag, great misgivings, and an excess of luggage, eases himself and his encumbrances down from his carriage onto a railway platform[...]*"(Coover 1991: 13).

The apparent seriousness represented by the Professor's status as an intellectual can be doubted even as early as in this introductory passage. This doubt is stimulated by the ambiguity of time expressed in indefinite terms such as "(19—)", "travels across [..] centuries" as well as by the imagery of weariness and quotidian (low) experience which is juxtaposed to the Professor's intellectual and academic status. At the same time, only a few lines further on, without any logical connection but through intertextual play, Coover's Pinocchio establishes his other, past, fairy tale and intertextual identity on the "Island of the Busy Bees" gaining his "*infamous nose*" (14), remembering "*his father's pride and temper*" (49) and "*his friend Eugenio*"(50). Such transgeneric and transspatial identities of the characters enable Coover, further on in the story, to undermine the seriousness of high art, high culture and high academic position not only by the depiction of the Professor's humiliation, but also by his playing with the idea of low and "high":

"*Seeming?..Growls Alidoro instantly, lapping his thighs, while Melampetta licks at his right nipple;[...] She moves into the thoratic cavity now, pushing provocatively at his knobby sternum, then works her way slowly down the hollow between his ribs..before returning to his abdomen[...] Alidoro, having nosed his thighs apart, is pressing toward his knees, panting havily. But this is a strange birth indeed, adds Melampetta. A son pregnant with his own mother!*" (67).

The Professor is not only exposed to humiliation here, meaning humiliation within the narrative conventions of a modern/postmodern novel in the contemporary world, but even his realization of his Pinocchio identity (on the level of narrative conventions of children's stories) is undermined by the intrusion of sexuality and physicality. Such a bizarre distortion is reminiscent of the grotesque, which evokes a strongly parodic effect. According to Christopher Baldick, the grotesque is characterized by

"*bizarre distortions, especially in the exeggerated or abnormal depiction of human features. The literature of the grotesque involves freakish caricatures of people's appearance and behaviour[...]*"(Baldick 1990: 93).

In this novel Coover's use of the grotesque, as mentioned above, intensifies the parodic effect and consequently the distance between the past and present, traditional and modern artistic representation. In addition to this, Coover's use of the grotesque is created through his juxtaposition of the ideal, platonic and spiritual, and on the other hand the sexual and perversely physical. While the dominant imagery from which Coover develops his exuberant linguistic play in his *Briar Rose* is that of innocence and experience, in *Pinocchio in Venice* the innocence and experience are extended further into spirituality and platonic beauty, and juxtaposed to physicality developed into its extreme forms of sexual and physical perversity. In its most extreme form this perversity manifests itself in the Carneval scene, in the Professor's (Pinocchio's) indulgence in sexuality as well as in the ironic depiction of the Madonna of the Organs, who is the exact opposite of all connotations the Holy Virgin normally evokes:

"[...]the monumental Madonna of the Organs for her part reaching into the scarlet folds of her glistening vagina with both hands and pulling out her ovaries which she proceeds to flick on their fallopian strings at the Count's shaft[...] the rest of her is more like an oversized walking anatomy lesson[...]in that not just her heart (which is bright green) is outside her body, but all her glands and organs are dangling from her generous flesh like Christmas ornaments: her spleen, kidneys, liver, brains, bladder, stomach, larynx, pancreas, and all the rest, her lungs worn like water wings, her mammaries like shoulder pads, her intestines looping from her rear like a long spongy tail or vacuum sweeper hose"(Coover 1991: 239-240).

This entirely physical, experiential, sexual, vulgar, perverse and naturalistic Madonna of the Organs is a parodic version of the traditional spiritual, transcendental, innocent, idealized and romantic Holy Virgin. The intent of this use of the grotesque and parodic is not to produce a ridiculing effect targetting the Christian religion or the Holy Virgin herself, but to point out the different sensibility of the postmodern period marked by the show-like and carnevalesque distortion of traditional cultural and religious icons by popular culture and media, and at the same time to evoke a critique of religious and intellectual bigotry and hypocrisy. At the same time, Coover points out the relativity and impossibility of any pure, innocent or idealized vision of the world conveyed through religion and puritan morality. Radical physicality, sexuality, perversity and obscenity of the Carneval section opposed to purity, innocence, spirituality evoked by religion suggests the impossibility and critique of the later values. In Coover's understanding, any of these visions of the world is adequate as well as inadequate are art forms representing them (fairy tale, children's stories for the former values, popular cultural forms for the later).

The carnival scene is the exact opposite of the innocence and purity, and the art forms originally representing them; both Professor and Pinocchio in one become the victims of their idealized vision of the world; Pinocchio's nose, within the framework of his fairy tale identity, becomes his sexual organ and thus his fairy tale identity becomes the object of Coover's parody, which evokes a critique of innocence and suggests the impossibility of any idealistic vision of the world. Similarly, the Professor's intellectualism within high culture and the whole intellectual tradition he represents are undermined through

Coover's depiction of his changed attitudes to sexuality. The Professor cohabits with his former student, and with the Madonna of the Organs as well as with his "supposed mother" known from Collodi's story as Blue Fairy:

"[...] he spoke to keep Bluebell's wildly bouncing breasts out of his mouth[...] he was lapping at them and gumming them and scrubbling his nose on them quite shamelessly"(Coover 1991: 267).

Thus the Professor becomes not only a symbolic but also allegorical representative of low and popular culture within the fairy tale genre. According to Christopher Baldick,

"In written narrative, allegory involves a continuous parallel between two (or more) levels of meanings in a story, so that its persons and events correspond to their equivalents in a system of ideas or a chain of events external to the tale[...]" (Baldick 1990: 5).

The Professor's breaking from the conventions of an idealized vision of the world, from morality, innocence and purity as well as from the art forms representing them, means a radical breaking from the possibility of realization of both traditional artistic forms and traditional moral values at present. Pinenut's changed views manifesting themselves in his physicality, sexuality and even perversity evoke a parodic effect associated with the Professor's originally high-intellectual, dignified status juxtaposed to his humiliated as well as physically perverse transspatial, transtemporal and transgeneric status. Thus from the point of view of social experience, by depicting Pinocchio in this way Coover criticizes the hypocrisy and falsehood of academic pretension and moral corruption, while on the other, metatextual level he calls into question traditional artistic representation. The Professor's act of cohabiting with real characters (his student) and fictional (Blue Fairy, Madonna of the Organs), as well as his sexual perversity, are gestures of radical protest against any possibility of purity and innocence and their artistic representation. Coover's use of parody and the grotesque suggests a distance between the past and present, beetween traditional and modern artistic representation. Parody, however incoherent on the structural level, undermines the narrative conventions of the fairy tale genre, but at the same time, through creating a distance as Linda Hutcheon would put it, it establishes a new meaning and consequently also a new kind of writing. As Tamás Bényei argues in his study of parody, the form used by Coover is

"[...] placed in a metapoetical context where, without losing its original meaning (the mocking imitation of another text or groups of texts), it acquires a number of other connotations (metafictional critique, self-referentiality, etc.) that have by now become part of the critical discourse on parody" (Bényei 1995:92).

Parodic distancing is further intensified by the metafictional elements and self-consciousness of Coover's protagonists regarding their identities. The Professor/Pinocchio realizes and is self-conscious of his double and schizophrenic identity in both (past/present) times, in both (traditional-modern; European-American) cultures:

"[...] as he himself had been a sort of walking parody of thought given form, assuming that what was in old Gepetto's pickled head was so noble a thing as to be called thought, he had been able to intuit (here, perhaps, the years in Hollywood helped) the hidden ironies in all ideal forms, and so began to perceive that thought's purity lay not so much in its forms as in its pursuit of those forms[...]" (Coover 1991: 177).

Thus he becomes a walking caricature of both cultures—traditional as well as modern and popular. This metafictional strategy, in which Coover's Pinocchio/Professor is self-conscious of both his past and present identities (fairy tale, contemporary world) as well as his parodic status in both discourses, makes both traditional (past, i.e.fairy tale) and contemporary (modern and popular, i.e. Hollywood) values and cultures relative, deprived of their ability to offer meaningful and objective messages about both worlds and both art forms representing them. This new kind of writing can formally be understood as a kind of metafictional writing which is conscious of the impossibility to create "an objective picture" of the world, as the traditional writing which it undermines used to do. At the same time, through emphasizing the relativity and plurality of meaning, through establishing a certain situation or meaning and then constantly undermining it, this kind of (postmodern) writing suggests a different poetics marked by the authors' attempts to point out the referential function of the language, and its relation to representation of external reality. Such a poetics creates an almost independent linguistic world, a linguistic entity. Thus the separation, the distance, the difference between the linguistic medium and its ability to represent outer experience is emphasized in this way. Such fiction, in Patricia

Waugh's view, *"[...] simply demonstrates the existence of multiple realities"* (Waugh 1984: 89).

This does not mean that the metafictional strategies used in Coover's novel are only a narcissistic play of signifiers without any reference to reality. This kind of writing

"[...] draws attention to the process of recontextualization that occurs when language is used aesthetically—when language is[...]used 'playfully'" (Waugh 1984:36). According Waugh, such metafiction

"[...] does not abandon 'the real world' for the narcissistic pleasures of the imagination. What it does is to re-examine the conventions of realism in order to discover —through its own self-reflection—a fictional form that is culturally relevant and comprehensible to contemporary readers. In showing us how literary fiction creates its imaginary worlds, metafiction helps us to understand how the reality we live day by day is similarly constructed, similarly 'written'" (Waugh 1984:18).

Conclusion

In this novel, Coover uses narrative strategies which evoke a parodic effect, the most significant of which are probably self-consciousness and metafiction understood in Patricia Waugh's terms. These strategies make readers aware of the fictitiousness of the works they are reading; they undermine the narrative conventions of traditional genres (fairy tales, children's stories), and present a critique of traditional artistic forms of representation and of the viability of the "objective" and unified vision of the world represented by these traditional genres. In Coover's *Pinocchio in Venice*, the metafictional elements are used in a different way compared with his novel *Briar Rose*. Coover's Pinocchio/Professor, travelling between the real contemporary and fantastic worlds, that is also between literary genres (fairy tale and novel), acquires an ambiguous, transgeneric, transspatial and transtemporal identity which radically upsets the stability of the subject and thus reveals the fictitiousness of the whole literary work. In this way these strategies point out the impossibility of linguistic and especially mimetic and objective representation of the world. In addition to this, the Professor's status is an iconic representative of the whole tradition of western cultural discourse and intellectualism. His subsequent humiliation in the different genres enables Coover to make a critique of hypocrisy, pretended intellectualism, moral and spiritual corruption, as well as of the distortion of the arts both in the past and at present. In the past because of the nature and intent of traditional genres to give a unitary, authoritarian and idealized vision of the world; and at present because of the influence of mass media and popular culture which produce a similar effect. In contrast and in addition to the parody used in *Briar Rose*, in *Pinocchio in Venice* Coover uses the grotesque, which intensifies both the parodic effect and his critique of contemporary social experience and the artistic forms representing it. The grotesque associated with Professor Pinenut's identity and character in *Pinocchio in Venice* broadens the difference between the physical and the spiritual, between the real and the fantastic, between the high and dignified and the low and quotidian, in terms of both life and literature. The famous Collodi story is used as a pre-text which Coover subjects to postmodern parody in order to undermine not only traditional genres, but especially traditional social and aesthetic experience, and the authoritarian, unitary vision of the world. Through his use of parody, grotesque and metafictional elements he offers a critique of false moral values and the literary genres representing them. At the same time, he offers a different, postmodern pluralistic, playful literary work producing different social and artistic sensibilities.

II.3.3 From Experience to Postmodern Sensibility (Robert Coover: *The DOOR: A Prologue of Sorts*, 1969)

Postmodern literary work calls into question the mimetic representation of reality, to which it often refers through the process of signification related to other literary works, myths and discourses. Such a depiction of reality does not mean that a postmodern literary work avoids referring to outer reality completely, but that it often refers to reality in a different way—through frequent reference to the way language creates the image of reality. Postmodern literary texts thus no longer primarily fulfill representational, informational or educational functions (Marčok 1995: 23), and they do not try to evoke an illusion of direct contact with or reference to external reality through language. This sub-chapter will analyze the narrative strategies Coover uses in his short story *The DOOR: A Prologue of Sorts* (1969) which undermine both the mimetic representation of reality and the illusion of direct contact with reality through language. Coover's *The DOOR: A Prologue of Sorts* is part of his short story collection *Pricksongs&Descants* (1969), in which he transforms, parodies and undermines famous myths, fairy tales, biblical stories and films.

The image of a door evokes an entrance to a house or a room, an enclosed object, and indicates a difference between the inside and outside, between the enclosed inner space of the room or the house and the outer space surrounding it. The motif of the door appears late on towards the end of the story, which means that it implies its meaning only after the whole text, the whole story has been read. Robert Coover does not want to evoke direct contact with reality through language, to evoke an illusion of imitation of reality and experience through language, but he modifies the idealized reality of three famous fairy tales, namely *Jack and the Beanstalk*, *Beauty and the Beast*, and *Little Red Riding Hood*. Using a palimpsestic narrative technique, the narrator intrudes directly into the structure of the famous fairy tale *Jack and the Beanstalk* and undermines its original meaning, especially the myth of Jack as a victor over evil (the giant) and the myth of children's independence from their parents, an independence associated with children's transition from childhood to adulthood, from innocence to experience. These are the connotations the original fairy tale evokes. At the same time, Coover undermines the symbolic and mythical meaning of the original fairy tale and plays with a variety of meanings and connotations associated not with direct representation of reality, but with the meaning evoked by the original fairy tale. In this way he offers a new meaning, especially through his depiction of the ambiguous identity of Jack; through breaking the linearity and chronology of the original pre-text; through intertextuality, metafiction and self-reflexivity; through the suppression of morality and didacticism and through the depiction of sexuality, eroticism and violence. Coover introduces Jack by means of the narrator's contemplative commentary at the beginning of the story, in the following way:

"*This was the hard truth: to be Jack become the Giant, his own mansions routed by the child he was. Yes, he'd spilled his beans and climbed his own green stalk to the clouds and tipped old Humty over, only to learn, now much later, that that was probably the way the Old Man, in his wisdom, had wanted it*" (Coover 1969:13).

In contrast to the original fairy tale, through direct "invasion" into this original tale, Coover establishes an entirely different identity for Jack. From the very beginning Jack is in the role of the malevolent and bloodthirsty giant, that is in the symbolic position of a representative of evil, but also of authority and experience, and in another, allegorical meaning also a representative of "new stories", being aware of the past stories, narratives and ways of writing of previous generations. The narrator's self-reflexivity and comments on his own role modifies his status to the position of a realistic observer of his own role. This enables him to maintain a certain distance from his own identity. According to Thomas Kennedy, Coover in this way

"*[...] plays with a surface realism of tone at once comic and convincing – a hallmark of Coover's power. We chuckle at his brooding Jack, turned giant in the woods, begrudgingly playing his part in the tale at the same time as we accept him as a psychologically 'real' character in a way impossible with the classic fairy tale form[...]*" (Kennedy 1992: 12).

Establishment of identity and situation and their constant undermining through self-reflexive and metafictional comments forms the basic compositional strategy of Coover's short story. In this way the author evokes a feeling of doubt, ambiguity and narrative insecurity in connection with both reality and meaning created in this way. The motif of Jack's cutting the tree and stalk creates the basic narrative situation in the first part of Coover's story. This process of cutting seen in intertextual and symbolic connections expresses the process of destruction of Jack's identity and its significance. In addition, the process of constant cutting alludes to his dissatisfaction with both his old and new identities. It expresses a protest against idealization, moralizing, didacticism, artificiality, shallowness, objectivity and verifiability. Jack cuts a tree on the top of which, as he finds out later, his mother sits. This symbolically alludes to his attempt to abandon childhood and to become independent, that is it signifies the process of transition from innocence to experience. Since in Coover's story Jack becomes a giant, he represents authority at the same time. This status of authority further acquires negative connotations since in the juxtaposition of the former and contemporary giants, the original giant represented evil. Jack's further cutting of the fallen tree, however, represents an attempt to overcome not only his old, but also his new identity, that is the identity of a representative of evil. It is a process of self-doubt which emphasizes the ambiguity in meaning of the "cutting" motif. Coover's apparent attempt to provide at least a fragment of plot through the cutting motif remains locked in the metatextual and intertextual situation of cutting itself, to which the narrator has a negative attitude, indirectly, through self-reflexivity and other motifs known from the original tale (climbing the beanstalk, Jack's mother, the giant). This negative attitude is the manifestation of dissatisfaction with any expression of authoritarian approach to the world represented by a clear and pseudo-objective vision of reality. In the first part of the short story, authority and authoritarianism are emphasized through the motifs of fatherhood and motherhood, as well as through constant implicit and intertextual allusions to the relationship between the current Jack and his original identity (his original identity represents authority, traditional and idealized vision of reality, whereas the current Jack represents a rejection of this identity). As Coover reveals later, Jack finally becomes father to a girl, which means he acquires both the biological and social authority of fatherhood, though he at the same time realizes its negative meaning, as seen through his self-reflexive comments. Coover implies negativity in the fatherhood role through the motifs of falsehood and hypocrisy associated with the father. The falsity and hypocrisy of (fatherhood) authority are expressed through the depiction of the father in the function of both educator and narrator of the stories (Jack/giant telling the stories to his daughter), that is to say, a narrator who provides his daughter with a certain picture of the world. Jack realizes his failure in the roles of both father and authoritarian (traditional, omniscient, in a God-like position), as well as narrator and mediator of truth. Coover shows this position of father and fatherhood, and Jack's relationship to his daughter in the following way:

"Because he'd given her her view of the world, in fragments of course, not really thinking it all out, she listening, he telling, and because of her gaiety and his love, his cowardly lonely love, he'd left out the terror[...](Coover 1969: 14)*[...]He'd willingly die to save her from death, live with all the terror if he could but free her from it"*(Coover 1969:15).

Coover points out the father's fairy tale, idealized vision of the world, and Jack, in his role of father, realizes the unreliability of such a model of the world despite the stimuli leading him to create it with regard to his daughter. This realization of the unreliability and hypocrisy of such a vision of the world is expressed through the narrator's attack on the idealization of reality mediated by fairy tales:

"[...] only kings could sleep and rise again, and all the kings were gone (Coover 1969:15)[...] Sooner or later, she'd know everything, know he'd lied. He'd pretended to her that there were no monsters, no wolves or witches, but yes, goddamn it, there were, there were.And in fact one of them got ahold of him right now, made him grab up his axe, dig ceremonially at his crotch, and return to his labors, and with a weird perverse insistence, made him laugh[...]"(Coover 1969:15).

Coover's Jack establishes his role of authority in different connotations but he denies it at the same time, which expresses a difference between idealized reality (fairy tales, parents' vision of the world presented to their children) and the "real", even brutally naturalistic reality which Jack, in his role of father, wants to protect his daughter from by giving her an idealized vision of the world. The symbolic meaning of evil represented by the giant from Jack's tales told to his daughter maintains the negative fairy tale meaning and the myth of evil, but Coover further develops the connotational contexts. This evil does not represent only general evil, but it is associated with the father as representative of the authority of adults, therefore symbolically expressing hypocrisy as well. In addition to this, the negativity of evil is associated with the unitary vision of the world, and authoritarianism in general.

In the first part of this short story, the father and mother do not represent Jack's biological parents, but the mother becomes a symbol, claiming her authoritarian role to express traditional values and connotations associated with the mother as a representative of love, goodness and the safety of motherhood. The mother represents a maternal image developed into a chain of symbols depicted in fairy tales and myths:

"There was his old mother up there, suffering continuance, preferring rot to obliteration, possessed like them all by a mad will, mindless and intransigent. Did he resent her? Yes, he did. There they all went, birthing hopelessly sentient creatures into the inexplicable emptiness, giving carelessly of their bellies, teats, and strength, then sinking away into addled uselessness, humming the old songs, the old lies, and smiling toothless enfuriating smiles" (Coover 1969:14-15).

Such a parodic depiction does not mean denigration of the mother's role as a parent, but in her role as a symbolic representative of authority and adulthood, that is to say, the mother evoking negative connotations associated with the motifs of lies and hypocrisy. The static situation of cutting the fallen tree to pieces, interrupted by intertextual and metafictional passages commenting on the role of authority and its meaning, passes smoothly into the two following sections in which Coover develops but also complicates his intertextual network. The second part of the story is reminiscent of fragmentary interior monologue of Little Red Riding Hood's grandmother that includes various allusions to the motifs known from the fairy tale Beauty and the Beast. This monologue is further interrupted by a fragmentary dialogue between Little Red Riding Hood and her grandmother. The last part introduces Little Red Riding Hood standing in front of the cottage door and contemplating both her fairy tale and "real life" roles. Finally, Coover reveals the reincarnated identity of Jack's daughter from the first part, indicating not a direct but rather a symbolic connection between the first and the third part of this short story (Jack's—that is the giant's—daughter from the first part becomes Little Red Riding Hood in the third part), by which he develops further contextual connections of both father's and her own identities. At the end of the first part, the narrator argues that *"He remembered the old formula: fill the belly full of stones"* (Coover 1969:15), which implies a connection with the original fairy tale. This also suggests a negation of the negative role of the representative of authority, especially through the motif of cutting, which is present in the second and third parts of the story as well. Through his cutting Jack suggests the motif and character of a woodcutter or a hunter who is a positive protagonist, a symbolic savior as in the original fairy tale of Little Red Riding Hood. Standing in front of the door, Little Red Riding Hood can hear cutting, which makes her hesitate about entering the cottage in the third part. This motif of cutting also symbolizes the distance between the original fairy tale, which gives an idealized and innocent picture of the world, and real-life experience, between the naive, innocent and idealized, and the contemporary postmodern and textual sensibility. As Larry McCaffery argues, this is a sensibility

"[...] saturated not only with self-consciousness but also with the realization that concepts such as play, games, fiction-making, artifice and subjectivity lie at the very center of what makes human beings civilized. Life-as-theater, man-as-fiction-maker or game-player – these can no longer be considered postures which we should avoid when engaged in 'serious' pursuits, but are now accepted as aspects of our basic nature" (McCaffery 1982:255).

In McCaffery's view, this meta-sensibility

"[...] is evolving into the characteristic sensibility of our age, the inevitable product of our heightened awareness of the subjectivity and artifice inherent in our systems, our growing familiriaty with prior forms, our increased access to information of all sorts" (McCaffery 1982: 255).

This distance between the past and the contemporary vision of the world, between past and contemporary sensibilities, is evoked in the second part of Coover's story, in which Beauty and the Beast as well as Little Red Riding Hood and her grandmother are depicted in parodic contexts, especially through the dialogue between Little Red Riding Hood and her grandmother. Parody appears in the grandmother's conflation of motifs from all the famous fairy tales, but the dialogue between Little Red Riding Hood and her grandmother is also about innocence and experience, the different sensibility of modern times, on the impossibility of any idealized, simplified and unitary vision of reality. Alluding to the motif of the Beast turned Prince from the original fairy tale, the grandmother argues that *"[...]my Beast never became a prince"*(Coover 1969:16). With this Coover suppresses the fantastic idealization of reality and through his narrator emphasizes the naturalistic "brutality"of reality. The incorporation of the original fairy tale Beauty and the Beast into Coover's short story points to the falsehood of the fairy tale, turning its idealization of reality into deception since the idealized Prince never comes. The grandmother further undermines the fairy tale idealization of innocence as she confronts Little Red Riding Hood with the reality of sensual experience:

"[she] don't understand! whose nose does she think she's twistin little cow? Bit of new fuzz on her pubes and juice in the little bubbies and off she prances into that world of hers that ain't got forests nor prodigies a dippy smile on her face and her skirts up around her ears well well I'll give her a mystery today I will if I'm not too late already and so what if I am?[...](Coover 1969:16) *[...] for listen I have suffered a lifetime of his doggy stink until I truly felt I couldn't live without it and child his snore would wake the dead though now I cannot sleep for the silence yes and I have pawed in stewpots with him and have paused to watch him drop a public turd[...] I have been split with the pain and terrible haste of his thick quick cock and then still itchin and bleedin have gazed on as he leapt other bitches at random and I have watched my own beauty decline my love and still no Prince no Prince an yet you doubt that I understand? and loved him my child loved the damned Beast after all"*(Coover 1969:17).

The grandmother thus acquires the identities of both the former Beauty from the Beauty and the Beast fairy tale and Little Red Riding Hood's grandmother. In contemporary terms she symbolically represents experience, but on another, symbolic level also awareness of the past traditional literary forms and genres, because her language and identity as an aged (former) beauty expresses disappointment not only over her fate, but also over her idealized status within the fairy tale genre. In this way, Coover presents a critique of the unitary vision of the world mediated by fairy tales and ultimately by any idealization of reality.

Little Red Riding Hood becomes entrapped in textual reality, representing an inventory of both original and modified versions of her character linked to the symbol of innocence and all the narratives and discourses mediating an idealized and innocent picture of the world. On the other hand, Little Red Riding Hood's new identity at the same time symbolically expresses experience, that is an awareness of the past which enables her to make an ironic smile at her current status and the meaning which she has traditionally been associated with. This can be seen in the following extract:

"She smiled faintly at the mockery of the basket she clutched. Well, it would be a big production, that was already apparent. An elaborate game, embellished with masks and poetry, a marshalling of legendary doves and herbs. And why not?[...] Even as the sun suddenly snapped its bonds and jerked westward, propelling her over the threshold, she realized though this was a comedy from which, once entered, you never returned, it nevertheless possessed its own astonishments and conjurings, its towers and closets, and even pathways, more gardens, and more doors"(Coover 1969:18-19).

In a similar way, Coover creates a status for Little Red Riding Hood as a character separated from the past, from childish naiveté and innocence, as well as from the simple childish perception of the world mediated by fairy tales:

"Old stories welled in her like a summation of an old woman's witless terrors, fierce sinuous images with flashing teeth and terrible eyes, phantoms springing from the sun's night-tunnels to devour her childhood[...]" (Coover 1969:18).

All the connotations of Little Red Riding Hood's experience come together in her position as a hesitant girl standing in front of the cottage in the third section of Coover's short story. In contrast to the original fairy tale, however, Coover lets his door open. The door thus represents a dividing line between childhood and adulthood, between innocence and experience, between naive and idealized and real visions of the world, between authority and submissiveness. Opening the door and crossing its threshold implies a change in Little Red Riding Hood's identity, as well as her realization of this change after crossing the threshold:

"She stared at the aperture and knew: not her. No. That much was obvious, an age had passed, that much the door ajar had told her" (Coover 1969:18).

Little Red Riding Hood's undressing, her crossing the threshold of the house, and subsequent closing the door does not represent a naive act of exposure to the danger, but a conscious act of the now experienced Little Red Riding Hood intended to deprive her of her former idealized and innocent identity, and all connotations she had previously evoked. It is also a step towards acquiring a new identity closer to experiential, authentic living and real life. The act of opening the door also signifies opening up space for the new intertextual sensibility of postmodern readers, who realize the power of language and its influence on their perception of reality. Opening the door also means entering into the world of intertextual imagination, a world of new stories, new literary forms and sensibility evoked not only by these new forms, but also by other stories included in this collection of Coover's short stories named *Pricksongs&Descants*. It is a world the narrator characterizes as

"[...] a comedy from which, once entered, you never returned, it nevertheless possessed its own astonishments and conjurings, its towers and closets, and even more pathways, more gardens, and more doors"(Coover 1969:19).

According to Thomas Kennedy, with this short story Coover

"[...] begins a marvelous series of prestidigitations functioning on a series of levels, promising the reader a baffling, comic and enlightening journey into the heart of the imagination that is metafiction" (Kennedy 1992:15).

Operating within the framework of famous fairy tales and stories, changing and altering their different motifs and characteristic features, Coover creates a metafictional situation par excellence which, as already mentioned, Patricia Waugh understands as

"[...] fictional writing which self-consciously and systematically draws attention to its status as an artefact in order to pose questions about the relationship between fiction and reality" (Waugh 1984:2).

This metafictional situation is a manifestation of the hypertextual sensibility of the postmodern period operating above the traditional textual reality, not by working with and altering the existing realities that traditional literary texts have always referred to, but by investigating the meaning these texts have produced. Coover uses the principle of hypertextuality in his short stories. In *The Art of Navigating Through Hypertext,* Jakob Nielsen writes:

"*Hypertext is non-sequential writing: a directed graph, where each node contains some amount of text or other information[...] [T]rue hypertext should also make users feel that they can move freely through the information according to their own needs. This feeling is hard to define precisely but certainly implies short response times and low cognitive load when navigating*"(Nielsen 1990:298).

The replacement of chronological plot with self-reflexivity and contemplation, coupled with the juxtaposition of innocence, idealization and sentimentality with vulgarity, brutality, sexual permissiveness and even perversity creates a parodic effect. It is not, however, a traditional coherent parody of a genre, but rather a means of establishing a situation which indicates a difference between the past and present as well as a difference from the traditional way of writing and perception of reality. It is a parody which, according to Linda Hutcheon,

"*[...] does not disregard the context of the past representations it cites, but uses irony to acknowledge the fact that we are inevitably separated from the past today —by time and by the subsequent history of these representations*"(Hutcheon 1991:226).

Hutcheon further observes that

"*Postmodern parody is both deconstructively critical and constructively creative, paradoxically making us aware of both the limits and the powers of representation—in any medium*" (Hutcheon 1991:228).

It is a form of parody which Jameson characterizes as blank and neutral (Jameson, 1991). Parody is a means which creates an ironic distance from the past, but also a postmodern sensibility of the perception of reality based on metatextuality. Parody focuses the reader's attention on the referential function of language and the way it mediates reality. In her book *Practising Postmodernism/Reading Modernism* (1992), Patricia Waugh argues that

"*The postmodern self-conscious awareness of the finitude of the material and the plasticity of the imagination (now producer of fictions by which to live rather than mediator of absolute vision) is often expressed through parody: a mode which explicitly speaks through the reformulation of an existing discourse. The materiality of language becomes the concern of theorist and imaginative writier alike*" (Waugh 1992: 11).

Such narrative techniques point out the artificiality, idealization and falsehood of myths, various fairy tales and stories, but on the other hand these techniques play a highly intellectual game with the reader which requires a certain intellectual knowledge and potential. Coover's use of postmodern parody, which is a manifestation of intertextuality showing the interconnection of texts and discourses rather than between text and reality, as well as his use of self-reflexivity and metafiction, focus the reader's attention on linguistic reality, on the process of creation of meaning in a literary work, while at the same time they cause the reader to become involved in the creation of this meaning. These narrative techniques reveal the complexity of the relationship between linguistic and external reality and they also relativize this relationship, thereby undermining traditional mimetic representation and the belief in the power of language to imitate and depict external reality. At the same time, these narrative strategies rely on the new sensibility of the postmodern period which is marked by an awareness of the relative inability of language to convey clear meaning, whether through general or artistic language.

II.3.4 Popular Culture, Media and Parodic Contexts of R. Coover's *For the Kiddies: Cartoon* (1987)

In a society Irving Howe characterized as "mass society"(Howe 1979:130), people become not only consumers of goods but also of media sounds and images, and at the same time they become objects of manipulation dominated by mass media, especially television, video and film, which provide consumers with a simplified, linear image of external reality. According to Gerald Graff, this is a society

"[...] where boredom is more conspicuous than poverty and exploitation, and where authority encourages hedonistic consumption and a flabby, end-of-ideology tolerance. Such a society does not present the type of sharp resistance requisite for individual self-definition"(Graff 1979: 213).

Transferring their picture of the world into people's consciousness, the media make the complicated world and the relationships in it linear and simplified (Newman, 1985), and this is especially typical of popular culture flattering the tastes of broad masses of people. Then there is commercial television in particular, aiming solely to gain commercial profit, which relativizes and deforms not only the picture of reality, but also the entire hierarchy of the value system.

It can be said that in the contemporary, postmodern period, images become the main tool and manipulator of people and their understanding of external reality. At the same time, images become the main medium contributing to the change of sensibility in people, and televison using the mediated image of reality *"[...] blurs the line between truth and fiction, between the truly earth-shattering and the trivial"*(Grenz 1996: 34). According to Grenz, furthermore,

"The screen thus becomes an embodied form of our psychic worlds. Living in the postmodern era means inhabiting a world created by the juxtaposition of diverse images. The world of the screen blurs undifferentiated images into a fragmented present, and postmoderns who are wedded to this world remain unsure that it is anything more than a blur of images" (Grenz 1996: 35-36).

A mediated, simulated image of reality (Baudrillard, 1988) and uncertainty about the relevant moral and value criteria are the main characteristics of the postmodern sensibility. In her essay *One Culture and the New Sensibility*, Susan Sontag understands this as a combination of sensibility and perceptivity, which is

"[...] rooted, as it must be, in our experience, experiences which are new in the history of humanity—in extreme social and physical mobility; in the crowdedness of the human scene (both people and material commodities multiplying at a dizzying rate); in the availability of new sensations such as speed (physical speed, as in airplane travel; speed of images, as in the cinema); and in the pan-cultural perspective on the arts that is possible through the mass reproduction of art objects" (Sontag 1978:296).

Many postmodernist literary works show this change in sensibility, a relativization of the value system as well as a different vision of reality created by the juxtaposition of different signs conveying and influencing people's perception of external reality. Robert Coover's short story collection *A Night in the Movies or, You Must Remember This* (1992) consisting of freely-interconnected parts which simulate, transform, deform and deconstruct film techniques and genres such as film commercials, newsreels, love, adventure and detective stories, comedies, westerns or cartoons is one example of such fiction. *Cartoon : For the Kiddies* is the title of one of these stories.

Two different ontological levels form the basic narrative and spatial situation in Coover's short story, that of the real and that of the cartoon (film, image). They do not evoke any illusion of difference, because both these levels overlap, supplant each other and even merge. Both levels are represented in external (reality) and internal (cartoon) space. The movements of the characters referred to as cartoon (dog, driver, unknown man, cop) and as real (cat, woman, man, real cop) are not movements between the inner (cartoon) and outer (reality) space, but the difference between reality and film is blurred, making these movements become signifiers in the sign system of the text.

The difference between both spaces and ontological levels is indicated only by the adjectives "real" and "cartoon" which are attributed to the characters. This manifests itself at the very beginning of the short story:

"The cartoon man drives his cartoon car into the cartoon town and runs over a real man. The real man is not badly hurt—the cartoon car is virtually weightless after all, it's hardly any worse than getting a cut lip from licking an

envelope—but the real man feels that a wrong has nevertheless been done him, so he goes in search of a policeman"(Coover 1992:135).

Creating such a juxtaposition of two ontological levels, Coover means to show the pointlessness of making a difference between these two worlds; indeed at the same time he suggests their equality. None of the characters in this short story is forced to step beyond the space between external reality and cartoon, since a transition between both worlds is depicted as natural and smooth, and all characters meet in the textual space. Depicting physical injury to a man, Coover implicitly demonstrates the negative influence of the visualised (film, image) world—the world of popular culture—on the real world. Such a strategy of erasing the boundaries between reality and fiction, between the real and the film world mediated by a constructed image of reality, between the fictional discourses of cartoon, literature and reality, Coover emphasizes the textuality of the perceived reality and shows the unimportance of the differences between the reality and film as perceived by people. Signs representing the world become quotable and, according to Anton Pokrivčák,

"the meaning[...] is formed by a random play of designators without the possibility to draw on any axiomatic system which would enable us to build a methodology of a truthful recognition of reality"(Pokrivčák 1997: 14).

In this way, according to Rifaterre and Pokrivčák, the character of literary signification changes in the sense that it becomes a relationship not between signs and reality, but between the signs themselves, which consequently makes this process semiotic rather than semantic (Pokrivčák 1997:14). In the subject's consciousness, both subject and objects are thematized, and become two constituting poles

"[...] which form a space between the meaning oscillating between them, a meaning which can never achieve its fulfillment, immanence, independence, eternality, because if this happened it would mean a cancellation of the condition of its own existence and its own death" (Pokrivčák 1997:23).

In this understanding, the world becomes "a sign construct"(Pokrivčák 1997: 23), *"a play of the so-called nonidentical signs, signs deprived of the possibility of their teleological fulfillment"* (Pokrivčák 1997: 23), or as Jacques Derrida puts it, "*There is nothing outside of the text*" (Derrida 1976:158).

As mentioned above, Coover emphasizes the textual character of perceived reality through the juxtaposition of the real and the cartoon world, as well through the depiction of their mutual interaction. This interaction is reminiscent of the combination of cartoon and feature films in which the characters from both real and cartoon worlds are on the stage or in the film rather than in reality, as for example in Spielberg's film *Who Killed Roger Rabbit?* (Kennedy 1992:85). In his short story Coover uses narrative techniques reminiscent of film, influencing the perception of reality through manipulation of the image of reality. In Coover's depiction of reality, however, the meeting and constant interplay of two different worlds and ontological levels evokes doubt about the possibility of identification of reality with fiction, which is further intensified by his use of humorous and even absurd, grotesque and parodic situations. Since the real man cannot find a real policeman after being run over by the cartoon car, he complains to the nearest cartoon policeman, while a real policeman is standing by the cartoon car with its cartoon driver, and a cartoon dog chases the cartoon policeman who is being chased by a real cat simultaneously. The cartoon policeman is further being chased by a cartoon woman. The real policeman shoots the real cat and is consequently seduced by the cartoon woman, who enjoys a love act with the dog, while the real man eventually takes the cartoon car. With the cartoon car shrinking to the size of a toy, the man subsequently discovers his real wife's infidelity with a cartoon man at home.

All these scenes are reminiscent of the technique of fast sequencing of images as used in a cartoon, aimed at evoking parallel linearity and emphasizing action and plot. Such a perception of reality is further evoked by Coover's depiction of the real characters, which produces a feeling of reduction of their physical nature. Thus these characters become signs in a chain of other sign connections, further creating textual space and textuality of the image. Literary text and literary representation of the film image of the cartoon merge into a textual "image" of reality. Depicting the interaction between cartoon and real world, Coover emphasizes the absurd grotesqueness following from the situational humor and shows the deformation and absurdity of this distorted vision of reality, human imperfection and the change in hierarchy of the human value system. At the same time, in this short story the meeting of the real characters with their cartoon counterparts produces a fantastic grotesque as understood by Silvia Pokrivčáková (2002:15), but in combination with different manifestations of grotesquerie it points to the new sensibility of the postmodern period, the imperfectness and inability of human reason to understand and explain the complicated chain of relationships concerning the position of people in the universe. This relativization of the hierarchy of values often manifests itself in open but also perverse sexuality in the story, as in the scene in which the cartoon woman seduces the real policeman:

"These breasts are nearly as large as the woman herself, and they have nipples on them that turn sequentially into pursed lips, dripping spigots, traffic lights, beckoning fingers, then lit-up pinball bumpers. The real policeman is not completely real, after all. He has cartoon eyes that stretch out of their sockets like paired erections, locking on the cartoon woman's breasts with their fanciful nipples. She takes her breasts off and gives them to the real policeman, and he creeps furtively away, clutching the gift closely like a fearful secret, his eyes retracting deep into his skull as though to empty it of its own realness, what's left of it" (Coover 1992:136).

Explicit but visually distorted sexuality, deformed by the depiction of a sexual act between the real man and cartoon woman, further results in the perversity of sexual contact between the cartoon woman and the dog:

"They ignore him [the cartoon man beating these two persons], cuddling up once more, the dog panting heavily after exerting himself, both mentally and physically, the woman erotically touching the dog's huge floppy tongue with the tip of her own"(Coover 1992 :137).

Finally, both the perversity of this erotic scene and also the distortion of reality as such culminate in a grotesque scene of marital infidelity between the real woman and cartoon man:

"At home he [the real man] shows his wife, lying listlessly on the sofa, the cartoon car, now no bigger than the palm of his hand, and tells her about his adventures[...] She lifts her skirts and shows him the cartoon man."He's been there all day." The cartoon man smirks up at him over his shoulders, making exaggerated undercranked thrusts with his tiny cartoon buttocks, powder white with red spots like a clown's cheeks. "Is he...he hurting you?" the real man gasps. "No, it just makes me jittery. It's a sort of like cutting your lip on the edge of an envelope," she adds with a grimace, letting her skirt drop[...]" (Coover 1992: 138).

Grotesque and absurd imagery resulting from the juxtaposition of reality and fiction evoking perversity on the one hand, while on the other suppressing the physical appreciation of the sexual act, shows up the artificiality of interaction between the created film world and external reality, and the difference in perception of reality produced by the cartoon image. In the context of sexually perverse connotations, such grotesque imagery reveals the different sensibility of the postmodern age, and the different understanding of both external reality and the hierarchy of values in the technologically advanced countries. This imagery is reminiscent of carneval grotesquerie which, according to Pokrivčáková,

"[...] is in direct opposition to the self-confident post-Englightenment rationalism and Cartesian identification of truth with human consciousness" (Pokrivčáková 2002: 26),

and it is further combined with satirical grotesque imagery. The satirical grotesque, according to Pokrivčáková, "reveals the pitfalls of some phenomena which it mocks [...]" (Pokrivčáková 2002: 20).

As Pokrivčáková further argues,

"More than any other trope, the grotesque builds its ontological potential on the de-objectivization, relativization or even subversion of values, that is on the mechanisms which have traditionally been an inseparable part of the operational inventory of all forms of reception theories"(Pokrivčáková 2002: 21).

According to Pokrivčáková then, the grotesque has

"[...] an ability to depict otherwise inexpressable and ungraspable aspects of the world and human existence" (Pokrivčáková 2002: 55).

These features of carnevalesque and satirical grotesque acquire the characteristic features of parodic grotesque (Pokrivčáková 2002: 55). Using parodic grotesque, Coover's short story acquires the character of postmodern parody of popular literature, film and entire popular culture, and gives a critique of the consumerist character of popular culture. As Tamás Bényei argues, it is a parody which

"[...] has changed its role: from exposer of exhausted forms and herald of literary change it seems to have evolved (or atrophied) into a signal of the problematic nature of originality and change itself"(Bényei 1995:95).

As mentioned above, in his short story *For the Kiddies!: Cartoon*, Coover uses narrative techniques reminiscent of the cinema, especially cartoons and popular films, and this manifests itself in his conflation of the real and cartoon worlds. The most common film techniques used in this story are the emphasis on action and plot, depthlessness, i.e. the absence of social and historical backgrounds for the characters, the emphasis on speed (fast sequence of scenes) reminiscent of film shots, as well as simple linearity, dynamism of action and dramatic episodes. To emphasize visuality and postmodern visual sensibility, in the composition of his short story Coover uses the imagery of focusing and distancing, as well as imagery evoking the dominance of one kind of world (and one ontological level) over the other (reality versus film, cartoon worlds). As can be understood from the above, this imagery of dominance manifests itself in the scenes in which the cartoon man injures the real man, the real policeman gives in to the sexual attractivity of the cartoon woman, the real woman to the sexual attractivity of the cartoon man, and the real cat is shot by the real policeman who is defending the cartoon characters. The cartoon car which the real man uses without realizing its cartoon nature finally shrinks to a minimum (Coover 1992:137). This imagery shows the dominance of the cartoon world, which is further supported by a scene in which the cartoon man ceremonially holds up the real cat—dead"(Coover 1992:137).

Through his emphasis on the image and metaphor of dominance, Coover emphasizes the dominance of a new visual sensibility and a new perception of the world, and at the same time demonstrates the absence of difference between different worlds or ontological levels, between reality and fiction. He also points out the textuality of perceived reality, which manifests itself for example in the sexual scene with the real policeman:

"The real policeman is not completely real, after all. He has cartoon eyes that stretch out of their sockets like paired erections, locking on the cartoon woman's breasts with their fanciful nipples"(Coover 1992:136).

Finally, the difference between both world is erased; they both merge, overlap and supplant each other *"[...] as though they were walking side by side down two different streets"* (Coover 1992:135), by which Coover no longer indicates a difference, but a linearity or similarity, a mutual co-existence and overlapping of both worlds. According to Kennedy, in this short story Coover deals with *"[...] how are we 'real' persons affected by our interchanges with "cartoon" (or fictional) characters"* (Kennedy 1992:86). This visuality expressed by narrative techniques and tropes such as parody and the grotesque, as well as through narrative techniques of film genres, shows a postmodern perception of reality which relativizes the unitary vision of reality previously promoted by fiction, evokes doubt about the possibility of full understanding of the world, and reveals the imperfectness of human existence. The imagery of sexual perversity and dominance suggests the manipulation of people by the media and popular culture, and offers a critique of the deformed vision of reality conveyed by the media that use the visual representation of reality. People become victims of such a perception of reality, they become clowns, jesters unable to distinguish reality from fiction, the truth from lies, and unable to identify stable moral criteria to judge the world. This manifests itself especially in the final scene in which new cartoon ears appear on the real man's head after he discovers his wife's infidelity. This scene is reminiscent of one from Collodi's famous story of Pinocchio, which puts a "real" person in the fantastic, fairy tale world and on a different ontological level as well, as in an absurd and grotesque position expressing the imperfectness of sensual and rational perceptions of reality. Coover's use of postmodern parody, irony and the grotesque presents a critique not only of traditional writing and mimetic representation of reality, but especially of the popular culture that cartoons and other popular films represent.

II.4 Popular Autobiography and Travel Book in One (Richard Brautigan's *An Unfortunate Woman: A Journey, 2000*)

The literary work of Richard Brautigan oscillates between romantic idealization and parodic metafictional paradox, between idealization of the private and secluded self and the violence of public life imposed on it, between humor and tragedy, between lyrical imagery, almost linear narration and fragmentary narrative strategies. In his works Brautigan treats many American "myths" (such as the American dream, the success story, heroism) related to American experience and American cultural identity. Neil Schmitz argues that Brautigan

"[...] is par excellence the 'reader of myths' whom Roland Barthes describes at length in Mythologies, the interpreter who reads the 'mythical signifier'"[...] as an "inextricable" whole made of meaning and form" (Schmitz 1973: 110).

Many critics have commented on Brautigan's romantic vision of the world (Alsen, 1996; Baštín, 1996); his recuperation of pastoral myths (Schmitz, 1973; Pütz, 1979), his emphasis on depiction of the secluded and alienated narrator (Schmitz, 1979; Clayton, 1971), his individualism and the symbolic power of imagination (Boyer, 1987) or his connection with counter-culture (Boyer, 1987; Clayton, 1971; Baštín, 1996). In my own book *Poetika americkej postmodernej prózy (Richard Brautigan a Donald Barthelme)[Poetics of American Postmodern Fiction: Richard Brautigan and Donald Barthelme]*, Prešov: 2001), I have emphasized the role and function of parody, popular culture and metafiction in Richard Brautigan's works.[1] In many of them, especially in his parodies of popular genres from the 1970's, Brautigan uses parody in order to criticize the role of popular culture and mass media in shaping and distorting people's perception and vision of the world.[2]

In his posthumously, but only recently published novel (Brautigan died in 1984, his novel *An Unfortunate Woman* was published in 2000) he used the form of a genre with a traditionally fixed structure—a journal, in which the narrator's strongly autobiographical entries (Brautigan's real journeys, his daughter, age, lecturing, local places where he lived and which he visited) are written in the poetic imagery with which the author treats the issues known from his earlier novels—nostalgia for youth, ageing, alienation, solitude, negative aspects of commercialized society and even death. The form of a journal, or *"a brief calendar map of one's journey through life"* (Brautigan 2000:99) as the unnamed narrator refers to it, enables Brautigan to stipulate the poetic framework through which he contemplates the passage of time and its role in the narrator's life. In contrast to Brautigan's earlier novel *The Tokyo-Montana Express* (1980), the narrator in this book seemingly gives a more chronological narration (the narrator's entries in the journal run from January 30, 1982 to June 28, 1982—that is until shortly before Brautigan's real death). This novel, however, is rather reminiscent of a traveller's journal or autobiography, describing the narrator recording journeys across the U.S.A., Canada, and Hawaii. In his study of American travel and autobiographical writing *Travel Writing and Autobiographical Studies* (2001), John D. Hazlett gives the basic features of travel writing, which are, in his view

"a. the fictionalization of the author-narrator,

b. the construction of the journey in a form that offers adventure or drama,

c. the conscious positioning of the author in relation to the "other" (which involves establishing distance or intimacy; meditations on national character; and a critique of U.S. culture), and finally

d. the conscious positioning of the autor in relation to previous writers and other travelers (which involves demonstrating his superiority to them)" (Hazlett 2001: 395).

Brautigan's narration does not give a detailed description of geographical locations, but focuses mostly on present or recent past events. The narrator in this novel is fictionalized and he offers a critique of U.S. culture, but Brautigan undermines the second aspect of Hazlett's characterization of travel writing (this novel is neither adventure nor drama), parodies the national character (Hazlett's third aspect of travel writing) and excludes the comments on previous writiers (the fourth aspect). The narrator, a 47 year-old writer reminiscent of Brautigan himself, argues that

"[...]one of the doomed purposes of this book is an attempt to keep the past and the present functioning simultaneously"(Brautigan 2000: 64).

This statement not only reveals one of the key themes of the book— time, but it also confirms the metafictional status of the narrator who, in contrast to

Brautigan's other book entitled *So The Wind Won't Blow it Away* (in which he uses the related genre of fictional autobiography based on the narrator's childhood), deals mostly with present events. In her study on autobiography *The Power of (Auto) Biography in Recent Literary Studies* (2001), Isabel Durán argues that

"*Autobiography—the story of a distinctive culture written in individual characters and from within—offers a privileged access to an experience (the American experience, the Black experience and so on) that no other variety of literature can offer. That is, autobiography renders in a peculiarly direct and faithful way the experience and the vision of a people—a group, a particular identity*" (Durán 2001: 382).

Although Brautigan's novel presents the narrator's experience as marginalized (because of his ageing, and because of his rejection of commercial and mainstream culture), he undermines the seriousness of this experience through playful parody. The narrator's awareness of his status and his way of addressing the reader suggests other relevant theme of the book:

"*Now I'll get back to the rest of this book, whose main theme is an unfortunate woman. I'm actually writing about something quite serious, but I'm doing it in a roundabout way, including varieties of time and human experience, which even tragedy cannot escape from*"(Brautigan 2000: 75).

Playing with both reader and time, in addition to the passage of time itself, the narrator develops other themes related to misfortune and its symbolic meaning such as solitude, ageing and death, which the woman who has hanged herself represents. This woman and another dying of cancer are mentioned in several places in the book (pp. 24; 90; 93) and represent, in Brautigan's understanding, not only death but also solitude and loneliness, as well as the lack of motivation for living a purposeful life. Brautigan further develops his imagery of death by introducing the cemetery (pages 23; 33), tombstones (36) and shrines (36). Brautigan's narrator mostly describes his boredom, his eating habits, and his observation of weather and nature:

"*Anyway, I had nothing to occupy myself with last night, so I made a huge pot of spaghetti sauce starting from scratch, slicing onions, mushrooms, a green pepper, etc. (97) [...] Being forty-seven years old hasn't slowed me* down that much, but the other 95 % of my life is very normal, quiet and often boring" (80).

The narrator's frequent interruptions of the linearity of his narration by referring to the momentary subject of his writing again refers to the lack of both inspiration and motivation, as if the narrator wanted to fill out the blank spaces in the notebook which must be completed willy-nilly:

"When I got this notebook to write about an unfortunate woman my plan was to end this journey when the notebook ended. There are 160 pages in the notebook. In the beginning I counted the words on each page after a day's writing. The first page has 119 words, the second 193[...]" (76),

and this manifests itself again, as if with relief, in the following extract:

"I'm now starting the last page (160) of this book. There are 28 lines to a page and I write on every other line, so I can add things in between the lines if I want to. That's 14 writing lines to a page times 160" (110).

For Brautigan's narrator, not only death but also life represent stillness, emptiness and solitude. Despite his detached, secluded and individualistic writing, in this case the fictional journal means for the narrator a constant attempt to establish communication with both natural and human worlds (women, lovers, friends, neighbours, his daughter) and to postpone death by writing a story (of his life), which is the scheme reminiscent of the Scheherezade story. Brautigan's narrator's attempts to establish contact with human beings fail very often not only because of the narrator's antipathy to some people (an Alaskan politician, a feminist student), but also because of his egocentrism and even narcissism, which is unable to develop deeper relationships either with men or with women. Although he has friends, they are either too far away from his residence (Chicago friends and others), or they are only formal partners for communication in his loneliness (his neighbors). His narcissistic ego does not allow him to overcome formal sexual experience and develop emotional relationships with either girlfriends or other women, including his daughter. He argues that

"I could not afford the luxury of a complicated love life. I had a simple love life and often when I have a simple love life, I don't have any love life at all. I sort of miss it, but the complications all return soon enough, and I find myself occupying sleepless nights, wondering how I lost control of the heart's basic events again" (Brautigan 2000: 21).

Brautigan's narrator is in the position of an eternal traveller observing life, but who is incapable of grasping either time or life in the position of real man or writer. He comments on his traveller's status in the following way:

"I guess that's what a passenger's supposed to do, pass from one place to another, but it doesn't make it any simpler. About all you can do is wish him luck, and hope that he has some slight understanding of what uncontrollably is happening to him" (20).

On the other hand, the narrator expresses his inability to control time both as an ageing man and a writer:

"Yes, it is difficult to keep the past and the present going on at the same time because they cannot be trusted to act out their proper roles. They suddenly can turn on you and operate diametrically opposed to your understanding and the needs of reality" (66).

For Brautigan, the narrator's inability to control the passing of time, life and even writing is a symbolic expression of his failure both to lead a purposeful life and to produce any successful writing. His narrator further argues that

"It becomes more and more apparent as I proceed with this journey that life cannot be controlled and perhaps not even envisioned and that certainly design and portent are out of the question. The process of being this book only accentuates my day-to-day helplessness" (59).

For the symbolic expression of such failure Brautigan uses not only these direct statements and the framework of the journal genre, but also the method and imagery of "displacement", "incompleteness" and the literary techniques which the narrator himself refers to as "[...] inconclusive fragments, sophomoric humor, cheap tricks, detailess details"(109). These methods and techniques enable him to undermine the traditional narrative and compositional techniques of the popular genres whose framework he uses (autobiography, diary, travel book), and at the same time symbolically to express the failure of the capacity of the individual and the writer to be successful and control both his life and writing. Displacement means the deliberate use of particular language, style, genre, events and situations set and made to work in inappropriate contexts. Incompleteness is related to events, actions and situations, both literal and symbolic, which begin or tend to begin, but which are interrupted and mostly never finished/completed. Thus for example, concerning displacement, Brautigan uses the form of a journal with exact dating reminiscent of a traveller's diary, in which however most of the described events and observations do not take place at the time they were recorded (see the dates), nor does the narrator's journal give the expected description of places he has visited. In the tourist paradise of Hawaii the narrator does not typically describe the wonderful scenery and the beaches, but he makes critical comments on the negative effects of commercialization (cars, pollution) and observes a cemetery instead. Thus the cemetery creates a displaced image of Hawaii in the context of traditional images and visions of this country. The narrator argues that

"*Most people when they come to Hawaii do not come for the cemeteries. They are interested in the sun and the beaches: two things that I've never really cared for, so I'm kind of displaced here in Hawaii, but I make do with what I have, and what I have right now is this Japanese cemetery to explore*"(Brautigan 2000: 28).

Alaska, like Hawaii, is not typically presented as a snowy country with polar animals, but is rather associated with consumer commodities (hot dogs, junk food), or with unsuccessful politicians. Displacement is also evoked by the parodic lovers among the soup cans in the supermarket, the movie theatres in big-city Chinatowns, and the narrator himself during his visit to his friends' place in Canada, when tragic events in the family make the narrator's visit undesirable.

Both Alaska and Hawaii lose their expected image and in both Brautigan's and the narrator's understanding suffer from growing technological progress and commercialization:

"*So much of America, even what were once unspoilable beautiful towns, look as if 'Los Angeles' had overflowed on them like a toilet bowl whose defecated contents all have something to do with the lifestyle of the automobile. I think the worst case of 'Los Angeles' automobile cultural damage I've ever seen is Honolulu*"(13).

Brautigan's fragmentary composition—part of which is his strategy of "incompleteness"—manifests itself not only in the unfinished, interrupted and fragmentary sentences, dialogues and conversations, but also in his depiction of incomplete events, situations and relationships, for example the relationship of the narrator to his lovers, friends, relatives and sexual partners (his love relations are mostly temporary or prematurely terminated; the sexual act with his partner cannot be completed because of his illness; his telephone conversation with his daughter neither improves nor re-establishes a good father-daughter relationship; his neighbors do not come; his travels never finish, and his journal remains incomplete). The narrator characterizes the book he is writing as *"[...] an unfinished labyrinth of half-asked questions fastened to partial answers"* (107), which are apparently left unfinished on purpose:

"There are ten writing lines left on this page and I have decided not to use the last line. I'll leave it to somebody else's life" (110).

All these techniques symbolically express the narrator's inability to cope with both reality and successful writing, an inability to control them and to produce a meaningful existence. Thus it is not only death, symbolically and yet paradoxically expressing stability, stillness and solitude, which is the central metaphor of Brautigan's book; it is also chaos, disorientation and misunderstanding leading to "failure". Brautigan's narrator becomes only a passive observer and recorder of events and life, both as a human being and a writer, since these events cannot be either controlled or predicted. As he himself argues:

"Also, I am the last person to know what's going on in my life, but I have a feeling that's maybe the way it is with everybody and belief in self-understanding is only a delusion" (99).

Thus, for Brautigan, life represents an unpredictable and uncontrollable flowing chaos, in contrast to death which represents stillness and loneliness, but quite paradoxically also an almost harmonious stability evoking the effects of a lyrical, though cold Poe-ish melancholy:

"A lot of the tombstones were piled in such a way that you couldn't see whose lives they represented[...] It was as if they never existed[...] A person couldn't just drive by one day as I had just done and get out of the car and walk among the dead, thinking about them, wondering who they were and how they had lived.

Being in the shrine, they were out of sight and out of mind. I had a feeling that the relatives who'd had them dug up and then put in the shrine did not visit their memories very often" (36).

For Brautigan, on the other hand, the natural world is poetic, idealistic and romantic and represents the desired harmony in communication between people that Brautigan's narrator so misses. Brautigan's narrator's desire for communication, for establishing contact between his secluded self and the rest of the world is expressed, for example, through the juxtaposition of romantic imagery with natural communication images:

"Today starts with me talking to a friend on the telephone last night.

Oh, yes, we're on the same back porch with no electrical storm in sight and the sun and the birds shining away in the sky and a few white clouds billowing about, seeming almost to be reflections coming off the snow in the mountains to the west, which go steplike miles to the Pacific Ocean far away and where I talked to a friend last night"(86-87),

or as it manifests itself in a different place in the book:

"I stared at the telephone, betrayed again by this strange instrument so far removed from nature. I've never seen anything in nature that looked like a telephone. Clouds, flowers, rocks, none of them resemble a telephone" (101).

In Brautigan's understanding, the human world, in contrast to nature, is rather spoilt, negative and excluded from natural harmony. Nature and the human world are very often marked by the negative effects of industrialization, not only in this but also in his other novels. Using fragmentary composition, the above methods of incompleteness and displacement along with frequent changing of the subject, often accompanied by lyrical imagery, undermine the narrative conventions of the genres whose narrative framework Brautigan uses (diary, autobiography, travel book) and create a parodic effect. This parody involves a critique of traditional literary forms and genres, as well as pointing out the negative effects of commercialization and a crisis in human relationships in the contemporary technologically advanced societies. At the same time, Brautigan's novel offers a playful, but also nostalgic contemplation on life, death and the passage of time, which means that he starts to develop a personal theme which later becomes general and universal. This strategy also undermines the traditional narrative strategies of autobiographies, diaries and travel books.

Although Brautigan's nostalgic and "serious" treatment of "life" and "death" is balanced by his use of humor together with playful but also ironic treatment of several issues such as love, women, human relationships and commercial culture, it is hardly enough for the production of a quality literary work. In this book Brautigan repeats some of his narrative and compositional strategies, as well as the eclectic motifs from his previous novels— love of (Japanese) women (*Sombrero Fallout: A Japanese Novel, 1976*; *The Abortion: An Historical Romance 1966, 1971*), nature, pastoral nostalgia, solitude, the contrast between physical phenomena and poetic imagination, and imaginary situations. This book does not represent the best of Brautigan's artistic achievements and however playful with words and poetic imagery, it reveals Brautigan's artistic creative crisis, which is also one of the subjects of the book. Brautigan's real creative crisis manifests itself, for example, in his frequent and pointless descriptions of the subjects he is writing or wants to write about, but which are suddenly interrupted without motivation. This can be seen, for example, in the scene with a spider on the narrator's arm, in which the subject is suddenly changed without any meaningful connection with the rest of the text:

"*He sure is small. He's about four times bigger than a period. Goddammit, he is spinning a web![...] I wish him all the luck in the world, and then blow him off my arm into the grass of the backyard, ultimately a better place than to live on my arm. I think the first time I took a shower with him at home on my arm with perhaps a few insects about the size of two periods in his web, it would be an irrevocable experience for him.*

Where was I before I noticed the spider setting up house-keeping on me? Oh, yes, I didn't go directly to the car after pouring myself a glass of wine. I walked over to my neighbours' house to see if they had gotten back from a month-long trip back East"(104).

This is nevertheless the most melancholic of Brautigan's books, in which the central symbol of death represents not only the lack of artistic motivation and people's inability to develop meaningful lives, but also portrays, as a result of this perhaps, the author's feelings shortly before his premature death.

CHAPTER III
POSTMODERNISM AND METAFICTION
III.1 Metafiction in Robert Coover's Fiction (*The Marker* and *The Hat Act, 1969*)

In a postmodernist literary work especially, the use of metafiction undermines the relation between the signifier and the signified, between reality and its artistic/literary representation. At the same time, the use of metafiction undermines traditional literary representation and offers a pluralistic, multidimensional vision of reality that problematizes an artistic work's claim to objectivity and truth. In my view, not all postmodern works necessarily include explicitly metafictional elements, but many authors use narrative techniques that are able to construct a postmodernist vision of the world. Linda Hutcheon sees metafiction mostly in its connection with history and its interpretation. She has coined the term historiographic metafiction that she understands as

"*those well-known and popular novels which are both intensely self-reflexive and yet paradoxically also lay claim to historical events and personages: The French Lieutenant's Woman, Midnight's Children, Ragtime, Legs, G., Famous Last Words*" (Hutcheon 1988: 5).

Hutcheon further argues that

"*In most of the critical works on postmodernism, it is narrative—be it in literature, history or theory—that has usually been the major focus of attention. Historiographic metafiction incorporates all three of these domains: [...] its theoretical self-awareness of history and fiction as human constructs (historiographic metafiction) is made the grounds for its rethinking and reworking of the forms and contents of the past*" (Hutcheon 1988: 5).

As can be seen from the above, Hutcheon identifies historiographic metafiction with the genre of the novel. At the same time, she emphasizes the role of narrative techniques in the artistic representation of history as well as the subversive function of the use of the "*paratextual conventions of historiography,*" and the whole narrative process of fiction. Thus despite the attribute historiographic, Hutcheon's understanding of metafiction is quite narrow. It does not consider the specificity of different kinds of metafictional elements within different kinds of postmodernist novels and postmodernist literature in general, and focuses on the unreliability of the representation of reality, especially history, in these postmodernist novels. In addition to this, Hutcheon argues that "*every representation of the past has specifiable ideological implications*" (121). On the one hand, this view brings her close to Hayden White's view she quotes that "*every representation of the past has specifiable ideological implication*"(White in Hutcheon 1988:120), and to his view that there is no difference between a historian's and an artist's presentation of events (White, 1978). On the other hand, these views themselves ideologize and politicize the understanding of fiction and thus blur the distinction between different kinds of discourses, especially between literature, arts and other written documents, between aesthetically quality art and junk, and popular fiction. Although it sounds formalistic, such blurring these distinctions eliminates the function of literature as a specific kind of discourse able to represent reality and cultural context in a specific aesthetic/artistic way. Speaking about the object rather than the method of representation of reality by specific artistic/literary means implies a necessary reduction and annihilation of this specificity, and an inevitable ideologization and sociologization of literary and artistic texts. Such a discourse thus necessarily becomes a discourse on the political, ideological, historical and sociological situation of the external condition rather than a literary discourse through which literature conveys a multi-dimensional vision of external reality by using a specific artistic language.

As has been quoted several times in this book, as distinct from Hutcheon Patricia Waugh understands metafiction as

"*a term given to fictional writing which self-consciously and systematically draws attention to its status as an artifact in order to pose questions about the relationship between fiction and reality. In providing a critique of their own methods of construction, such writings not only examine the fundamental structures of narrative fiction, they also explore the possible fictitiousness of the world outside the literary/fictional text*" (Waugh 1984:2).

Waugh further emphasizes a diversity of metafiction:

"*Metafiction is thus an elastic term which covers a wide range of fictions. There are those novels at one end of the spectrum which take fictionality as a theme to be explored[...] whose formal self-consciousness is* limited. At the center of this spectrum are those texts that manifest the symptoms of formal and ontological insecurity but allow their deconstructions to be finally recontextualized or 'naturalized' and given a total interpretation [...] Finally, at the furthest extreme that, in rejecting realism more thoroughly, posit the world as a fabrication of competing semiotic systems which never correspond to material conditions[...]" (Waugh 1984: 18-19).

In the same book, Patricia Waugh further gives several signs and examples of metafiction the most important of which are concerned with the relationship between fiction and reality, the arbitrary status of the language and paradoxical of the author, foregrounding the fictiousness of fiction and reality, and intertextuality (Waugh, 1984).

In my view, in Coover's short stories *The Marker* and *The Hat Act* (1969), three of the above aspects of metafiction, that is, foregrounding the relation between fiction and reality; foregrounding the fiction of fiction and reality; and the intertextuality (through parody) dominate. These metafictional elements not only problematize a clear, unified and authoritarian vision of the world; they also undermine the mimetic representation of reality and the belief in the ability of language as a sign system to produce a meaningful, clear and understandable vision of the world. These metafictional elements also problematize several myths associated with western culture. In Coover's *The Marker,* Coover emphasizes the ambiguous connection between fiction and reality (point 4), although it mostly manifests itself not in the juxtaposition of fictional characters and historical figures, but in the depiction of the fictional and (possibly) imaginary characters, reality and fiction. Three basic narrative situations represent four kinds of "reality" in this short story:

1. The seeming reality of Jason and his wife preparing for the sexual act
2. Jason's disorientation in respect of reality—the appearing and disappearing wife, his own uncertainty about his position resulting in the love act which turns out to be with a dead and rotting woman, evoking doubt about the reality of the event
3. The intrusion of the policemen into the scene (emphasizing the confusion between this fiction and reality) who make claims on reality through their discovery of a dead woman (dead for three weeks) as well as through a physical act of freeing Jason from the rotten body

4. The police officer's comments on tradition and innovation (reality and fantasy) creating metatextual reality.

The first of these "kinds of reality" (point one) evokes the semblance of a real, truthful, objective, undeniable reality—Jason is described as fleshy, vivid,

"tall and masculine, about 35, with strong callused hands and a sensitive nose"(Coover 1969:88),

and his wife as *"beautiful, affectionate"*(Coover 1969:88), emotional, attractive, and erotic. In addition to this, "*her motion exists within the motion itself and not in her deliberations*"(Coover 1969:88). In this way Coover evokes the illusion of reality as really lived, experienced, and perceived. At the same time, however, Jason holds a book *"he has doubtless been reading"*(Coover 1969: 88). The juxtaposition of the book and Jason's wife alludes to a possible parallel between mimetic representation of reality a reader reading about Jason makes and possible mimetic nature of the book Jason had been reading before being tempted by his wife. Thus Coover depicts Jason as doubly entrapped in his illusion of the possibility of both mimetic perception and the representation of reality. Jason believes in the possibility of real physical sexual act and, if we believe in the parallel between his vision of reality and the book he is reading, in the mimetic representation of reality through literary art (the book he is reading).

2. Coover further uses the imagery of darkness and light to problematize both a general and specifically Jason's vision of reality. Light, representing physical reality, a clear vision, and a belief in the mimetic (truthful, objective, verifiable) representation of it disappears with Jason's snapping out of the light into darkness. Darkness problematizes clear and verifiable reality, obscures the difference between the real and the imaginary, and evokes uncertainty about the clear vision of the world. In the darkness, Jason's wife turns out to be her abstract image. She

"[...] fades slowly (as when, lying on a beach, one looks at the reflection of the sun on the curving back of the sea, then shuts tight his eyes, letting the image of the reflected sun lose its brilliance, turn green, then evaporate slowly into the limbo of uncertain associations), gradually becoming transformed from that of her nude body crackling the freshness of the laundered sheets to that of Beauty, indistinct and untextured, as though still

emerging from some profound ochre mist, but though without definition, an abstract Beauty[...]" (Coover 1969:88);

Jason loses his orientation towards physical objects (bed, chest of drawers) and is unable to turn on the light, thus remaining entrapped in darkness, the symbolic representation of uncertainty, of the impossibility of a clear vision of reality in irrational abstraction, all of which undermine both the vision of reality and, symbolically, a belief in the ability of art to represent reality mimetically. Jason wants to have a control over events, over physical reality, and over his own senses conveying his perception of the external world. This also manifests itself in Coover's depiction of the sexual act. The sexual act resulting in orgasm as the culmination of physical pleasure is a metaphor for a belief in the physical world, in man's ability to perceive, understand, control and explain it. Despite turning his wife into an abstraction, an image, Jason understands her as a physical being, and his endeavor to gain control over physicality and reality manifests itself in his belief in his wife's real presence (through the realization of the sexual act). This sexual act, however, evokes grotesque, ironic and parodic connotations. The narrator comments on it in the following way:

"[...] the experience, the anxiety of it and its riddles, seems to have created a new urgency, an almost brutal wish to swallow, for a moment, reason and its inadequacies, and to let passion, noble or not, have its hungry way. He is surprised to find her dry, but the entry itself is relaxed and gives way to his determined penetration. In a moment of alarm, he wonders if this is really his wife, but since there is no alternate possibility, he rejects his misgivings as absurd" (Coover 1969:90).

Jason's endeavor to control loses the object of his control since there is nothing to be controlled, and since the sexual act without orgasm as the culmination of physicality and experience loses its meaning. The imagery of disgust and decay (of Jason's wife) becomes the imagery of the deviation, perversity and decay of rational, experiential vision of the world represented by Jason and his own understanding of reality. His wife is suddenly rotten and dead for three weeks,

"Her eyes are open[...] staring up at him, without meaning[...] the flesh of her face is yellowish[...]her mouth is open in a strangely cruel smile[...] her gums have dried and and pulled back from her teeth[...] her blonde hair[...] is

splayed out over the pillow like a urinal mop spread out to dry[...] There is a fuzzy stuff like mold around the nipples of her shrunken breasts" (Coover 1969:90-91).

The absurdity of Jason's belief in the ability of reason to perceive, control, and understand the physical world is further emphasized literally by Jason's being stuck in his wife's body and, figuratively, in this belief itself, symbolically in an objective reality which can be controlled, perceived and lived. The narrator says: *"Jason tries desperately to get free from her body, but finds to his deepest horror that he is stuck!"*(Coover 1969:91). These are characteristics typical of a rational understanding of the world, that is, for the mimetic artistic representation of reality. Thus this becomes also a belief in realistic, mimetic art implying the illusion of the possibility of this kind of art (fiction) and reason to represent, control and depict reality objectively. This all, however, takes place in darkness, evoking uncertainty and breaking Jason's illusion about reality and realistic representation.

3. The image of light and the arrival of policemen on the scene may seemingly represent a return to actual reality and belief in objective knowledge of the external world, which is symbolically alluded to by the narrator:

"At this moment, the lights come on and the police officer and his four assistants burst into the room.

'Really!' cries the police officer, pulling up short. 'This is quite disgusting!'" (Coover 1969:90).

The light illuminates darkness and establishes a clear vision of reality and the world, which stands for the symbolic representation of the revelation of "truth". This revealed truth might be either Jason's perversity or even a deviation—understood exeggeratively as a criminal act by the police, or as his obsession by the belief in experience, rationality and mimetic art. The seriousness of realistic and mimetic vision at this level of reality is undermined by policemen's untraditional behavior—their punishment of Jason and the seemingly unmotivated comments by one of them on tradition, which evokes a grotesque and parodic effect. This parody is

"[...] a kind of [...] rereading of the past that both confirms and subverts the power of the representations of history [...] Irony makes [...] intertextual references into something more than simply academic play or

some infinite regress into textuality: what is called to our attention is the entire representational process—in a wide range of forms and modes of production—and the impossibility of finding any totalizing model to resolve the resulting postmodern contradictions" (Hutcheon 1991:226).

Grotesque and parodic effects, used for the function of re-reading past reality and past literary representational forms, manifest themselves in a following scene:

"[...] the police officer, without ceremony, pulls Jason's genitals out flat on the tabletop and pounds them to a pulp with the butt of his gun" (Coover 1969: 91).

This scene suggests a parody of the hard-boiled school of detective novels, but Coover subverts the meaning of this parody. It is not a traditional parody of the genre, the detective story, but turns out to be a parody of the mimetic representation and traditional forms of writing that Jason represents. The cruel act of crushing Jason's genitals seems to be the police officer's punishment of reality and perversity in the same (perverse) way, but it also metaphorically represents his attempt to violate, break and undermine literary and artistic tradition. As Andersen comments:

"Jason represents every reader whose vision has been limited by an adherence to traditional artistic forms [...] The young man's aesthetic sterility is represented by his penis which he has a difficult time removing from the corpse [...] Readers who reject alternative possibilities are making love to dead corpses" (Andersen in Kennedy 1992: 35).

This is further intensified by the police officer's comments, reminiscent of those of a hard-boiled detective, although on a topic unrelated to the criminal act or investigation of the genre.

4. These comments represent a different kind of reality represented in this short story. The police officer argues that he is not "[...] in the strictest sense, a traditionalist" (Coover 1969:91), and he claims that

"I mean to say that I do not recognize tradition qua tradition as sanctified in its own sake. On the other hand, I do not join hands with those who therefore deem it of terrible necessity that all custom be rooted out at all costs. I am personally convinced [...] that there is a middle road, whereon we recognize that innovations find their best soil in traditions, which are justified in their own turn by the innovations, which created them. I believe, then, that *law and custom are essential, but that it is one's constant task to review and revise them*" (91).

The police officer by both his acts and comments becomes an innovator and a representative of a breaker with tradition on two ontological levels: on the one hand, he breaks the conventions of a policeman sticking to law (punishing Jason), thus becoming both a representative of a new kind of detective from those of the hard-boiled detective novels, which were themselves innovative at a certain period, but rather traditional from the contemporary perspective. On the other hand, his traditionality, however, is further undermined by the police officer's metafictional comments on the understanding of tradition, which subvert the seriousness of his status as a police officer in the story in which Jason appears. Thus the police officer is placed within two, or even three discourses, three ontological levels: on a seemingly realistic level of Jason's story if we take the story literally, mimetically, if we believe Jason's story and the arrival of the police; on a metafictional level associated with the parodic context of hard-boiled detective stories; and on the meta-metafictional level associated with the police officer's comments not only on direct reality (traditional detective behaviour), but especially on reality conveyed through literature, through art, through a mediated reality. Coover finally turns the reader's attention from the nature and conventions of the detective novels to the metafictional context thus further parodying and undermining this genre—a corpse is removed, investigation is aimless since the revelation of the perverse sexual act (necrophilia) is unmotivated, Jason remains officially unpunished, and finally no investigation is initiated. The police officer's final words concern a book (more specifically a marker), representing reality mediated through literary art. Finally, Jason's attempt to continue with his reading the book through asking the police to put the marker back is an allusion to his attempt to continue to be a mimetic, realistic, literal reader:

"*The marker!*" *Jason gasps desperately [...]*" (Coover 1969: 92), but *"[...] the police officer does not hear him, nor does he want to*" (92).

The literal reading of the story as a story of sexual perversity (un)punished by the police does not make any sense, since copulation with a dead and decaying corpse in a way described by Coover is impossible, and so both the criminal act and the police investigation are absent, which all undermine the logic and rationality of a traditional detective story. Thus the story, if not read as Jason's fantasizing on reading and love, can be read as an allegory on the conflict between traditional and innovative writing/literature and, at the same time, as a critique of traditional writing and mimetic artistic representation. In addition to this, the story turns out to be a parody of both traditional detective stories and mimetic art (literature) that are based on rationalistic, experiential and logical understanding of physical reality. As can be seen from the above, Coover's problematization of the relation between fiction and reality through the juxtaposition of different ontological levels, through his use of parody, grotesque, and intertextuality creates a metafictional effect. Through such a use of metafiction, Coover points out the "exhaustion" of traditional literary forms based on a belief in unproblematic and unitary vision of reality through mimetic art, and he thus undermines the myth of the western rationalistic tradition associated with Western thinking and understanding of the world. At the same time, Coover offers a new, playful, parodic and problematic vision of reality giving a pluralistic vision of the world and several interpretative opportunities. And last, but not least, the parody of the hard-boiled detective story genre may be understood as a kind of cultural criticism associated with American cultural identity since John Cawelti argues that popular literary genres he calls formulas

"[...] are always ways in which specific cultural themes and stereotypes become embodied in more universal story archetypes" (Cawelti 1976:6).

Through the use of parody and grotesque, not only this genre, as a typical genre of American cultural tradition emphasizing a certain roughness, violence, and illegal practices of the legal representatives (of law, the detectives) is undermined and criticized, but Coover's story undermines the whole myth these genres have created about (American) cultural identity as well.

The Hat Act

The construction of different ontological levels as well as Coover's use of metafiction in the short story *The Hat Act* are slightly different from his story *The Marker*. As distinct from *The Marker*, any direct metafictional comments on literature, arts or representation are absent in *The Hat Act*. The depiction and the manipulation of reality is represented by a magician. On the other hand, drawing on Waugh's theory, in this story Coover, as in *The Marker,* problematizes the relation between fiction and reality by the juxtaposition of reality and illusion (fantasy), rationality and irrationality as well as through blurring the distinction between magic (fantasy) and reality. The distinction between reality and magic represents a distinction between a rational, clear and verifiable reality and its artistic (illusionist) representation by the magician, controllable by reason, logic and experience. A magician is in the position of the controller of his magic and of the audience, an illusion maker, a manipulator of the "narrative of magic" which brings him success with an audience expecting him to be in this position as the controller of reality. The stability of this position as well as the clear vision of reality is undermined in a moment when the magician loses control over both the audience and his magic, magic turning out to be uncontrollable and magical even for the magician. This evokes chaos in connection both with traditional expectations and in all the characters' vision of reality. The narrator describes the magician's act in the following way:

"*Magician withdraws eighth hat from seventh, ninth from eighth, as rabbits extract other rabbits from other hats. Rabbits and hats are everywhere. Stage is one mad turmoil of hats and rabbits*" (Coover 1969: 241).

This act evokes laughter in the audience, which can be still in keeping with the status of a magician in the role of a clown, but the magician's function as a controller (of the audience, entertainment, even the magic) is undermined by his following inability to control both his magic and the audience. His behavior is

"*[...] a desperate struggle. At first, it is difficult to be sure he is stuffing hats and pitching rabbits faster than they are reappearing. Bows, stuffs, pitches, smiles, perspires*" (Coover 1969: 241).

The chaos and confusion are further intensified by the magician's further inability to control his own magic, which is just tricks, manipulations within reality:

"*[Magician]...attempts tentatively to stuff first [hat] into second, but in vain. Attempts to fit second into first, but also without success. Smiles weakly at audience. No applause [...] Trembling with anxiety, magician presses out first hat, places it brim up on table, crushes second hat on floor [...] Loud booing. Freezes. Pales. Returns to table with both hats [...]"* (Coover 1969:242).

The magician, in the position of both controller (traditional magician) and entertainer (traditional entertainer of masses) is unable to fulfill either of these roles. The control, as Coover suggests by his depiction of the magician's subsequent acts, is possible only through belief in fantasy and its control. Both a magician (doing fantastic, irrational, impossible and fantastic magic) and the audience (demonstrating its belief it by applauding) symbolically represent a shared in the possibility of control over fantasy and illusions, or, in other words, a belief in the ability of the human mind and reason to control fantasy and imagination. This manifests itself in Coover's depiction of the magician's fantastic magic (his disappearance in the hat, the extraction of his lovely assistant from it) culminating in his trick with his own body after being snapped by the volunteers from the audience:

"Magician's neck stretches, snaps in two: POP! Large men tumble apart, rolling to opposite sides of stage, one with body, other with hat containing magician's severed head. Screams of terror [...] Decapitated body stands [...] Zipper in front of decapitated body opens, magician emerges. He is as before..." (Coover, 1969:244).

The same trick (fantasy?) repeats with the large men, a boy and the magician's assistant. The audience and the magician represent two different visions and ontological levels of reality. While the magician is able to continue keeping control over both reality and fantasy, the audience believes in physical reality, its graphic representation, and is unable to grasp the magician's trick. This means that while the audience is initially unable to notice a trick and the manipulation of reality (thus becoming representative of rationality, experience and logic) the magician's position of both a manipulator, magician, and a controller seems to be exaggerated and emphasized by his status as the controller of irrationality and imagination. The belief in his ability to control his tricks, imagination and fantasy is, however, undermined and parodied by Coover's depiction of the confusion between reality and fantasy as perceived by the magician. The repeated tricks, with the violent death of men, a boy and a lovely assistant suggest both the belief of the audience in this unreal and, consequently, the entertainment it produces. On the other hand, a belief in the magician's magic, in his manipulation, in the real existence of his acts perceived as such by the audience is further undermined by Coover's depiction of his magician's ability to control both reality and fantasy, resulting in terror and death:

"*He is perspiring. Fumbles inside hat. Withdraws nude hindquarters of lovely assistant [...] Tugs desperately on plump hindquarters, but rest will not follow [...] Is becoming rather frantic [...] Gritting teeth, infuriated, hurls hat to floor, leaps on it with both feet. Something crunches. Hideous piercing shriek. Screams and shouts. Magician, aghast, picks up hat, stares into it. Pales [...] Magician huddles miserably over crushed hat, weeping convulsively. First large man and young country boy enter timidly [...] from wings. They are pale and frightened. They peer uneasily into hat. They start back in horror [...] They clutch their mouths, turn away, and vomit[...] Large man and country boy tie up magician, drag him away*"(Coover 1969: 254-255).

As Thomas E. Kennedy argues, the magician's tricks

"*[...] begin to seem no mere sleight-of-hand or illusion but true magic, crossing the borders of natural law, plunging beyond the limits of what mortal man can do*" (Kennedy 1992: 64-65).

In this sense, the audience can represent both the object of entertainment and a belief in physical reality, as well as in the ability of the magician to manipulate it through tricks, which means that the audience still believes in physical reality appreciating the ability of a magician to create the illusion about it, his facility of manipulation, although within rational verifiable external reality. The magician, on the other hand, becomes an object of his own manipulation, but at the same time, a representative of the failure of imagination and manipulation of reality. He, as well as his audience, according to his behavior and response to his own violence, seems to believe in its physical reality (a death of woman), but, at the same time, the end of this story may suggest everything he has created including the death of a young woman is also only an illusion, a fantasy. If we accept this as truth, then the meaning of the magician's status can be symbolically opposite—a magician is as much a winner as the imagination and art (represented by him) is since he has created the illusion of death, not its real existence. The ambiguity of such interpretation, Coover's use of the manipulation of different kinds of reality (magician's magic, fantasy) along with his use of parody creates a metafictional aspect of this short story. Parody can be traced on both levels— on the level of objective, physical reality and on the intramural level of narrative techniques of fiction. Thus, on the one hand, the story can be read as a parody on traditional forms of entertainment represented by folk magicians (his magic does not work and evokes chaos, violence and eventually death), and, on the other, as a parody of traditional mimetic genres (possibly of popular culture?). In addition, Kennedy comments on another possible reading of this story, which produces, in my view, an allegorical meaning. He argues that

"Like a magician, a fiction writer is an illusionist. But the "true" magician involves himself in more than sleight-of-hand, just as the "true" artist seeks to deal profoundly with reality rather than merely entertain. The tool is the same. Both magician and writer work with the imagination, an orderly intentional mental process, and the creative faculty of the human mind, the formative power" (Kennedy 1992:65).

This interpretation suggests a critique of popular culture intended as a form of entertainment which manifests itself especially in the final ironic scene with a boy from the audience setting up a placard against the table which reads:

"THIS ACT IS CONCLUDED
THE MANAGEMENT REGRETS THERE
WILL BE NO REFUND" (Coover 1969:256).

In this way Coover's use of metafictional elements here, similarly in his short story *The Marker*, establishes the illusion of reality and, consequently subverts it, thus blurring the boundaries between fact and fantasy, realistic and fantastic, rational and irrational, mimetic and innovative. In this way metafiction undermines the traditional rational/mimetic expectations of Western rationality, mind and art, these characteristics formerly creating a myth of Western rationality and the Enlightenment belief in the possibility of rational and objective understanding of reality. At the same time, Coover undermines the entertainment function of popular culture and art as seemingly accessible to broad audiences. This is achieved through Coover's use not only of metafiction, but also of irony and parody.

III.2 Allegorical Metafiction— Paul Auster's *The Locked Room* (1985)

In his short stories and novels discussed in the previous chapter, Robert Coover uses the metafictional elements that break ontological certainty and reveal the fictitiousness of these works through the use of fictional and fantastic elements. The use of these elements obscures the boundaries between different ontological worlds, between reality, fantasy and fiction. These improbable, fantastic/fictional elements are, for example, copulation with a dead and rotting body (in Coover's story *The Marker*), the magician's vivifification of dead bodies (in Coover's short story *The Hat Act*), or the manipulation of time, as in sci-fiction, and the juxtaposition of real, historical, autobiographical and fictitious characters in Vonnegut's novel *Timequake,* which will be discussed in the next chapter. As distinct from the above metafictional short stories and Vonnegut's novel, the metafictional principles in Auster's short novella *The Locked Room* are based on entirely different narrative techniques. The fictitious status of a novel as revealed by metafictional techniques is alluded to, commented on and emphasized, conveyed through the depiction of the fantastic, sci-fiction, fictional elements, through the explicit ontological uncertainty through the juxtaposition of ontologically incompatible worlds depicted as equal, but especially through the thematization of writing and reading and through allegory.

The Locked Room, the last part of Paul Auster's *The New York Trilogy*, consisting of three short novels, or rather novellas, shows similarities to but also differences from other two. *The Locked Room* shares similarities with the other two, *City of Glass* and *Ghosts*, in the author's thematization and treatment of writing, reading, fiction and reality, in the depiction of loneliness and alienation of the individual in a chaotic urban environment, and in the author's use of the motifs of the double (Doppelgänger), mystery and a search, all producing various connotations associated with both real life and fiction. It is, on the other hand, different particularly in the exclusion of a detective story model its consequent parody of the narrative pattern of the novel. On a basic level, the narrative pattern of *The Locked Room* is reminiscent of a psychological novel about the relationship of two friends, complicated by the love relationship and later marriage of one of them, an unnamed narrator, with the other one's (Fanshawe's) wife whose husband (Fanshawe) had suddenly disappeared and is believed dead. In addition to this, it can also be understood as the story of a quest for and an attempt at reconciliation with the past and lost friendship. However, this realistic pattern is complicated by a thematization of writing and reading which manifests itself through Auster's depiction of characters, his use of intertextual and intratextual elements including the metacommentary on fiction, writing techniques and literature in general.

In this Auster novel, the unnamed narrator is a writer as well as Fanshawe's lost friend, and the dominant theme of this novel circles around the discovery and reconstruction of Fanshawe's manuscripts and the narrator's commentary on these manuscripts, which is supplemented by the quotations from, paraphrasing of and the commentaries on various literary and non-literary doccuments (Fanshawe's, his mother's and sister's letters and diaries). In addition to this, the narrator is not only a writer, but he also represents writing himself by his oral reconstruction of Fanshawe's life, and by simultaneously writing his biography. Both the narrator and Fanshawe may represent different aspects of writing, different approaches to life and society, creating a certain symbolic asymmetrical construction of two personalities. During childhood and maturation as well as during the narrator's and Fanshawe's friendship Fanshawe dominates by being a class leader, popular and a famous sportsman (baseball player), while the narrator's personality is suppressed and represents the inferior partner in the friendship and an admirer of Fanshawe's success. Fanshawe, as the narrator sees, him

"was too (good?) at games for that, too central a figure among us to retreat into himself [...] He was the best baseball player, the best student, the best looking of all the boys. Any one of these things would have been enough to give him special status—but together they made him seem heroic, a child who had been touched by the gods. Extraordinary as he was, however, he remained one of us" (Auster 1990: 253).

The narrator thus represents a supplementary, physically and perhaps also emotionally different, suffering and introverted counterpart to Fanshawe, creating two symbolic aspects of one personality to which the narrator alludes at the very beginning, saying

"He was the one who was with me, the one who shared my thoughts, the one I saw whenever I looked up from myself"(Auster 1990: 235).

Thus the narrator's classmates from basic and high schools including the narrator himself understand Fanshawe as an ideal to be achieved, a perfect friend, sportsman, and hero who, however, never boasted and paraded his success since, as the narrator comments,

"If he did well, it was always in spite of himself, with no struggle, no effort, no stake in the thing he had done" (Auster 1990: 251).

Fanshawe becomes a certain embodiment of the success in his childhood which is reminiscent of the success story as part of the concept of the American Dream. It is exactly this success (in sport, friendship, writing) which is envied by Fanshawe's friends but which is put in an ironic context by Auster. Fanshawe's path to success is unproblematic, natural, and spontaneous and his success is not the main aim of his life, and through this the very nature of the American Dream is undermined. Despite his success, however, Fanshawe is not an aggressive and ambitious boy striving to achieve. He is rather shy, calm, secluded, reticent and rejects all material and other luxury his success can bring. In addition to this, Fanshawe

"had never had any regular work [...] nothing that could be called a real job. Money didn't mean much to him, and he tried to think about it as little as possible" (Auster 1990:241).

Thus Fanshawe's rejection of material prosperity, success and fame is also associated with his writing. For him, writing is a matter of spiritual concentration and activity, not a way to achieve success with readers; his writing becomes his main aim in itself, not a path to success and material prosperity, to the fulfilment of the American Dream. As his wife comments on his writing,

"He had never tried to publish. At first, when he was very young, he was too timid to send anything out, feeling that his work was not good enough. But even later, when his confidence had grown, he discovered that he preferred to stay in hiding. It would distract him to start looking for a publisher, he told her, and when it came right down to it, he would much rather spend his time on the work itself" (Auster 1990:242).

Auster's construction of Fanshawe's character thus shows the parodic and ironic reversal of the idea of the American Dream of success. For Fanshawe, success is not the main aim or the path to a career and material prosperity, but a route to spontaneous life and spirituality represented by writing. Auster's depiction of Fanshawe represents first the achievement of all possible kinds of success (being a school hero, successful sportsman, a husband to a beautiful, attractive and loving wife, later also a successful writer), and then the rejection of all of this, represented by Fanshawe's indifference to money, financial security, stable work, success (the publication of his works), and the escape from his wife to seclusion, loneliness and to spiritual asylum. This rejection and escape represent a metaphorical rejection of physicality, success and the version of the American Dream Fanshawe's schoolmates and friends represent. These characters, including the unnamed narrator who is Fanshawe's childhood friend, create a counterpart to Fanshawe and main elements in Auster's assymetrical construction of the protagonists. They represent other, more typical, but also more negative aspects of the myth of the American Dream and the consequences it can bring. Success, fame and material prosperity associated with writing or real life in general becomes, in opposition to Fanshawe, the main aim of his life, and a success a matter of envy. As he comments,

"Especially as we grew older, I do not think I was ever entirely comfortable in his presence. If envy is too strong a word for what I am trying to say, then I would call it a suspicion, a secret feeling that Fanshawe was somehow better than I was" (Auster 1990: 247) [...] I would get so close to Fanshawe, would admire him so intensely, would want so desperately to measure up to him— and then, suddenly, a moment would come when I realized that he was alien to me, that the way he lived inside himself could never correspond to the way I needed to live. I wanted too much of things, I had too many desires, I lived too fully in the grip of the immediate ever to attain such indifference. It mattered to me that I do well, that I impress people with the empty signs of my ambition: good grades, varsity letters, awards for whatever it was they were judging us on that week. Fanshawe remained aloof from all that, quietly standing in his corner, paying no attention" (Auster 1990: 251).

The narrator thus becomes the exact opposite of Fanshawe with his approach to success, being interested in *"the empty signs of his ambition"*, rather in the nature of success and what it brings. As opposed to Fanshawe, success for him is more a matter of hard work, endeavour and ambition than talent and spontaneity, especially in respect of writing. The narrator comments on his own writing in the following way:

"*I had written a great many articles, it was true, but I did not see that as a cause for celebration, nor was I particularly proud of it. As far as I was concerned, it was just a little short of hack work[...] It was simpler to go on writing articles in any case. By working hard, by moving steadily from one piece to the next, I could more or less earn a living—and, for whatever it was worth, I had the pleasure of seeing my name in print almost constantly[...] I was not quite thirty, and already I had something of a reputation. I had begun with reviews of poetry and novels, and now I could write about nearly anything and do a creditable job. Movies, plays, art shows, concerts, books, even baseball games—they had only to ask me, and I would do it. The world saw me as a bright young fellow, a new critic on the rise, but inside myself I felt old, already used up. What I had done so far amounted to a mere fraction of nothing at all. It was so much dust, and the slightest wind would blow it away*" (Auster 1990: 244-245).

The characters represent two extremes of personality, two different principles through which Auster addresses the idea of success, the American Dream, and writing. Fanshawe represents honesty, spontaneity, a rejection of material and public aspects of fame and success, freedom through spirituality and seclusion, and writing as a matter of talent and gift, while the narrator is a representative of the superficial, public and commercial aspects of success, including the American Dream and writing. Writing as represented by the narrator becomes rather a matter of hard work and practise than talent and spontaneity. Both the characters, however, create two aspects of one allegorical personality, two sides of life, success, and writing. Envy, ambiton and an attempt to achieve success (American Dream) manifests itself in Auster's further construction of his unnamed narrator. His marrying Fanshawe's wife (and thus getting the desirable woman), living with his mother, and writing a biography of him is a metaphorical compensation for his friend's success, a way to achieve an ideal in a different way, through his following and imitating Fanshawe's life.

According to Craig Owens,

"In allegorical structure [...] one text is read through another, however fragmentary, intermittent, or chaotic their relationship may be; the paradigm for the allegorical work is thus the palimpsest [...] Conceived in this way, allegory becomes the model of all commentary, all critique, insofar as these are involved in rewriting a primary text in terms terms of its figural meaning" (Owens 1992: 54).

Owens further observes that

"Allegorical imagery is appropriated imagery; the allegorist does not invent images but confiscates them. He lays claim to the culturally significant, poses as its interpreter[...] He does not restore an original meaning that may be have been lost or obscured[...] Rather, he adds another meaning to the image. If he adds, however, he does so only to replace; the allegorical meaning supplants an antecedent one; it is a supplement" (Owens 1992:54).

Depicting the character and constructing the story, Auster uses symbolic imagery to produce the allegorical effect associated with writing. Writing as a theme is derived from the primary content of the story, it can be identified and derived from this basic meaning through the re-construction of Auster's symbolism and imagery. This allegorical meaning is not subordinate meaning, it is equivalent to the primary meaning, it becomes its supplement and replacement. As has been mentioned above, on the primary, basic level the novel *The Locked Room* can be read as a psychological modernist novel on the married life and crisis of a middle aged man, with mystery, detective and Gothic elements (the disappereance of Fanshawe, his mysterious letters, the unnamed narrator's search for him, the depiction of fear and psychological depression of the narrator). Systematically using the symbolism and imagery of writing, as well as the motif of the doppelganger Auster turns the readers's attention to the process of reading, writing, and interpretation, in their various aspects, as well as to the relationship between life and its artistic/linguistic representation. The basic narrative line circles around the reconstruction of Fanshawe's life and his literary works by different protagonists (his wife, an unnamed narrator, his sister and mother), although this is set within the story of a middle-aged couple (the unnamed narrator and Fanshawe's wife). In addition to this, most of the protagonists themselves become in a direct or inderect way writers, either telling the stories or or writing about the stories. In this Auster novel the idea of telling, of the narrative, is central to the artistic process, highlighted by the protagonists' role as commentators on and intepreters of both life and literary and artistic works. These metacommentaries force the reader to realize the fictitious status of the flow of narration reconstructing both Fanshawe's personality and his work In addition, the juxtaposition of these commentaries and the unnamed narrator's voice pretending to reconstruct both his and Fanshawe's lives, become equal, become the equivalent aspects of the process of telling understood as an artistic activity.

The narrator's status as teller, reconstructor and especially interpreter is emphasized at the very beginning of Auster's novel, evoking a similarity with and an intertextual allusion to E.A. Poe's short story *The Fall of the House of Usher*. The unnamed narrator, like the narrator in Poe's story, receives a letter from his childhood friend's wife (from Roderick Usher in Poe's story) asking him about Fanshawe, and inviting him to come to discuss the value of literary and other works Fanshawe wrote but never published. The unnamed narrator's reading of Fanshawe wife's letter becomes an act of reading and interpretation, as well as an attempt to reconstruct the meaning and reveal the truth. He comments in the following way:

"Seven years ago this November, I received a letter from a woman named Sophie Fanshawe. "You don't know me," the letter began, "and I apologize for writing to you like this out of the blue. But things have happenned, and under the circumstances I don't have much choice [...]

The explanation came in the second paragraph, very bluntly, without any preamble. Fanshawe had disappeared, she wrote, and it was more than six months since she had las seen him[...] This letter caused a series of little shocks in me" (Auster 1990: 235-236).

This position of a narrator as both an interpreter and creator of the story is supported by his retelling of Fanshawe wife's life and her relationship to Fanshawe from a position of a third person, an omniscient narrator which allots him a position of the teller and reconstructor of other man's story, an interpreter, but especially a creator of the new narrative which is supported by his omniscient (God-like) position, as can be seen from the following example:
"With the baby in her lap, she told me the story of Fanshawe's disappearance.

They had met in New York three years ago. Within a month they had moved in together [...]" (Auster 1990:238).

The narrator's omniscient position is reminiscent of a narrator in the realistic tradition who tries to imitate and copy reality to evoke the illusion of truthfullness and objectivity of the physical reality through its imitation. Such a position, however, implies his status as derivative and secondary since he only retells Fanshawe wife's story. The idea of derivativeness and secondariness is further supported by the narrator's position (occupation) as a reviewer (reviewing as an act not of primary creation, but of commenting on the already created work), and further by his status of an inferior friend (weaker, less successful), and the replaced husband of Fanshawe's wife and a father to his child, and later by his position as the author of Fanshawe's biography. Thus the narrator's status (as reviewer, biographer, reconstructor of Fanshawe's life) limits him to this derivative, secondary position since in this role he must heavily rely on facts and on imitation, not on the creation of reality. At the same time, this position suppresses any creativity and freedom the narrator could gain as an independent writer of fiction. It is through the deployment of an unnamed narrator that Auster constructs this derivativenness in opposition to originality, creativity and spontaneity. The unnamed narrator's realization of his status results in his attempt to escape from this derivativenness and inferior position with an act of liberation. The early traces of the narrator's attempt to become creative rather than derivative, that is original, are expressed through his attempt to find the other, figurative and symbolic meaning of the factographic document which Fanshawe's letter represents. As the narrator, having read this letter comments on it:

"I read the letter over and over, trying to pull it apart, looking for an opening, a way to read between the lines—but nothing came of it. The attempt to get inside it. In the end I gave up, put the leter in a drawer of my desk, and admitted that I was lost, that nothing would ever be the same for me again" (Auster 1990:282).

The last sentence does not only indicate a possible change of the narrator's situation (because the allegedly dead Fanshawe has sent him a letter confirming he is alive), but figuratively also a change of his status as an inferior and derivative supplement to Fanshawe. This stems exactly from the realization of his inability to be creative, to find a figurative meaning, a meaning "between the lines", which is a manifestation of the realization of his position. The process of growing independence, abandonement of the inferior position, and gaining a status of the original, creative author continues and manifests itself in a following scene where the narrator comments on his status as both a derivative and creative writer:

"*There was never any discussion of telling the truth. Fanshawe had to be dead, or else the book would make no sense. Not only would I have to leave the letter out, but I would have to pretend that it had never been written. I make no bones about what I was planning to do. It was clear to me from the beginning, and I plunged into it with deceit in my heart. The book was a work of fiction. Even though it was based on facts, it could tell nothing but lies. I signed the contract, and afterwards I felt like a man who had signed away his soul*" (Auster 1990: 291).

Thus the narrator reveals his future position as a writer of fiction, however heavily it might rely on facts. Writing biography could mean to use, as Hayden White says, the same narrative method both historians and fiction writers use (White, 1978) but the presence of a living subject of the narrator's study (and his narration—Fanshawe) can always deny the treatment of his life and facts, which means that the objective truth cannot be proved, and the biography must necessarily become a fictional work. Thus the narrator realizes his future position as an author of fiction rather than faction and his status changes from a passive reader to an active interpreter and finally a creative author himself. This realization and the revelation of the narrator's status as a creative author fully manifests itself in Auster's depiction of the narrator later in his part-time job as a census-taker. Doing this job he is transformed from the position of recorder and interpreter of reality to the position of a creator, a constructor of reality through fiction, as he applies the principles of fictional narration to a situation which demands only recording. Manipulating facts and figures to satisfy the governmental research (Auster 1990:292-293) he becomes a creative author (inventor rather recorder) who realizes the pleasure of creative writing, as manifested in the following scene:

"*My field work had turned into desk work, and instead of an investigator I was now an inventor [...] I don't know how many people I invented—but there must have been hundreds of them, perhaps thousands[...] I would sit in my room[...] filling out questionnaires[...] I went in for big households—six, eight, ten children—and took special pride in concocting odd and complicated networks of relationships, drawing on all the possible combinations: parents, children, cousins, uncles, aunts, grand-parents[...]Most of all, there was the pleasure of making up names. At times I had to curb my impulse towards the outlandish—the fiercely comical, the pun, the dirty word—but for the most part I was content to stay within the bounds of realism. When my imagination flagged, there were certain mechanical devices to fall back on: the colors (Brown, White, Black...), the Presidents (Washington, Adams...), fictional characters (Finn, Starbuck...)"* (Auster 1990: 294).

These comments are the proof of the narrator's transformation from a recorder/interpreter to an author of fiction realizing and endulging in his role and commenting on the narrative method he uses. The pleasure of writing and of creating reality manifests itself in his further comments on his falsification and manipulation of the census data:

"That was on one level. At the heart of it was the simple fact that I was enjoying myself. It gav e me a pleasure to pluck names out of thin air, to invent lives that had never existed, that never would exist. It was not precisely like making up characters in a story, but something grander, something far more unsettling" (Auster 1990: 294).

This realization of creativity, authenticity becomes the realization of the truthfullness and value of the story telling, art and fiction which, in the narrator's view, can represent reality not only more truthfully, but they can even influence reality itself literally. As he comments,

"Everyone knows that stories are imaginary. Whatever effect they might have on us, we know they are not true, even when they tell us truths more important than the ones we can find elsewhere. As opposed to the storywriter, I was offering my creations directly to the real world, and therefore it seemed possible to me that they could affect this real world in a real way, that they could eventually become a part of the real itself. No writer could ask for more than that" (Auster 1990:295).

The narrator's vision of story-telling as creating reality provides a metaphor not only for the importance of creative writing, but also of the equivalence of reality and fiction. Fiction is thus not understood as a separate, desolate, different activity, but as equal to human life. The narrator's status as a creator rather than imitator of reality, an author rather than a recorder, is further supported by the play with and the mystification of his identity after his separation from his wife for some time, going to France to trace the places Fanshawe had formerly visited. He calls a Tahitian prostitute Fayaway, a character from Melville's novella *Typee*, and himself Melville (the American author) and uses Melville's story to explain his background to Fayaway. Finally, he identifies an American coming to the bar as Fanshawe and behaves to him as if to the real Fanshawe, his old friend. Confusing his own identity with fictional characters and creating a new identity as an American stranger, he represents the act of writing, realizing his creative potential as a writer, celebrating the pleasure of writing, of creating stories. As he says:

"*My happiness was immeasurable. I exulted in the sheer falsity of my assertion, celebrating the new power I had just bestowed upon myself. I was the sublime alchemist who could change the world at will. This man was Fanshawe because I said he was Fanshawe, and that was all there was to it*" (Auster 1990: 348).

The narrator's position becomes now a position of a creator, an alchemist creating things out of nothing. Despite his absence, Fanshawe becomes a manipulator of the narrator's life (his carefully planned escape, the anticipation of the narrator's later marriage with his wife, and organizing their meeting through his letters) just as a writer of fiction manipulates with his characters. As Chris Pace argues, Fanshawe

" *[...] has become a character in a work of fiction by Fanshawe; actions that previously seemed acts of free choice or of the will become, in light of Fanshawe's letter, scripted and planned by Fanshawe from the start[...] The narrator's life has become so entwined with Fanshawe's that he no longer has a life that is truly his own; he is now nothing more than a character in one of Fanshawe's creations [...]"* (Pace).

The narrator's realization of Fanshawe's plotting and manipulation together with his mystification of reality becomes an act of liberation, an act giving him the status of authorial independence, creativity and originality. At the level of physical reality, the narrator's life, this leads initiallly plan to his plan to find and kill Fanshawe and to escape from his family to finally be rid of Fanshawe's influence, but then to his awareness of the derivativeness of this plan, and his own position as the victim, the subject of Fanshawe's plot. As he says,

"There were times when little scenes would flash through my head—of strangling Fanshawe, of stabbing him, of shooting him in the heart—but others had died similar deaths inside me over the years, and I did not pay much attention to them. The strange thing was not that I might have wanted to kill Fanshawe, but that I sometimes imagined he wanted me to kill him" (Auster 1990: 317).

The narrator's transition from a dependent, derivative and uncreative reader to a creative, independent and original author is fully manifested in the final scenes of the novel during his meeting with Fanshawe. The narrator is given a journal to read by Fanshawe and is informed it is the last of Fanshawe's work, but starting to read he comments:

"I read steadily for almost an hour, flipping back and forth among the pages, trying to get a sense of what Fanshawe had written. If I say nothing about what I found there, it is because I understood very little. All the words were familiar to me, and yet they seemed to have been put together strangely, as though their final purpose was to cancel each other out[…] I lost my way after the first word, and from then on I could only grope ahead, faltering in the darkness, blinded by the book that had been written for me [...]

I wandered out to the tracks several minutes in advance. It was raining again, and I could see my breath in the air before me, leaving my mouth in little burst of fog. One by one, I tore the pages from the notebook, crumpled them in my hand, and dropped them into a trash bin on the platform. I came to the last page just as the train was pulling out" (Auster 1990: 370-371).

Despite his realization of Fanshawe's influence on his life and writing, the narrator again starts to take up the derivative, secondary position as a reader and interpreter, as well as the victim of his plans. But then his refusal to read, interpret, and even to deal with Fanshawe's final book becomes an act of final liberation from his influence on his life (he refuses to kill him) and in writing, and, at the same time, a beginning of his creative role whether as a creative reader or an author. This position of a creative rather than derivative reader manifests itself in the narrator's discovery of Fanshawe's trick—Fanshawe's "notebook", faction rather than fiction, which gives a reconstruction of his life and which he is asked by Fanshawe to read as an example of such a genre, becomes a different kind of writing when read by the narrator, not only difficult to interpret but also to read. The narrator thus rejects his inferior status as reader and interpreter and, as summarized in the final paragraph, becomes free and independent both as man and author, about to start a new career and life His change in status is expressed through the metaphor of the departing train suggesting a new way, a new path, and a new and different future. Pace argues that

"*The narrator reclaims his identity, finally, by reclaiming his creative power. At the same moment that he comes closest to a severe mental breakdown and even death, the narrator rediscover his power as a creator, as an author [...] Once the narrator realizes that he is going to recover from his wounds, that he has faced his enemy and survived, then he is truly freed from the power that Fanshawe had over him. His creator is not dead, but he no longer has any power over his creation. The narrator has escaped from the locked room at last [...]*" (Pace).

As Pace comments further, on the last scene in Auster's *The Locked Room*, after throwing away Fanshawe's book,

"*There remains no more trace of Fanshawe, and the story is now ended on the narrator's terms[...]*(Pace).

This final scene thus means

"*the completion of his [the narrator's] relationship with Fanshawe—he has turned the tables and taken control by creating a fiction about the fiction that Fanshawe created. Now the narrator is the creator and Fanshawe is the character. It is now the narrator who is able to decide where things end and where they begin, and it is Fanshawe who is now trapped inside someone else's fiction*" (Pace).

It is not only writing, but also death and killing which play a significant role in Auster's construction of meaning and his allegorical play with words. The narrator's intentions to kill Fanshawe's mother, and people with whom he had something in common (a prostitute, an unknown American in France) and Fanshawe himself are, on the basic level, intentions to become a free and independent physical being in a real life. His final rejection of killing Fanshawe at the end of the book is a manifestation of the narrator's awarenes at last of Fanshawe's power as plotter and manipulator, but also of his own independence. As Pace argues, the narrator,

"*[...] once he becomes conscious that he is a character in Fanshawe's artifice of self-annihilation, can take control of his life again by refusing to* complete the structure that Fanshawe has crafted around him[...] Just as the narrator has taken back control of his life despite the continued existence of Fanshawe, so can the rest of us become more aware of our creative powers over our own lives despite the existence of fate and circumstance" (Pace).

Secondly, the narrator, at the same time, is initially a reviewer and an author in a traditional style, and his intention to kill Fanshawe may symbolize an attempt to kill, destroy and control creativity and new, different kinds of writing, different from his own. One of Fanshawe's last novels is entitled *Neverland* and is referred to as

"Not[...] typical novel [...] Not [...] typical anything [...] But Fanshawe's book stands out. There's something powerful about it, and the oddest thing is that I don't even know what it is" (Auster 1990: 271),

as a publisher says in his final words. And the narrator comments on the last of Fanshawe's notebooks/books in the following way:

"Each sentence erased the sentence before it, each paragraph made the next paragraph impossible[...] He had answered the questions by asking another question, and therefore everything remained open, unfinished, to be started again [...] It is as if Fanshawe knew his final work had to subvert every expectation I had for it [...] I felt there was something too willed, something too perfect, as though in the end the only thing he had really wanted was to fail— even to the point of failing himself" (Auster 1990: 370).

The comments on Fanshawe's books as untraditional, subversive, using the method of a mirroring and self-reflexive structure, is reminiscent of the narrative strategies of the postmodernist fiction which Fanshawe's book seems to be. The narrator, however, initially represents writing based on the mimetic (traditional, imitative) principle of traditional writing. Despite this his work is mostly reviews, essays and an intended biography. Thus the narrator's intention to kill Fanshawe represents the struggle and failure of traditional writing against innovative and postmodernist writing and the creative potential of such writing represented by both Fanshawe (who is not killed) and the narrator, who eventually becomes a symbolic and potential author and creator. It is neither the narrator nor Fanshawe who wins at the end, but creative imagination and story telling represented by both these characters at the end of the book. As Pace argues,

"Once the narrator realizes that he is going to recover from his wounds, that he has faced his enemy and survived, then he is truly freed from the power that Fanshawe had over him. His creator is not dead, but he no longer has any power over his creation. The narrator has escaped from the locked room at last" (Pace).

Thirdly, the imagery of death may refer to the traditional and new status of the creative reader, which can enable him/her realize his/her creative potential and become a partner in the construction of the author's meaning, rather than passive receiver of the, let us say, only primary meaning of the literary text. The narrator's intentions to kill Fanshawe's mother, an unknown American in France, and finally Fanshawe, represent the "mimetic" reader of reality. These murderous intentions imply the application of principles of physical reality (the narrator's belief that killing the controllers can remove control itself), but the narrator's realization of Fanshawe's control and manipulation as well as the his final rejection of killing him implies the realization of the existence of another reality, that constructed by the work of art, by fiction. In other words, the narrator's transition from a potential murderer to a saver of the future victims (by his refusal to kill them), and finally to a creator of stories (telling his version of the encounter with Fanshawe, that is also Fanshawe's story) is a transition from a traditional, simplistic reader to a creative reader, a reader participating in the authors's construction of the plot and its meaning. It is exactly the type of reader required particularly by the postmodernist fiction Auster's *The Locked Room* and the whole *New York Trilogy* represents. Also, it is the position of the reader post-structuralist theories emphasize. Alan Bilton referring to Richard Rorty and his understanding of the construction of meaning argues that

"Meaning is wholly linguistic. Which is not to say that real snakes don't exist or that they don't slither—only that the meaning of the words 'slither'or 'snake' is wholly a linguistic matter, separate from the actual living thing" (Bilton 2002: 71).

In additon to this, Dragana Nikolic observes that in postmodernism
"The meaning has become whatever one wishes it to become, the result of endless play of signification. The relation between signifier and signified is not defined as a unity that is outside the text, it is rather manifested as the arbitrary relation between the word and its concept" (Nikolic).

Auster's narrator from *The Locked Room* also represents not only a creative, but at the end also a post-structuralist reader and interpreter of reality as manifested in his realization of the position of the traditional reader, consequently the creator of new (linguistic, textual) reality and meaning. In other words, now he is the one who gives meaning to the text, and the world, through the creation of his own story/ies, not an author as in traditional Aristotelian poetics (see Nikolic).

Thus in opposition to Coover's short stories discussed above, Auster's thematization of writing and reading as analyzed here creates a metafictional effect and what Craig Owens called an allegorical impulse (Owens, 1992). The thematization of writing is further achieved by Auster's use of intertextual and intratextual elements and the allusions to and comments on writing: (Fanshawe is a character from the first novel by Nathaniel Hawthorne, who, as the main character in the short story *Wakefield*, mysteriously disappears despite leading quite a comfortable life with his wife, and lives an isolated and lonely life in seclusion. Fayaway, a Tahitian girl the narrator meets, is a character from Melville's fiction, the narrator in France claims that his name is Melville; the detective Sophie, Fanshawe's wife had hired to find him, is named Quinn, the name of the detective from the first part of *The New York Trilogy* (*The City of Glass*). Throughout the whole novel a metacommentary on, and the interpretation of, various discourses such as Fanshawe's and his sister's letters, diary, his own as well as the narrator's reviews and works occurs.

It can also be said that Auster's thematization of writing is achieved through his use of the allegorical principle. On the primary level, *The Locked Room* can be read as a modernist psychological novel on friendship and love, or on the relation between an artist and life, or as a story of a romantic retreat of an artist from reality. However on the allegorical level (postmodern allegory in Owens's understanding, not a traditional allegory) it is a story of the relationship between the traditional and post-structuralist/postmodernist and creative reader, between the author and his work, between traditional and innovative writing, between real physical and linguistic/textual reality which are all the issues of post-structuralism and postmodern writing. Auster's depiction of the narrator's search for Fanshawe, who is a writer, is a symbolic search for the author and meaning, and a deliberate separation and retreat of Fanshawe from the family and especially from his work symbolically shows the problematization of the author and the authorship. Despite the narrator's attempt to find the meaning in Fanshawe's work through the reconstruction of his life and a search for him (that is for the subject), the author (subject) is missing, "decentred", and the meaning can be constructed not by finding the author, but by constructing meaning by a creative reader, which the narrator gradually becomes. In other words, a text and its meaning can exist without the presence of an author, the author, as Roland Barthes would say, is dead (Barthes, 1977), and meaning is created through a creative reading of the text and through the analysis of the relationships between different texts, rather than between an author and his text. In Derriderian terms, the meaning can be anywhere (Derrida, 1972) depending on the reader's ability to reconstruct and justify it. As Nikolic argues, referring to Auster's depiction of Fanshawe and his deliberate escape and both literal and symbolic separation from his work,

"The more the poet watches the outside, the more he becomes aware that the world does not correspond to a definite pattern of knowledge. The meaning has become whatever one wishes it to become the result of endless play of signification. The relation between signifier and signified is not defined as a unity that is outside the text, it is rather manifested as the arbitrary relation between the word and its concept [...] In a constant shifting of meaning, the words do not point to something outside the language, rather meaning is achieved through their endless interaction and combination. Meaning has become the activity of reading, a matter of interpretation, as the text shifts away from the author" (Nikolic).

Auster points out these ideas through his depiction of the relationship between Fanshawe and the narrator, between the narrator and his and Fanshawe's writing. The narrator's realization of his own status as a creator and his final rejection of killing Fanshawe is the realization of the meaninglessness of identifying the author (subject) with his work as well as the realization of the independence of the literary text and its meaning from the author, or from the meaning the author might have intended. Bertens argues,

"[...] 'decentring' of the subject and the infinite deferment of meaning are central to poststructural postmodernism" (Bertens 1991: 133).

Like Bertens, Foster identifies a poststructural postmodernism which, in his view, *"assumes 'the death of man' not only as original creator of unique artifacts but also as the centered subject of representation and history"* (Foster 1984: 67).

In Foster's view, it

"launches a critique in which representation is shown to be more constitutive of reality than transparent to us" (Foster 1984:67).

Thus it can be said Auster's metafiction employed in his *The Locked Room* is mostly based on an allegorical principle. This allegory points out poststructuralist concerns with the relationship between an author and his work, reality and fiction, the nature of the writer (subject) and artistic meaning which qualifies this work, should we use Bertens' and Newman's terminology, a poststructuralist postmodernism. In addition to this, Auster's use of the doubles in the narrative structure shows different kinds of people and writers who are constructed in a way which gives a critique of some of the basic aspects of American cultural identity, that is a critique of the success story, the American Dream. This is manifested through Auster's depiction of Fanshawe as a successful and later potentially rich author because of the success of his books, and in his consequent rejection of this status by his denying the enjoyment both of life and of the material prosperity his writing could bring him. Nina Vietorová argues that

"Certain 'subjects'—'problems' seem to employ Auster's attention more than others, namely his concentrated interest in the position of man in the world, our feeling of being lost, our tendency, intention to be anonymous, locked in oneself, isolated from the environment of the outer world. For Auster as a typical postmodern writer of a broad spectrum of interests the loss or split of identity represents priority" (Vietorová 2003: 14).

On the other hand, the narrator's enjoyment of life, sex and physical reality to which he eventually returns after a voluntary separation from his wife and family, and his final meeting with Fanshawe is the manifestation of the opposite aspects of the very personality associated with success and the American Dream. The narrator's return to reality means a return to the physical, material and consumerist world, a turning back to confirm the American Dream. But since the ending is open and Fanshawe continues to live in isolation, rejecting physical reality, success and American Dream. His deliberate escape and isolation from all advantages and success it could bring him represents a rejection and a critique of the American Dream.

III.3 Crossing the Genres— Fact or Fiction? Kurt Vonnegut's *Timequake* (1997)

As distinct from Coover's short stories, Kurt Vonnegut's most recent novel *Timequake* (1997) represents an entirely different kind of metafictional writing. As I have mentioned earlier, by metafiction I do not mean a genre or a sub-genre of the novel, but what Patricia Waugh characterizes as

"[...] tendency within the novel which operates through exaggeration of the tensions between and oppositions inherent in all novels; of frame and frame-break, of technique and counter-technique, of construction and deconstruction of illusion"(Waugh 1984: 14).

In the short stories by Coover discussed above, the author establishes the narrative situation which is reminiscent of mimetic writing, and develops metafictional strategies which play with the figurative meaning of narrative events on the symbolic and allegorical level (*The Hat Act*). The metafiction is developed through the use of these techniques in combination with the juxtaposition of reality and fiction (the symbol of the book, reading and the juxtaposition of probable and improbable events); especially in his short story *The Marker*. In Vonnegut's novel *Timequake* a metafictional effect is achieved by the radical breaking the conventions of the chronological narrative (and thus both real, historical and a fictional time); by the radical fragmentation stemming from this subversion of time resulting in the creation of hypertextual blocks; by the intensive intertextuality; by breaking the boundaries between different ontological worlds, fact and fiction as well as between the genres by the inclusion of different genres, literary techniques, and styles; and by metacommentaries and the inclusion of the text within a text which André Gide characterizes as mise-en-abyme:

" *taking the term from the practise in heraldry where one quadrant of a coat of arms reduplicates in miniature the structure of the entire coat of arms in which it appears*" (Gide in Stonehill 1988: 8-9).

This is a technique reminiscent of the inclusion of stories within the stories Patricia Waugh understands, along with characters reading about their own fictional lives, self-consuming worlds and others as one of the framing devices (1984: 30). Waugh understands framing as the construction of frames, established order, system both in life and literature (Waugh 1984: 28). She argues that

"*Contemporary metafiction, in particular, foregrounds 'framing' as a problem, examining frame procedures in the construction of the real world and of novels*" (Waugh 1984:28).

As Waugh further observes,

"*Contemporary metafiction draws attention to the fact that life, as well as novels, is constructed through frames, and that it is finally impossible to know where one frame ends and another begins*" (Waugh 1984:29).

Such narrative strategies creating metafictional effects enable Vonnegut to construct a world, which forces a reader participate in its construction and in both the reading and the writing processes. It is a world in which personal confessions, factography, literature, art and the narrator's metacommentary on them establish a hypertextual structure through which Vonnegut plays with a reader and undermines both a unified vision of the world and literary methods of writing, especially This is a play on Wittgensteinian understanding of language games which, according to Waugh,

"*[...] deny the reader access to a centre of orientation such as a narrator or point of view, or a stable tension between 'fiction', 'dream', 'reality', 'vision', 'hallucination', 'truth', 'lies', etc.* " (Waugh 1984: 136).

In Waugh's view, with the use of these language games,

"*Naturalized or totalizing interpretation becomes impossible. The logic of everyday world is replaced by forms of contradiction and discontinuity, radical shifts of context which suggests that 'reality' as well as 'fiction' is merely one more game with words*" (Waugh 1984:136-137).

This chapter will analyze Vonnegut's use of narrative techniques creating metafictional effects, especially the thematization of time resulting in its fictionalization, and the use of intertextuality as an important metafictional and fictionalizing device in Vonnegut's novel *Timequake*.

Chronology/Time

As the title of Vonnegut's novel suggests, time is the central metaphor through which the author develops his untraditional vision of the world. In his study of fantasy, Gerald Hoffmann identifies objective and subjective time in fiction. In his view,

" 'Objective' clock-time is regular, uniform, quantitative, irreversible, while subjective mind-time is relative, multiform, reversible and characterized by its (mental) organization into past, present and future, the first and the last of which the mind can actualize through memory and forecast"(Hoffmann 1982:324).

As he further observes,

"The modernists devaluated mechanical time and emphasized mind-time, but in so doing they only shifted the base of 'reality' from the outer to the inner world without abandoning the concept of reality" (Hoffmann 1982: 324).

In his study of *The Fantastic in Fiction*, Gerald Hoffmann further introduces the term "cognitive and emotive models of meaning" of time and identifies of these (Hoffmann 1982: 325). In his view, one is the time which

"[...] appears as cosmic order, and man develops, in view of the circular course of nature, a mythic religious feeling for rhythmical phases. The universal course of time is here the eternal recurrence of the same, the all-embracing value of persistence in succession" (Hoffmann 1982: 325).

In Hoffmann's view, modernists such as Virginia Woolf, Joseph Conrad, James Joyce or D.H. Lawrence

"[...] reverted to a cosmic-cyclical time concept in order to transfer time from the worn-out linear concept of progress and usefulness to a universal power beyond human reach" (Hoffmann 1982: 325).

The second kind of time, in Hoffmann's view, can be understood as

"Time as succession with its aspects of past, present and future [which] forms the basis of cause-and-effect structures which rationalize change; and its linear sequence is the foundation of the notion of progress and the teleological conceptions of history" (Hoffmann 1982: 325).

This time is, in Hoffmann's view, typical of 19th century sensibility and realistic writing (Hoffmann 1982: 325). Finally, Hoffmann distinguishes psychic-existential notion of time. As he observes referring to this notion of time,

"Time is here a continuum experienced in a stream of consciousness that incessantly shifts present to the past and future and back, connecting hopes and fears with remembered or projected instants of time" (Hoffmann 1982: 327).

What is essential for this kind of mental time, typical for modernism is, according to Hoffmann,

"the cancellation of chronological sequence; the experience of the simultaneity of past, present and future; and—especially important for modernism—[...] 'epiphany' (Hoffmann 1982: 327), which *"[...]overcomes the fleeting and meaningless stream of mechanical time through psychic duration"* (Hoffmann 1982: 327).

This understanding of time is undermined by postmodern fiction, and the differences between subjective and objective times as well as cognitive and emotive models of meanings as characterized above, are erased and become. As Hoffmann observes,

"The postmodern author[...] renounces the difference between the two concepts, or, one should rather say, he renders both irreal and fantastic by making them relative, contingent and irrelevant, so that they lose their distinguishing and interpretative function for defining the real and the true. This arbitrary mingling of objective and subjective time concepts can destroy the illusion of reality, but also the existence of a character" (Hoffmann 1982: 324).

In his novel *Timequake*, Vonnegut undermines both subjective and objective time as well as all three cognitive and emotive models of meaning which are typical of 19th and early 20th century sensibility and, at the same time, of realistic and modernist writing. The concept and the image of the timequake enables a narrator with strong autobiographical characteristics to operate between past and present over a time span of about 10 years, with many flashbacks to different periods, and to manipulate the characters' lives and events through these shifts in time. Erasing the differences between past, present and future, between subjective and objective time, between time for the narrator and time in other characters' books (Kilgore Trout's book commented upon by the the autobiographical narrator reminiscent of Vonnegut himself), and a transgeneric time on different ontological levels (as presented in *Timequake* through a narrator, in the books/stories written by Kilgore Trout, an imaginary author included and commented upon by a narrator in the novel, and the time of Vonnegut's life itself), Vonnegut undermines the importance of time and makes it all fictional, constructed and irrelevant. This fictiousness is further supported by the construction of the logical impossibility and irrationality associated with this narrative flow, especially through Vonnegut's inclusion of the fantastic, the sci-fiction element, that is shifts in time making the characters return to the past and live their lives again. The narrator, referring to himself as Junior, argues that

"*The premise of Timequake One was that a timequake, a sudden glitch in the space-time continuum, made everybody and everything do exactly what they´d done during a past decade, for good or ill, a second time[...] I had the timequake zap everybody and everything in an instant from February 13th, 2001, back to February 17th, 1991. Then we all had to get back to 2001 the hard way, minute by minute, hour by hour, year by year, betting on the wrong horse again, marrying the wrong person again, gettting the clap again. You name it!*" (Vonnegut 1997: 12-13).

This narrative frame suggests a linearity and chronology through the imagery of continuity and repetition (minute by minute, hour by hour) through which the author seemingly suggests a reminescence on and the recuperation of the past historical events, characters' and Vonnegut's lives which, however, turns out to be Vonnegut's ironic, parodic and playful reconsideration of the position of a man, human beings, writer and the writing/artistic process in history, society and the universe. In addition to this, such a play with time and events includes the commentary on the ecological and nuclear threat, consumerism and other issues related to contemporary US. and other societies. An illusion of a chronological time and linearity is subverted, however, as early as in the preface in which the narrator pretends to play the role of Vonnegut being a writer himself who comments on the subsequent events and authors from the book. This narrator offers a pseudo-modernist reminiscence and a flash-back (1952, November 11,1996) writing from the perspective of November 12, 1996. This is, however, undermined by the inclusion and comments on the time (year 2001, and a time shift between 2001-1991) of the following novel, and other stories (Kilgore Trout's) written between 1931-2001, as well as by the narrator's/Vonnegut's imaginary vision of his future life (in 2010). Despite exact dating of the events in the *Prologue*, the meaning of this exactness suggesting chronology is undermined not only by the metafictional and intertextual inclusion of the comments on *Chapter I* and what follows, and Kilgore Trout's fiction, but also by the subversion of the reality of the presented events, characters and setting. This results in the total suppression of the importance of the meaning of time. The narrator, pretending to be Kurt

Vonnegut (a real, existing figure) and the narrator of the book which follows "Prologue" says that in this following book he is

"[...] on the beach at the writers' reatreat Xanadu in the summer of 2001, six months after the end of the rerun, six months after free will kicked in again" (Vonnegut 1997: xiv) and that he

"[...] was there with several fictitious persons from the book, including Kilgore Trout" (Vonnegut 1997:xiv).

The narrative strategy in the above extract shows how the author nullifies the meaning of subjective, objective, linear, cyclical, mythical and other times, rendering them meaningless. It emphasizes not only the uselessness and unimportance of categorization of time typical of Western rational thinking, but also fictitiousness, literarinness, artistry, artificiality of the presented events, characters, and setting since Kilgore Trout "*doesn't really exist*" (Vonnegut 1997: xiii). It means that the narrator of the book that follows could not possibly have met with him. Such a fictionality is juxtaposed with real historical events in a different time period in comments by a narrator reminiscent of the real Vonnegut (the first chain reaction of uranium on Earth in 1942, a Nobel Peace Prize for Andrei Sakharov 1975, an honorary doctorate for Sakharov by Staten Island College in New York City in 1987, a gathering at the university to commemorate the fiftieth anniversary of the detonation of the first atomic bomb over the city of Hiroshima in 1995), and further, to metafictional elements, especially the comments on Kilgore Trout's stories, which represent different ontological worlds. Such a depiction of time loses its base in truth since all times, as I have suggested, are fictional, created and constructed by language. Vonnegut's undermining of time through undermining the veracity and credibility of the presented events and characters; through the inclusion of fantastic elements (the timequake); through the juxtaposition of incompatible ontological worlds the boundaries between which are erased (the world of fantasy, the world of the real life, and a world of fictional discourses) is taken further by the inclusion of hypertextual teachniques based around comments on different historical, autobiographical (of Vonnegut, a real person) and fictional (books) events. This enables Vonnegut to create both fictional and real-life "frames"(Waugh 1984: 28) which refer to both fiction and life experience, and which further create a postmodern collage of time entirely different from all the times and traditional meanings of it characterized above.

Vonnegut's postmodern collage in this novel produces an effect of simultaneity of time since all parts of the collage can produce their own meaning and cannot be explained

"under the aegis of an explanatory rationale, be it that of history, myth, or psychology" (D'haen 1986: 220)

as in realistic or modernist writing. As Theo D'haen further argues, these parts create only fragments which

"[...] are not part of larger wholes as these larger wholes are only fragments of metanarratives which the Postmodernist no longer believes in"(D'haen 1986: 220).

This postmodernist collage further creates the effect of multiplicity which can be achieved, according to D'haen by

"[...] juxtaposing various kinds of images or materials, provided they come from sufficiently divergent origin" (D'haen 1986: 220).

Vonnegut's construction of time based on postmodernist collage, fragmentation and multiplicity erases the differences between different kinds of time and makes all kinds of time equally important. The differences between objective and subjective, mechanical and cyclical, cosmic, linear-historical, psychic-existential as well as between cognitive and emotive models of meaning are unidentifiable and unimportant. These narrative strategies then render all time fictional and constructed, and underline the important role of language in creating separate fictional reality through time. Time becomes

"[...] relative contingent and irrelevant" (Hoffmann 1982:324), and all kinds of time *"[...] lose their distinguishing and interpretative function for defining the real and the true. This arbitrary mingling of objective and subjective time concepts can destroy the illusion of reality [...]"* (Hoffmann 1982: 324).

Intertextuality and Hypertextuality

Intertextuality is one of the most important elements of metafiction within postmodernist fiction which foregrounds the fictionality and autonomy of the artistic/literary worlds and the difference between physical reality and the artistic/literary reality which constructs such a world through language. Manfred Pfister argues that

"*Postmodernist intertextuality within a framework of poststructuralist theory means that here intertextuality is not just used as one device amongst others, but is foregrounded, displayed, thematized and theorized as a central constructional principle*" (Pfister 1991:214).

Intertextuality, however, should not be understood as a single connection between texts (Mai 1991:31); it can take many different forms and modes all of which emphasize this connection. The main aim of such a deployment of metafiction is not to imitate, but to creatively and playfully transform the original meaning of the pretexts and the cultural codes they had produced, and to evoke a contemporary sensibility, as well as to re-consider both literary (artistic) traditions and the cultural, historical, political and social experience of people as well as a linguistic (artistic) representation of this experience. Intertextuality can manifest itself as a quotation, paraphrasing of or the allusion to other literary and non-literary texts or genres, but also as a parody or collage (Pfister 1991:208).

In Vonnegut's novel *Timequake,* a complex labyrinth of intertextual forms and techniques creates a separate, playful and fictional world through which the author comments on different issues related to the contemporary postmodern world and its sensibility (ecological threat, consumerism, beaurocracy, sex, visual culture), and through which he re-considers both his life and the American literary tradition. The very Prologue to Vonnegut's novel breaks the conventions of "Prologues" by breaking the boundaries between fictional (literary), fantastic and real worlds and characters. This enables the author to create apparently two ontological worlds with several "levels" of reality, namely the real physical world represented by biographical (comments on real historical personalities's lives – J. Brahms, E. Hemingway, N. Hawthorne, T. S. Eliot, H. D. Thoreau, political representatives) and autobiographical levels (a narrator pretending to be Vonnegut, a writer, his parents and family), and an apparently fictional world represented by Kilgore Trout's fiction and life. What dominates in the narrative structure this work is the autobiographical mode emphasizing the autobiographical narration, as a writer and artist, but also as husband, brother, father, which is juxtaposed with the narrator's comments on the life and work of Kilgore Trout, a fictional writer who appeared in previous Vonnegut novels. The commentaries on both the narrator's and Trout's lives and works are, however, fragmented, and ironic, and create a parodic effect. The aim of both irony and parody aim is not to ridicule particular works or styles, but to point out a playful imagination associated with contemporary sensibility, as well as to produce a self-mockery, a self-parody of the narrative voice in its function as autobiographical narrator. These self-parodic narrative techniques evoke a distance of the narrators from the presented events and comments, undermine and relativize the seriousness of presented ideas, and emphasize the role of playful imagination in the perception and construction of the world.

The very beginning of Vonnegut's novel *Timequake (Prologue)* introduces subsequent intertextual techniques used in the novel through which the author breaks the ontological boundaries between different (real physical, and fictional) worlds, and which relativize the seriousness and undermine traditional mimetic representation of reality. Junior, the narrator does not speak about reality, but uses an intertextual commentary on Ernest Hemingway's story *The Old Man and the Sea* and his own work which follows. The commentary on Hemingway's story allows the narrator to make a connection between the historical and physical (both writers—Vonnegut and Hemingway, and a fisherman, the narrator's friend) and fictional worlds (their works).

The narrator after commenting on the plot of Hemingway's story says:

"*I was living in Barnstable Village on Cape Cod when the story appeared. I asked a neighboring commercial fisherman what he thought of it. He said the hero was an idiot. He should have hacked off the best chunks of meat and put them in the bottom of the boat, and left the rest of the carcass for the sharks[...] And then I found myself in the winter of 1996 the creator of a novel which did not work, which had no point, which had never wanted to be written in the first place.* Merde! *I had spent nearly a decade on that ungrateful fish, if you will. It wasn't even fit for shark chum.*

I had recently turned seventy-three. My mother made it to fifty-two, my father to seventy-two. Hemingway almost made it to sixty-two. I had lived too long! What was I to do?

Answer: Fillet the fish. Throw the rest away" (Vonnegut 1997:xi-xii).

The intertextual technique used in the above extract (comments on both the narrator's and Hemingway's works) shows the difference between physical reality and art (literature) through the treatment of the idea of usefullness. The narrator/writer represents a world of art, the imagination and reality conveyed through language while the fisherman represents a physical world of practical utility. The fisherman's is a logic of utility distant and different from art, which is why, applying the logic of this utilitarian approach, he rejects the behaviour in Hemingway's novella as that of a fisherman, as a real and practical being. This fisherman (the narrator's friend) is unable to see the different ontological status of a work of fiction, the figurative meaning of Hemingway's protagonist not as a real but as literary, fictional character and understands the fisherman's behaviour in Hemingway's story as useless and purposeless. On the other hand, the autobiographical narrator (reminiscent of a writer, Vonnegut) understanding his writing in terms of the real fisherman's logics of utility, but rejecting his novel as unsuitable even for the sharks as a food (utility), creates a humorous, ironic and parodic transformation of the seriousness of this statement. Thus his understanding of art is the understanding of an artist aware of the working of different rules in the world of fiction and art, different from the reality represented by a fisherman, his friend. It is an understanding of art in a Wildean sense as perfectly useless and inadequate for life. At the same time, a depiction of different logics/world views creates a parody on both simplified (superficial) understanding of literature and of traditional literature based on the mimetic representation of reality. This parody and self-parody of the narrator's own work creates a distance from the seriousness of the presented events and thus offers a playful intertextual game for a reader, involving him or her in constructing and supplementing the meaning of the work he/she is reading. In addition to this, the relativization of the "truthfullness" and objectivity conveyed through the self-parody results in the comparison of its usefulness to human life with that of a fish. The narrator's comments question the usefullness of human life, measured in terms of the utility of a practical product (the fish), effectively an ironic expression of the impossiblity of measuring the immeasurable, applying the logic of real life to the logic of fiction.

The strategy of the juxtaposition of intertextual elements from real historical and literary documents and quotations fropm real historical figures (Sakharov and others) with fictional documents (Kilgore Trout's story, the autobiographical narrator's intratextual comments on his previous works) results in the erasure of the boundaries between reality and fiction which are erased, creating the spatial form (Frank, 1968) and equality of both ontological levels, both discourses. At the same time, this technique reveals these levels, linguistic status, the status of fictionality and separatedness from the rules governing real life. As can be seen from the above extract, the humorous, ironic and parodic effect in such a use of intertextuality is achieved by the deliberate misapplication of the rules and value systems of real life to the rules of the fictional world of literature and art. This is an intertextual strategy which dominates the structure of Vonnegut's novel. It can be seen not only from the above extract from the *Prologue*, but it manifests itself in the whole of the novel. At the very beginning of Chapter One, Vonnegut's narrator gives quotations or pseudoquotations from Mark Twain's essays, the Bible, Henry David Thoreau's works, and later from the works of Gunter Grass, Bernard Russell, Nietzsche, Sigmund Freud and other well-known authors, philosophers and other personalities, as well as a meta-commentary on the works of American and other authors. As in the above extract, these intertextual strategies are further developed into the comments and generalizations on various aspects of human life which as in the following example:

"Jesus said how awful life was, in the Sermon on the Mount: "Blessed are they that mourn," and "Blessed are the meek," and "Blessed are they which do hunger and thirst after righteousness."

Henry David Thoreau said most famously, "The mass of men lead lives of quiet desperation."

So it is not one whit mysterious that we poison the water and air and topsoil, and construct ever more cunning doomsday devices, both industrial and military. Let us be perfectly frank for a change. For practically everybody, the end of the world can't come soon enough" (Vonnegut 1997: 2).

The (pseudo) quotations from the Bible and Thoreau have an authoritative and overtly moralising tone, which is hen transferred to the moralistic commentary of the autobiographical narrator on the nuclear threat and pollution in the contemporary modern world. At the same time, the importance of the preservation of human life is emphasized here. This is in keeping with this section's serious, moralistic tone, but in contrast to the concluding section of this chapter which shifts the idea of the importance of human life into a parodic context:

"The African-American jazz pianist Fats Waller had a sentence he used to shout when when his playing was absolutely brilliant and hilarious. This was it: "Somebody shoot me while I'm happy!"

That there are such devices as firearms, as easy to operate as cigarette lighters and as cheap as toasters, capable at anybody's whim of killing Father or Fats or Abraham Lincoln or John Lennon or Martin Luther King, Jr., or a woman pushing a baby carriage, should be proof enough for anybody that, to quote the old science fiction writer Kilgore Trout, "being alive is a crock of shit" (Vonnegut 1997: 2-3).

The seriousness of the moralizing tone is undermined by the mockery of living and of human life through Waller's and Kilgore Trout's quotations, producing the parodic effect. It is a parody dependent on doccuments and discourses emphasizing the importance and seriousness of human life and thus the importance of human beings in the universe. Trout's and Waller's quotations emphasize the unimportance, uselessness and absurdity of striving for survival and life, and the importance of enjoying life through human activity itself, be it sport, writing or any other. This rejection of the seriousness of death and an emphasis on the enjoyment of life manifests itself in the following extract where Vonnegut gives a parodic transformation of the Biblical allusions:

"I will say, too, that lovemaking, if sincere, is one of the best ideas Satan put in the apple she gave to the Serpent to give to Eve. The best idea in that apple, though, is making jazz" (Vonnegut 1997: 84).

A similar strategy of presenting the quotations or pseudoquotations in ironic and parodic contexts, offering a commentary on various aspects of life, can be seen in the following example in which the seriousness of Sigmund Freud's theories is subverted by ironic generalizations of his ideas and, subsequently, on women's talkativeness:

"Sigmund Freud said he didn't know what women wanted. I know what women want. They want a whole a lot of people to talk to" (Vonnegut 1997: 83).

These intertextual strategies further enable Vonnegut to resent a critique of contemporary consumerist life and popular culture, and a self-ironic mockery of the idea of success and the process of its achievement, and, in a playful way, to comment on the issues related to life in a technologically advanced civilization. The strategies also allow a reconciliation with the passing of time, ageing, the vanity of human life, fate, and the position of a writer and an artist during a period of changed sensibility in the postmodern era. The narrator himself is a victim of such a critique of consumerist culture in the passage in which this narrator calls television a *"cathode-ray tube"* (Vonnegut 1997: 22) or *eraser* (Vonnegut 1997: 193), and in which he expresses a nostalgia over the passing of time and the change of sensibility in mass society (Howe, 1979):

"The minds of children in intellectually humble American homes back then weren't swamped with countless stories from TV sets. They heard or read only a few stories, and so could remember them, and maybe learn something from them. Everywhere in the English-speaking world, one of those was 'Cinderella.' Another was 'The Ugly Duckling'" (Vonnegut 1997:36)[...]

In the early days of television, when there were only half a dozen channels at most, significant, well-written dramas on a cathode-ray tube could still make us feel like members of an attentive congregation, alone at home as we might be. There was a high probability back then, with so few shows to choose from, that friends and neighbors were watching the same show we were watching, still finding TV a whizbang miracle.

We might even call up a friend that very night, and ask a question to which we already knew the answer: "Did you see that? Wow!"

No more" (Vonnegut 1997: 22).

In Vonnegut's fictitious author's view, such a sensibility is impossible in postmodern society where mass media, popular culture and the image have replaced both the spoken and the written word and have erased imagination. This manifests itself in Trout's depiction of the Booboolings in his sci-fiction story. These people are reminiscent of contemporary people:

"When the bad sister was a young woman, she and the nuts worked up designs for televison cameras and transmitters and receivers. Then she got money from her very rich mom to manufacture and market these satanic devices, which made imaginations redundant. They were instantly popular because the shows were so attractive and no thinking was involved[...] New generations of Booboolings grew up without imaginations. Their appetites for

diversions from boredom were perfectly satisfied by all the crap Nim-nim was selling them. Why not? What the heck.

Without imaginations, though, they couldn't do what their ancestors had done, which was read interesting, heartwarming stories in the faces of one another" (Vonnegut 1997: 18).

Intertextuality is further manifested in the inclusion of framing devices, especially *"stories within stories [...], characters reading about their fictional lives [...]"* (Waugh 1984: 30) or the mise-en-abyme technique characterized at the beginning of this sub-chapter. In Vonnegut's novel *Timequake,* many characters read and comment on their own fictional lives or the fictional lives of other fictional characters from other fictional books, all of which is juxtaposed to the narrator's comments on his own life and the life of real historical personalities who are very often famous people such as artists, writers, philosophers or politicians. Stories within stories are represented particularly by the inclusion of comments on, quotations and fragments from real writers, Vonnegut himself, and the fictional character Kilgore Trout. The Kilgore Trout stories commented by the autobiographical narrator are mostly either sci-fiction, fantastic or postmodern (although this word is never mentioned) stories, breaking the boundaries between real, fictional, historical and fantastic ontological worlds while parodying literary conventions and evoking the idea of the absurdity of human life. This can be seen in the following extract in which the narrator comments on the Trout's first story which

"[...] was set in Camelot, the court of King Arthur in Britain: Merlin the Court Magician casts a spell that allows him to equip the Knights of the Round Table with Thompson submachine guns and drums of 45- caliber dumdums.

Sir Galahad, the purest in heart and mind, familiarizes himself with this new virtue-compelling appliance. While doing so, he puts a slug through the Holy Grail and makes a Swiss cheese of Queen Guinevere" (Vonnegut 1997: xiii).

The narrator's comments here reveal the postmodern and parodic character of Trout's story, a parody of the medieval Arthurian romances. These comments are further supplemented by both the narrator's, and Kilgore Trout's intratextual comments on their own works, works and writing techniques of different authors, but on also their own writing methods through which they both reject traditional mimetic representation of reality through art and literature, and offer a postmodern and playful imagination as characteristic of their own works. Kilgore Trout comments on his writing technique in the following way:

"'In my entire career as a writer,' said Trout in the former Museum of the American Indian, 'I created only one living, breathing, three-dimensional character. I did it with my ding-dong in a birth canal [...]' He was referring to his son Leon [...]

'If I'd wasted my time creating characters,' Trout said, 'I would never have gotten around to calling attention to things that really matter: irresistible forces in nature, and cruel inventions, and cockamamie ideals and governments and economies that make heroes and heroines alike feel like something the cat drug in.'

Trout might have said, and it can be said of me as well, that he created caricatures rather than characters. His animus against so-called mainstream literature, moreover, wasn't peculiar to him. It was generic among writers of science fiction'" (Vonnegut 1997: 63).

These comments show the rejection of the mimetic, realistic tradition associated with "the three-dimensional", convincing, vivid characters typical for this kind of writing, and a clear rejection of the mainstream literature. At the same time, they emphasize the parodic, playful and caricaturesque nature of Trout's, the autobiographical narrator's and the real Vonnegut's works and writing techniques. The characters from Vonnegut's novel, especially autobiographical Junior as well as Kilgore Trout and his characters, are what Aleid Fokkema calls borderline characters. Fokkema characterizes these characters in the following way:

"The borderline character has an accessible self, its thoughts and feelings are expressed in the novel in which it appears, and biological, social and desriptive codes will be used to signify it. But simultaneously that accessible self is determined by language. Moreover, the codes may have been used ironically, and there is a certain ontological instability because the logical code and the principle of coherence are violated. Hovering between intertext and reference, these postmodern characters occupy a place on the borderline which is both specific (neither realist nor exclusively "metafictional") and imprecise [...]" (Fokkema 1991:187).

As Fokkema further observes,

"The postmodern 'borderline' character which is both signified according to some established literary conventions and tied up in intertextual references, linguistic structures, and discourses, is representational in that it represents a concept about the world of human culture. Such postmodern characters are not mimetic because they represent universal human beings, but because an understanding is offered of contemporary western culture[...] of which discourses, other fictions, earlier conventions, and certain hierarchical power relations are part" (Fokkema 1991:189-190).

Vonnegut's depiction of borderline characters then does not abandon reality entirely, but emphasizes the linguistic and cultural nature of our perception and vision of the world through various discourses, images, signs and role models.

Here, mainstream means traditional, popular and common writing and it alludes to the whole literary canon and traditional writing the rejection of which is specified in the autobiographical narrator's (Junior's) comments:

"Highly literate people once talked enthusiastically to one another about a story by Ray Bradbury or J. D. Salinger or John Cheever or John Collier or John O'Hara or Shirley Jackson or Flannery O'Connor or whomever, which had appeared in a magazine in the past few days.

No more"(Vonnegut 1997: 15).

This extract shows both the narrator's and Vonnegut's rejection of the whole tradition not only of the realistic, but also the American modernist canon represented by most authors mentioned above. Not only these authors, but also formulaic (Cawelti, 1976), popular and kitschy literature are rejected through the rejection of the narrator's book characterized as a Gothic novel (Vonnegut 1997: 208), and through the mocking irony the narrator uses to desribe the Gothic novel. He says:

"I asked him [his friend and a fellow-writer] for a definition of a Gothic novel. He said, 'A young woman goes into an old house and gets her pants scared off.'

Borden and I were in Vienna, Austria, for a congress of PEN[...] when he told me that" (Vonnegut 1997: 208).

A rejection of seriousness is developed into a rejection of both the statement and its serious tone through self-irony, producing caricaturesque effects. This self-irony manifests itself throughout the whole novel through the constant ironic allusions to the uselessness and unimportance of literature, art and writing, very often through the imagery of the death of authors either imaginary or real. The rejection of traditional writing in the above extract is followed by the narrator's (and Vonnegut's) comments on his own writing techniques which are entirely different and characterized as follows:

"All I do with short story ideas now is rough them out, credit them to Kilgore Trout, and put them in a novel. Here's the start of another one hacked from the carcass of Timequake One [...]" (Vonnegut 1997: 15).

This extract shows eclecticism, fragmentation, intertextuality, metafiction and playfulness based on breaking the boundaries between different realities (reality, ideas-abstraction, world fiction/s) all being basic characteristics of postmodern literature and of Vonnegut's work.

As has already been mentioned, all these intertextual techniques alluding to or representing different styles, genres, kinds of literature (personal and official letters, quotations from biographies, literary, religious and philosophical as well as realistic, autobiographical, romantic, Gothic, sci-fiction and postmodernist works) merge and create hypertextual blocks which erase any idea of continuity, stability, any claims for truthfullness and objectivity typical of realistic and modernist vision of the world, and recuperate for us, unlike Trout's Booboolings, the power of imagination and playfullnes, diversity and pluralistic vision of the world as an alternative to both contemporary cultural products and everyday life. It is a hypertextuality characterized by Michael Rifaterre as *"the reader-generated loose web of free association"* (Rifaterre 1994:781) which involves a reader in the construction of a story and a world through fiction, and which enables a reader to start from any page, any hypertextual block. These hypertextual blocks thus become axiologically, semantically and ontologically all equal, all emphasizing the power of playfullness and imagination represented by fiction and reading as the only alternative to the contemporary consumerist culture as well as the alternative to traditional and popular writing and popular culture. Within the use of such narrative techniques, language loses its detachability from context (Waugh 1984: 37), which

"results in a failure to distinguish between hierarchies of messages and contexts" (Waugh 1984: 38).

Intertextuality, hypertextuality and the narrative techniques mentioned above all create a metafictional effect in which different worlds and ontological levels merge

"*and the relationship between them—between 'play' and 'reality'—is the main focus of the text*" (Waugh 1994: 38).

Conclusion

In his short stories *The Marker* and *The Hat Act* above, Coover achieves a metafictional effect through either emphasizing the incompatibility of the real and fictional (and fantastic) worlds, parody (*The Marker*), or through playing with the idea of manipulation (with the perception of reality) and illusion represented by a magician (*The Hat Act*). As distinct from these stories, in Vonnegut's novel *Timequake* the metafictional effect is achieved by the thematization of time and the radical fragmentation of the narrative structure through the inclusion of metacommentaries on life, fictional works and writing techniques; by the juxtapositon of different ontological worlds (reality, the world of fiction, fantasy) the boundaries among which are erased; by the intensive use of intertextuality creating hypertextual blocks of different styles, genres, discourses as well as a postmodernist collage; by a radical subversion of the seriousness of given statements through the use of parody, irony, self-parody and a self-irony. Intertextuality, often manifesting itself in the use of numerous quotations and paraphrases from different real and fictititous characters' books, biographies, and utterances gives a pluralistic and disunified vision of the world by offering various interpretative possibilities. In his study *Intertextualities* Heinrich Plett argues,

"*As there is a multiplication of quotations, so there is also a multiplication of contexts. The structural result of this procedure can be termed collage[...]*" (Plett 1991:11).

All these metafictional strategies undermine traditional realistic and modernist writing and offer a vision of the world characteristic of the postmodernist period, that is one influenced, shaped, and manipulated by various discourses, images, and sign structures. Metafictional strategies enable Vonnegut to relativize the seriousness of death, the passing of time, ageing, topical issues such as a threat of a nuclear disaster, violence, air-pollution, and consumerism of popular and other cultures. At the same time, there is a nostalgic tone towards past sensibility, and some aspects of past culture which are evoked. Moreover, through the thematization of literature, art, writing through various metacommentaries, intertextuality including quotations, allusions, paraphrazes and comments, Vonnegut emphasizes the power of the "playful" manipulation of readers through this postmodern metafictional literature and literature and art in general, as an alternative to the chaotic, absurd, manipulated and violent world.

NOTES
Notes to Chapter I

[1] Beebe, Maurice. "Ulysses and the Age of Modernism." *James Joyce Quarterly* 10 (1972): 172-188.
Beebe, Maurice. "What Modernism Was." *Journal of Modern Literature* 3 (1974): 1065-1084.
Howe, Irving, ed. *The Idea of the Modern in Literature and the Arts*. New York: Horizon, 1977.
Howe, Irving. *Celebrations and Attacks: Thirty Years of Literary and Cultural Commentary*. New York: Horizon, 1979.
Le Roy, Gaylord, and Ursula Beitz. "The Marxist Approach to Modernism." *Journal of Modern Literature* 3 (1974): 1158-1174.
Spender, Stephen. *The Creative Element: A Study of Vision, Despair and Orthodoxy among some Modern Writers*. London: British Book Center, 1954.
Spender, Stephen. *The Struggle of the Modern*. Berkeley and Los Angeles: University of California Press, 1963.

[2] Linda Hutcheon gives characteristic features of postmodernist poetics; Brian McHale, drawing on Jakobson's theory of the dominant, sees a difference between modernism and postmodernism as a difference between the epistemological and ontological "dominant" within the literary work, and he gives the inventory of postmodernist strategies; Patricia Waugh identifies and analyzes metafiction and metafictional strategies and understands them as typical postmodernist strategies; see these authors' works in the Works Cited section below

[3] see Hassan, Ihab. "Toward a Concept of Postmodernism." *Postmodernism: A Reader*. Ed. Thomas Docherty. New York, London, Toronto, Sydney, Tokyo, Singapore: Harvester Wheatsheaf, 1993. 146-156.

[4] see Hutcheon, Linda. *A Poetics of Postmodernism: History, Theory, Fiction*. New York and London: Routledge, 1988; McHale, Brian. *Postmodernist Fiction*. London and New York: Routledge, 1987. Waugh, Patricia. *Metafiction. The Theory and Practise of the Self-Conscious Fiction*. London and New York: Routledge, 1984.

[5] Irving Howe considers such novels as *The Assistant* by B. Malamud; *The Catcher in the Rye* by J.D. Salinger; *A Walk on the Wild Side* by N. Algren; *The Adventures of Augie March*; *Henderson the Rain King* by S. Bellow; and *The Field of Vision* by W. Morris to be postmodern

[6] see Trachtenberg, Stanley in the Works Cited section; and, for example, Couturier, M., Regis, D. *Donald Barthelme*. London: Methuen, 1982; Gordon, L. *Donald Barthelme*. Boston: G.K. Hall, 1981; Molesworth, Ch. *Donald Barthelme's Fiction: The Ironist Saved from Drowning*. Columbia, MO: University of Missouri Press, 1982, and many others

Notes to Chapter II.1.1

[1] As I have mentioned, Christopher Morris sees the intertextual connection between Doctorow's novel *Welcome to Hard Times* and Dickens' *Hard Times*; on the other hand, stretching of the sign Welcome to Hard Times across the main street of the town in the story is understood as a reference to a sign evoking the question of referentiality and representation. Morris thus asks the question *"do titles, textual signs, refer to 'signifieds' or to other signs?"*(Morris 1991: 27), although he does not further explain metafictional associations related to the title

Notes to Chapter II.1.3

[1] Fiedler, Leslie. "Cross the Border—Close That Gap." *Post-Modernism. American Literature Since 1900*. Ed. Marcus Cunliffe. London, 1975. 344-366.

[2] see, for example, D'haen, Theo. "Popular Genre Conventions in Postmodern Fiction: The Case of the Western." *Exploring Postmodernism*. Calinescu, M. and Fokkema, D. Eds. Amsterdam/Philadelphia: John Benjamins, 1987. 161-174.

Notes to Chapter II. 3. 1

[1] Durusoy, Gertrude. "A Comparative Study of Books for Children as Popular Culture." *Popular Culture(s).* Eds. Büken, Gulriz, Raw, Laurence, and Isci, Gunseli Sonmez. Izmir: The British Council in Association with the American Studies Association of Turkey and Ege University, 1999.141.

[2] In Ray B. Browne's understanding, popular culture has become *"a growth and extension of folk culture"* (Browne 1999:16). Browne, R.B. "The Arts and Cultures." *Popular Culture(s).* Eds. Büken, Gulriz, Raw, Laurence, and Isci, Gunseli Sonmez. Izmir: The British Council in Association with the American Studies Association of Turkey and Ege University, 1999.16.

[3] see Sontag, Susan. "One Culture and the New Sensibility." Sontag, Susan. *Against Interpretation and Other Essays.* New York: Octagon Books, 1978. 293-304.

Notes to Chapter II.4

[1] my papers on Richard Brautigan, for example

"Travelling, Displacement and Romantic Identity in Brautigan's Novels *A Confederate General from Big Sur, The Abortion: An Historical Romance 1966*, and *The Tokyo-Montana Express*." *Teacher Training Curriculum Innovation.* Prešov: Department of English Language and Literature, Faculty of Humanities and Natural Sciences, Prešov University, 1998. 68-73.

"Brautigan's Parodical Vision of History (*A Confederate General from Big Sur*)." *Problemi romano-germanskoj filologii.* Uzhgorod: Zakarpatia, 1999. 140-144.

"Brautigan's Parody in *The Abortion: An Historical Romance 1966.*" *European, British and American Studies at the Turn of the Millennium. Acta Facultatis Philosophicae Universitatis Ostraviensis.* Ostrava: University of Ostrava, 1999. 49-56.

"Richard Brautigan's Parody of Popular Genres (*Dreaming of Babylon: A Private Eye Novel 1942*)". *ZENAF Conference Proceedings.* Frankfurt: Centre for North American Studies, 2000. 125-133.

[2] I mean especially his novels *The Hawkline Monster: A Gothic Western,* 1974; *Willard and His Bowling Trophies: A Perverse Mystery,* 1975; *Dreaming of Babylon: A Private Eye Novel 1942,* 1977

WORKS CITED

Alsen, Eberhard. *Romantic Postmodernism in American Fiction*. Amsterdam-Atlanta, GA: Rodopi B.V., 1996.
Auster, Paul. *The New York Trilogy. City of Glass.Ghosts.The Locked Room*. New York: Penguin Books USA, 1990.
Baldick, Chris. *The Concise Oxford Dictionary of Literary Terms*. Oxford: Oxford, University Press, 1990.
Barth, John. "The Literature of Exhaustion." *Atlantic Monthly*, Vol. 220, August 1967. 29-34.
Barth, John. *Essays and Other Non Fiction*. New York: G.B. Putnam's Sons, 1984.
Barthelme, Donald. *Paradise*. New York: G.P.C.Putnam's & Son, 1986.
Barthelme, Donald. *Snow White*. New York: Atheneum, 1986.
Barthes, Roland. "The Death of the Author." *Image-Music-Text.* London: Fontana, 1977. 142-148.
Baštín, Štefan. "Richard Brautigan as a Neo-Romantic Rebel and an Exponent of the Counterculture." *Zborník Filozofickej fakulty Univerzity Komenského— PHILOLOGICA*. Bratislava: FF UK, 1996. 135-142.
Baudrillard, Jean."The Evil Demon of Images and the Precession of Simulacra." *Postmodernism: A Reader.* Ed. Thomas Docherty. New York, London, Toronto, Sydney, Tokyo, Singapore: Harvester Wheatsheaf, 1993. 194-199.
Baudrillard, Jean. "On the Murderous Capacity of Images." Available at <*http://www.uta.edu/english/apt/collab/texts/precession.html*>
Baudrillard, Jean. *Selected Writings*. Ed. Mark Poster. Stanford: Stanford University Press, 1988.
Bényei, Tamás. "Ironic Parody or Parodistic Irony? Irony, Parody, Postmodernism and the Novel." *Hungarian Journal of English and American Studies* 1.1(1995): 89-124.
Bertens, Hans. "Postmodern Culture(s)." *Postmodernism and Contemporary Fiction.* Eds. Smyth, Edmund J. London: B.T. Batsford Ltd., 1991. 123-137.
Bilton, Alan. *An Introduction to Contemporary American Fiction*. Edinburgh: Edinburgh University Press, 2002.

Boyer, Jay. *Richard Brautigan*. Boise: Boyse State University, 1987.

Bradbury, Malcolm. "An Age of Parody: Style in Modern Arts" *Encounter* 55.1 (1980): 36-53.

Brautigan, Richard. *The Hawkline Monster: A Gothic Western*. New York: Pocket Books, 1976.

Brautigan, Richard. *An Unfortunate Woman: A Journey*. New York: St. Martin's Press, 2000.

Calinescu, Matei. "Parody and Intertextuality." *Semiotica* 65: 1-2 (1987): 183-190.

Cawelti, John. *Adventure, Mystery and Romance: Formula Stories as Art and Popular Culture*. Chicago and London: University of Chicago Press, 1976.

Clayton, John. "Richard Brautigan: The Politics of Woodstock." *New American Review* 11 (1971): 56-68.

Connor, Steven. *Postmodernist Culture. An Introduction to Theories of the Contemporary*. Oxford: Blackwell. Second Edition, 1997.

Coover, Robert. *Pricksongs & Descants*. New York and Scarborough, Ontario, Plume, 1969.

Coover, Robert. *A Night at the Movies, or, You Must Rember This*. Normal, Il.: Dalkey Archive Press, 1992.

Coover, Robert. *Spanking the Maid*. New York: Grove Press, 1982.

Coover, Robert. "ADVENTURE! Shootout at Gentry's Junction." Coover, R. *A Night at the Movies or, You Must Remember This*. Normal, Il.:Dalkey Archive Press, 1992. 53-73.

Coover, Robert. *Pinocchio in Venice*. New York: Linden Press, 1991.

Coover, Robert. *Briar Rose*. New York: Grove Press, 1996.

Coover, Robert. *Ghost Town*. New York: Henry Holt and Company, 1998.

Coover, Robert. "Lucky Pierre in the Doctor's Office". *Playboy Stories. The Best of Forty Years of Short Fiction*. Ed. Alice K. Turner. New York, London, Ringwood, Toronto, Auckland, Harmodsworth: Penguin, 1994. 553-561.

Coover, Robert. "Klikař Pierre u doktora." *Playboy Stories. Nejlepší povídky za čtyřicet let trvání časopisu Playboy*. Ed. Alice K. Turner. Praha: Mustang, 1996. 673-686.

Cuddon, J. A. *Dictionary of Literary Terms and Literary Theory*. London: Penguin, 1991.

Dawson, Nicholas. "An Examination of the Identity of Author and Character and Their Relationship Within the Narrative Structure of Paul Auster's New York Trilogy." Available at <http://www.bluecricket.com/auster/articles/dawson.html>

Derrida, Jacques. *Of Grammatology*. Baltimore and London: The John Hopkins University Press, 1976.

Derrida, Jacques. "Structure, Sign, and Play in the Discourse of the Human Sciences". *The Structuralist Controversy: The Languages of Criticism and the Sciences of Man*. Eds. Macksey, Richard, Donato, Eugenio. Baltimore, 1972. 247-265.

Derrida, Jacques. "Structure, Sign, and Play in the Discourse of the Human Sciences." *Twentieth-Century Literary Theory. A Reader*. Ed. K.M. Newton. Houndmills, Basingstoke and London: MacMillan, 1988. 149-154.

D'haen, Theo. "Popular Genre Conventions in Postmodern Fiction: The Case of the Western." *Exploring Postmodernism*. Calinescu, M. and Fokkema, D. Eds. Amsterdam/Philadelphia: John Benjamins, 1987. 161-174.

D'haen, Theo. "Postmodernism in American Fiction and Art". *Approaching Postmodernism*. Eds. Fokkema, Douwe, Bertens, Hans. Amsterdam-Philadelphia: John Benjamins, 1991. 211-232.

Doctorow, Edgar Lawrence. *Welcome to Hard Times*. New York: Random House, 1960.

Doctorow, Edgar Lawrence. *Vítajte v ťažkých časoch*. Bratislava: Slovenský spisovateľ, 1989.

Docherty, Thomas, ed. *Postmodernism: A Reader*. New York, London, Toronto, Sydney, Tokyo, Singapore: Harvester Wheatsheaf, 1993.

Durán, Isabel."The Power of (Auto)Biography in Recent Literary Studies." *Power and Culture in America: Forms of Interaction and Renewal*. Eds. Celada, Antonio R., García, Daniel Pastor, Gonzáles de La Aleja. Salamanca: Spanish Association for American Studies, 2001. 381-390.

Durusoy, Gertrude. "A Comparative Study of Books for Children as Popular Culture." *Popular Culture(s)*. Eds. Buken, Gulriz, Raw, Laurence, and Isci, Gunseli Sonmez. Izmir: The British Council in Association with the American Studies Association of Turkey and Ege University, 1999. 141-152.

Eco, Umberto. "Budú knihy nahradené elektronickými médiami? Knihy, texty a hypertexty [Books, Texts and Hypertexts]". *Dominofórum* 48 (2000): 16-17.

Federman, Raymond, ed. *Surfiction.* Chicago: The Swallow Press, 1974.

Federman, Raymond. *Self-Reflexive Fiction*, 1988.

Federman, Raymond. "Surfiction—Four Prepositions in Form of an Introduction." *Surfiction.* Ed. Federman, Raymond. Chicago: Swallow Press, 1975. 5-15.

Fiedler, Leslie. *Waiting for the End: The American Literary Scene from Hemingway to Baldwin.* Harmondsworth: Penguin Books, 1964.

Fiedler, Leslie. A *Fiedler Reader.* New York: Stein and Day, 1977.

Fiedler, Leslie. "Cross the Border—Close That Gap". *Post-Modernism. American Literature Since 1900.* Ed. Marcus Cunliffe. London, 1975. 344-366.

Fiedler, Leslie. "Cross the Border— Close That Gap: Post-Modernism. Cunliffe, Marcus. Post-Modernism." *American Literature Since 1900.* London, 1993. 329-351.

Fokkema, Aleid. *Postmodern Characters: A Study of Characterization in British and American Postmodern Fiction.* Amsterdam-Atlanta: Rodopi, 1991.

Fonda, M. "Introduction to Freud's Theories." Available at Fonda, M. <*http://www.clas.ufl.edu/users/gthursby/fonda/freud.html*>

Foster, Hal. "(Post)Modern Polemics." *New German Critique* 33 (1984): 67-79.

Foucault, Michael. "What is an Author?" Foucault, Michael. *The Foucault Reader.* New York: Random House, 1984. 101-120.

Fowler, Roger, ed. *A Dictionary of Modern Critical Terms.* London and New York: Routledge, 1995.

Frank, Joseph. "Spatial Form in Modern Literature." Frank, Joseph. *The Widening Gyre: Crisis and Mastery in Modern Literature.* Bloomington and London: Indiana University Press, 1968. 3-62.

Freud, S. in Fonda, M. "Introduction to Freud's Theories". Available at <*http://www.clas.ufl.edu/users/gthursby/fonda/freud.html*>

"General Issues and Signs of Metafiction". Avialable at <http://www.eng.fju.edu.tw/Literary_Criticism/postmodernism/metafiction. htm#Waugh>

Gilbert, Sandra M., Gubar Susan. *The Madwoman in the Attic. The Woman Writer and the Nineteenth-Century Literary Imagination.* New Haven and London: Yale University Press, 1984.

Graff, Gerald. "Babbitt at the Abyss". *Literature Against Itself: Literary Ideas in Modern Society.* Chicago and London: The University of Chicago Press, 1979. 207-240.

Grenz, Stanley J. *A Primer on Postmodernism.* Grand Rapids, MI: Eerdmans Publishing Co., 1996.

Grmela, Josef. "Metamorfózy americkej literárnej tvorby po 2. sv. vojne." Grmela, J., Grmelová, A., Malinovská, Z., Šimon, L., Žitný, M., Sisák, M., Valcerová, A. *Vývinové problémy svetovej literatúry po roku 1945.* Prešov: FF UPJŠ, 1994. 17-31

Grmela, Josef, Grmelová, Anna. *Theory of Literature for Students of English: An Introduction.* Prešov: FF UPJŠ, 1989.

Grünzweig, Walter, Maierhofer, Roberta, Wimmer, Adi, eds. *Constructing the Eighties.Versions of an American Decade.* Tübingen: Günter Narr Verlag, 1992.

Hammel, William, ed. *The Popular Arts in America: A Reader.* New York-Chicago-San Francisco-Atlanta: Harcourt Brace Jovanovich, Inc. Second Edition, 1972.

Hassan, Ihab."Toward a Concept of Postmodernism." *Postmodernism: A Reader.* Ed. Thomas Docherty. New York, London, Toronto, Sydney, Tokyo, Singapore: Harvester Wheatsheaf, 1993. 146-156.

Hauer, Tomáš. *S/krze postmoderní teorie.* Praha: Karolinum, 2002.

Hazlett, William."Travel Writing and Autobiographical Studies." *Power and Culture in America: Forms of Interaction and Renewal.* Eds. Celada, Antonio R., García, Daniel Pastor, Gonzáles de La Aleja. Salamanca: Spanish Association for American Studies, 2001. 391-395.

Herzogenrath, Bernd. *An Art of Desire: Reading Paul Auster.* Amsterdam-Atlanta: Rodopi, 1999.

Hodrová, Daniela, ed....*na okraji chaosu...: Poetika literárního díla 20. století.* Praha: Torst, 2001.

Hoffmann, Gerald."The Fantastic in Fiction: Its Reality Status, its Historical Development and its Transformation in Postmodern Narration". *Real* 1(1982): 267-364.

Hoffmann, G., Hornung, A., Kunow, R. "'Modern', 'Postmodern' and 'Contemporary' as Criteria for the Analysis of 20th Century Literature." *Postmodernism in American Literature.* Eds. Manfred Pütz, Peter Freese. Darmstadt: Thesen Verlag, 1984.12-37.

Homans, Peter. "Puritanism Revisited: An Analysis of the Contemporary Screen-Image Western." *The Popular Arts in America: A Reader.* Ed. Hammel, William. New York-Chicago-San Francisco-Atlanta: Harcourt Brace Jovanovich, Inc. Second Edition, 1972. 97-112.

Homoláč, Jiří. *Intertextovost a utváření smyslu v textu.* Praha: Karolinum, 1995.

Howe, Irving. "Mass Society and Post-Modern Fiction." *The American Novel Since World War II.* Ed. Alfred Kazin. New York: Fawcett World Library, 1979. 124-141.

Hutcheon, Linda. "Parody Without Ridicule: Observations on Modern Literary Parody."*Canadian Review of Comparative Literature* 5: 2 (1978):201-211.

Hutcheon, Linda. *A Theory of Parody.* New York and London: Methuen, 1985.

Hutcheon, Linda. *A Poetics of Postmodernism: History, Theory, Fiction.* New York and London: Routledge, 1988.

Hutcheon, Linda. "The Politics of Postmodern Parody." *Intertextuality.* Ed. Plett, Heinrich F. Berlin-New York, Walter de Gruyter, 1991. 225-236.

Jackson, Rosemary. *Fantasy: The Literature of Subversion.* London and New York: Routledge, 1981.

Jameson, Frederick. *Postmodernism, or, the Cultural Logic of Late Capitalism.* Durham: Duke University Press, 1991.

Jařab, Josef. "Poesie a krutost nečítankové skutečnosti." *Od Poea k postmodernismu.* Praha: Odeon, 1993. 489-493.

Jencks, Charles. *What is Post-Modernism?* London: Academy Editions, 1986.

Kennedy, Thomas. E. *Robert Coover: A Study of the Short Fiction.* New York, Twayne Publishers, 1992.

Klages, Mary. "Postmodernism". Available at
<*http://www.colorado.edu/English/ENGL2012Klages/pomo.html*>

Klages, Mary. "Psychoanalysis and Sigmund Freud." Available at <http://www.colorado.edu/English/ENGL2012Klages/freud.html>
Kolář, Stanislav. *Evropské kořeny americké židovské literatury*. Ostrava: Ostravská universita, 2000.
Kristeva, Julia. "Narration et transformation". *Semiotica* 1(1969): 422-448.
Lauzen, Sarah E. "Notes on Metafiction: Every Essay Has a Title". *Postmodern Fiction: A Bio-Bibliographical Guide*. Ed. McCaffery, Larry Westport: Greenwood Press, 1986. 93-116.
Lye, John."Modernism." Available at <http://www.brocku.ca/english/courses/2F55/modernism.html>
Lyotard, Francois. "Answering the Question: What is Postmodernism?" *Postmodernism: A Reader*. Ed. Thomas Docherty. New York, London, Toronto, Sydney, Tokyo, Singapore: Harvester Wheatsheaf, 1993. 38-46.
Mai, Hans-Peter. "Bypassing Intertextuality. Hermeneutics, Textual Practise, Hypertext." *Intertextuality*. Ed. Plett, Heinrich F. Berlin: Walter de Gruyter, 1991. 30-59.
Maltby, Paul. *Dissident Postmodernist: Barthelme, Coover, Pynchon*. Philadelphia: University of Pennsylvania Press, 1991.
Mánek, Bohuslav. "Science Fiction and Science in Contemporary Poetry in English". *6th Conference of British, American and Canadian Studies (Proceedings)*. Prešov: Prešovská univerzita, 2000. 16-22.
Marčok, Viliam. *Tri aspekty postmodernej literárnosti*. Bratislava: Metodické centrum mesta Bratislavy, 1995.
Marsden, Michael. Nachbar, Jack."The Modern Popular Western Radio, Television, Film and Print." available at <http://www2.tcu.edu/depts/prs/amwest/html/wl1263.html>
Marx, Bill. "Coover Rides Again Satirical *Ghost Town*." *The Boston Globe*. September 3 (1998): E3.
McCaffery, Larry. *The Metafictional Muse: The Works of Robert Coover, Donald Barthelme, and William H. Gass*. Pittsburgh: The University of Pittsburgh Press, 1982.
McCaffery, Larry, ed. *Postmodern Fiction: A Bio-Bibliographical Guide*. New York, Westport, Conn., London: Greenwood Press,1986.
McGrath, P. "The Puppet's Progress." *The Washington Post*. January 6 (1991): 11.

McHale, Brian. *Postmodernist Fiction.* London and New York: Routledge, 1987.
McLuhan, Marshall. *Jak rozumět médiím.* Praha: Odeon, 1991.
McWilliams, Dean. "The Changing Image of America in American Literature." *Romania and America: Cross-Cultural Perspectives.* Bucharest: American Library, 1979. 125-131.
Michalovič, Peter. *Orbis terrarum est speculum ludi.* Bratislava: Sorosovo centrum súčasného umenia, 1999.
Morris, Christopher. *On the Fiction of E.L.Doctorow.* Jackson and London: University Press of Mississippi, 1991.
Newman, Charles. *The Post-Modern Aura: The Act of Fiction in an Age of Inflation.* Evanston: Northwestern University Press, 1985.
Newman, Michael. "Revising Modernism, Representing Postmodernism: Critical Discourses of the Visual Arts". *ICA Documents* 4. *Postmodernism* (1986): 32-51.
Nielsen, Jakob. "The Art of Navigating through Hypertext." *Communications of the ACM 33* (March 1990): 296-310.
Nielsen, Jakob. "The Art of Navigating Through Hypertext." Available at <http://jefferson.village.virginia.edu/elab/hfl0039.html>
Nikolic, Dragana. "Paul Auster's Postmodernist Fiction: Deconstructing Aristotle's 'Poetics'". Available at <http://www.bluecricket.com/auster/articles/aristotle.html>
Nixon, Howard L.II. *Sports and the American Dream.* New York: Leisure Press, 1984.
Nye, Russel. "The Popular Arts and the Popular Audience." *The Popular Arts in America: A Reader.* Ed. Hammel, William M. New York-Chicago-San Francisco-Atlanta: Harcourt Brace Jovanovich, Inc. Second Edition., 1972. 7-14.
Owens, Craig. "The Allegorical Impulse: Toward a Theory of Postmodernism." Owens, Craig. *Beyond Recognition: Representation, Power, and Culture.* Berkeley, Los Angeles, Oxford: University of California Press, 1992. 52-87.
Pace, Chris. "Escaping from the Locked Room: Overthrowing the Tyranny of Artifice in Paul Auster's New York Trilogy" Available at http://www.bluecricket.com/auster/articles/thesis.html

Peprník, Michal. *Směry literární interpretace XX. století.* Olomouc: FF UP, 2000.
Pfister, Manfred. "How Postmodern is Intertextuality?" *Intertextuality.* Ed. Plett, Heinrich F. Berlin: Walter de Gruyter, 1991. 207-224.
Plett, Heinrich F. "Intertextualities." *Intertextuality. Intertextuality.* Ed. Plett, Heinrich F. Berlin: Walter de Gruyter,1991. 3-29.
Poe, Edgar Alan. "The Fall of the House of Usher." *Edgar Alan Poe: Complete Tales & Poems.* New Jersey: Castle Books, 2002. 171-184.
Poirier, Richard. "The Politics of Self-Parody." *Partisan Review* (1968): 339-353.
Pokrivčák, Anton. *Literatúra a bytie.* Nitra: FHV UKF, 1997.
Pokrivčáková, Silvia. *Karnevalová a satirická groteska.* Nitra: Garmond, 2002.
Pospíšil, Tomáš. *The Progressive Era in American Historical Fiction: Dos Passos' 42nd Parallel and Doctorow's Ragtime.* Brno: Masarykova Universita, 1998.
Procházka, Martin. "American Literature: Beginnings to 1914. Revolution&the Early Republic." Procházka, Martin, Quinn, Justin, Ulmanová, Hana, Roraback, Eric. *Lectures on American Literature.* Praha: Karolinum, 2002. 46-56.
Procházka, Martin, Quinn, Justin, Ulmanová, Hana, Roraback, Eric. *Lectures on American Literature.* Praha: Karolinum, 2002.
Pütz, Manfred. *The Story of Identity: American Fiction of the Sixties.* Stuttgart: Metzler, 1979.
Rifaterre, Michael. "Intertextuality vs. Hypertextuality." *New Literary History* 35 (1994): 779-788.
Rose, Margaret. *Parody/Metafiction.* London: Croom Helm, 1979.
Rose, Margaret. *Parody: Ancient, Modern, and Post-Modern.* Cambridge: Cambridge University Press, 1993.
Rowe, John Carlos. "Postmodernist Studies". *Redrawing the Boundaries.* Eds. Stephen Greenblatt, Giles Gunn. New York: MLA Press, 1992. 179-208.
Ruland, Richard, Bradbury, Malcolm. *Od Puritanismu k postmodernismu: Dějiny americké literatury.* Praha, Mladá fronta, 1997.

Russell, Charles. "Individual Voice in the Collective Discourse". *Postmodernism in American Literature: A Critical Anthology*. Eds. Manfred Pütz and Peter Freese. Darmstadt: Thesen Verlag, 1984. 205-214.

Schmitz, Neill. "Richard Brautigan and the Modern Pastoral." *Modern Fiction Studies* 19 (1973): 109-125.

Seaboyer, Judith. "Robert Coover's Pinocchio in Venice: An Anatomy of a Talking Book." *Venetian Views, Venetian Blinds: English Fantasies of Venice*. Eds. Manfred Pfister and Barbara Schaff. Amsterdam-Atlanta: Rodopi, 1999. 237-255.

Sim, Stuart, ed. *The Routledge Companion to Postmodernism*. London: Routledge, 2001.

Slethaug, Gordon E. "The Hawkline Monster: Brautigan's 'Buffoon Mutation.'" *The Scope of the Fantastic: Selected Essays from the First International Conference on the Fantastic in Literature and Film*. Eds. Collins, Robert A., Pearce, Howard. Westport, Connecticut: Greenwood Press, 1985. 137-145.

Smith, Henry Nash. *Virgin Land: The American West as Symbol and Myth*. Cambridge, Mass.: The Belknap Press of Harvard University Press, 1950.

Smith, Henry Nash. "The Myth of the Garden and Turner's Frontier Hypothesis." *American Literature, American Culture*. Ed. Hutner, G. Oxford-New York: Oxford University Press, 1999. 349-357.

Smyth, Edmund J., ed. *Postmodernism and Contemporary Fiction*. London: B.T. Batsford Ltd., 1991.

Sontag, Susan. "One Culture and the New Sensibility." Sontag, Susan. *Against Interpretation and Other Essays*. New York: Octagon Books, 1978. 293-304.

Sontag, Susan. *A Susan Sontag Reader*. Harmondsworth: Penguin, 1983.

Spencer, Lloyd. "Postmodernism, Modernity, and the Tradition of Dissent." *The Routledge Companion to Postmodernism*. Ed. Sim, Stuart. London: Routledge, 2001.158-173.

Spender, Stephen. *The Creative Element: A Study of Vision, Despair and Orthodoxy among some Modern Writers*. London: British Book Center, 1954.

Stevenson, Randall. "Postmodernism and Contemporary Fiction in Britain." *Postmodernism and Contemporary Fiction*. Ed. Smyth, Edmund J. London: B.T. Batsford Ltd., 1991. 19-35.

Stonehill, Brian. *The Self-Conscious Novel: Artifice in Fiction from Joyce to Pynchon*. Philadelphia: University of Philadelphia Press, 1988.

Thomson, Philip. "The Grotesque." Methuen Critical Idiom Series, 1972. Available at
<*http://www.mtsu.edu/~english/Grotesque/Major%20Practitioners/Theorists/Thomson/thomson3.html#disharmony*>

Trachtenberg, Stanley. *Understanding Donald Barthelme*. Columbia: University of South Carolina Press, 1990.

Turner, Frederick Jackson. *The Early Writings of Frederick Jackson Turner, with a List of All His Works Compiled by Everett E. Edwards and an Introduction by Fulmer Mood*. Madison, Wisconsin, 1938.

Varsava, Jerry., A. *Contingent Meanings: Postmodern Fiction, Mimesis, and the Reader*. Gainesville: Florida State University Press, 1990.

Vietorová, Nina. *Some Aspects of English 20th Century Literature*. Bratislava: Lingos, 2002.

Vietorová, Nina. *Postmodern Shifts in American Postmodern Fiction*. Bratislava, 2003.

Vilikovský, Pavel. "Doslov." Doctorow, Edgar L. *Vítajte v ťažkých časoch*. Bratislava: Slovenský spisovateľ, 1989. 185-187.

Vonnegut, Kurt. *Timequake*. New York: K.P. Putnam's Sons, 1997.

Waugh, Patricia. *Metafiction. The Theory and Practise of the Self-Conscious Fiction*. London and New York: Routledge, 1984.

Waugh, Patricia. *Practising Postmodernism/Reading Modernism*. New York: Routledge, 1992.

White, Hayden. *Tropics of Discourse: Essays in Cultural Criticism*. Baltimore, Md.:John Hopkins University Press, 1978.

Willis, Lonnie L. "Brautigan's The Hawkline Monster: As Big As the Ritz." *Critique: Studies in Modern Fiction* 23.2 (1981-82). 37-48.

Yanc, Jeff. "The Western Novel Goes to Hell in Robert Coover's *Ghost Town*" October 29 (1998). Available at
<*http://multihome.www.desert.net/tw/10-29-98/book2.htm.*>

Žilka,Tibor. *Postmoderná semiotika textu*. Nitra: FF UKF, 2001.

Jaroslav Kušnír (Ed.)

Ideology and Aesthetics in American Literature and Arts

ISBN 3-89821-513-X

Paperback, October 2005, € 24,90

Available at every bookstore
or directly from

ibidem

Jaroslav Kušnír is the editor of the forthcoming book entitled *Ideology and Aesthetics in American Literature and Arts*. This book will also be published by *ibidem*-Verlag and includes contributions by African, East and West European, Asian and North American scholars which deal with and compare ideological and non-ideological approaches to the analysis of literary, artistic as well as popular works (popular music) mostly by American authors. Most of the essays deal with a way various aspects of American identity are depicted, represented, treated, ideologized and aestheticized in different literary genres, forms of art and media. The contributions offer multidisciplinary, cross-cultural and comparative perspectives and represent a diversity of scholarly voices ranging from the general discussion on the relationship between ideology and art (Anton Pokrivčák), ideology and multiculturalism (Cristina Garrigós). They also give the analysis of poetry (Pokrivčák, Obododima Oha), postmodern fiction (Pi-Hua Ni, Cristina Garrigós), drama (Zoe Detsi-Diamanti, Csaba Csapó) as well as the comparative analysis of the depiction of the identity of North American Indians in such different media as literature and film (Michal Peprník). In addition to this, the book includes the analysis of Black rap music (Wojciech Kallas).

***ibidem*-Verlag**
Melchiorstr. 15
D-70439 Stuttgart

info@ibidem-verlag.de

www.ibidem-verlag.de
www.edition-noema.de
www.autorenbetreuung.de

www.ingramcontent.com/pod-product-compliance
Lightning Source LLC
Chambersburg PA
CBHW051643230426
43669CB00013B/2416